Decolonizing Contemporary Gospel Music Through Praxis

Bloomsbury Studies in Black Religion and Cultures

Series Editors: Anthony B. Pinn and Monica R. Miller

Bloomsbury Studies in Black Religion and Cultures advances innovative scholarship that reimagines and animates the global study of black religions, culture, and identity across space and time. The series publishes scholarship that addresses the mutually constitutive nature of race and religion and the social, cultural, intellectual, and material effects of religio-racial formations and identities. The series welcomes projects that address and foreground the intersectional and constitutive nature of black religions and cultures and privileges work that is inter/transdisciplinary and methodologically intersectional in nature.

African Spirituality, Politics and Knowledge Systems
Toyin Falola

Black Transhuman Liberation Theology
Philip Butler

Innovation and Competition in Zimbabwean Pentecostalism
Edited by Ezra Chitando

Speculations on Black Life
Edited by Darrell Jones, Monifa Love and Anthony Pinn

Religion and Inequality in Africa
Edited by Ezra Chitando, Loreen Maseno and Joram Tarusarira

Decolonizing Contemporary Gospel Music Through Praxis

Handsworth Revolutions

Robert Beckford

BLOOMSBURY ACADEMIC
LONDON • NEW YORK • OXFORD • NEW DELHI • SYDNEY

BLOOMSBURY ACADEMIC
Bloomsbury Publishing Plc
50 Bedford Square, London, WC1B 3DP, UK
1385 Broadway, New York, NY 10018, USA
29 Earlsfort Terrace, Dublin 2, Ireland

BLOOMSBURY, BLOOMSBURY ACADEMIC and the Diana logo are trademarks of
Bloomsbury Publishing Plc

First published in Great Britain 2023
Paperback edition published in 2025

Copyright © Robert Beckford, 2023

Robert Beckford has asserted his right under the Copyright, Designs and Patents Act, 1988,
to be identified as Author of this work.

For legal purposes the Acknowledgements on p. ix constitute an extension of
this copyright page.

Series design by Maria Rajka
Cover image courtesy of Faisal Abdu'Allah and Kofi Allen

All rights reserved. No part of this publication may be reproduced or transmitted in any
form or by any means, electronic or mechanical, including photocopying, recording, or
any information storage or retrieval system, without prior permission in writing from the
publishers.

Bloomsbury Publishing Plc does not have any control over, or responsibility for, any third-
party websites referred to or in this book. All internet addresses given in this book were
correct at the time of going to press. The author and publisher regret any inconvenience
caused if addresses have changed or sites have ceased to exist, but can accept no
responsibility for any such changes.

A catalogue record for this book is available from the British Library.

Library of Congress Control Number: 2023933729.

ISBN: HB: 978-1-3500-8173-4
PB: 978-1-3504-1059-6
ePDF: 978-1-3500-8175-8
eBook: 978-1-3500-8176-5

Series: Bloomsbury Studies in Black Religion and Cultures

Typeset by Deanta Global Publishing Services, Chennai, India

To find out more about our authors and books visit www.bloomsbury.com and
sign up for our newsletters

For Micah and Mahli

Contents

Acknowledgements ix

Introduction: Soulful contemporary gospel music and the soul of the Gospel of Jesus 1

Part I Theoretical moorings

1 Groovement: Bridge the gap 15
2 Warrior charge: Confronting the coloniality within contemporary gospel music 30
3 Testimony: Categories for Black Christian decolonial thinking 45

Part II Colonial thought in Black British gospel music

4 Roots Manuva: Colonial Christianity in the songs of the Windrush generation 63
5 Vybz Kartel: Coloniality in the golden age of contemporary gospel music 80

Part III Decolonial methods

6 Handsworth revolutions: Delinking contemporary gospel music from colonial Christianity 97
7 Black voices at the Royal Wedding: Translating decoloniality into music production 114

Part IV Production tools

8 West Indian front room crossover 121
9 The Black vernacular 137
10 Dangerous memories 150

Part V Impact

11 Mercy, Mercy Me 165

Conclusion: Resurrection revolution 172

Notes	175
Bibliography	201
Index of songs	218
Index	241

Acknowledgements

So many people to thank! This book would not have materialized without the creative genius of the music producer Tony Bean. I am also indebted to Bev Thomas, the anti-racist educator, who did much of the initial negotiation between myself and the Bible Society to realize the production of the *Jamaican Bible Remix* album. All the Birmingham-based musicians on the album gave their time for minimal remuneration. I cannot thank you enough: Soweto Kinch, Witness Dis, Darren Elision, Justice Williams, Jerome Buckner, Abigail Kelly, Juice Aleem and Marlene. Thanks also to Professor William Henry, from the University of West London, who made a DJ-ing 'comeback' on the track 'Pay Back'. Credit is also due to the film-makers who produced the album's music videos. Thank you to Lensi Photography, Remi Love, Daniel Anderson, Husnaa Anderson and Mandisa Gordon. I am also grateful for the support of the Bible Society and my former colleagues in the Department of Theology and Religious Studies at Canterbury Christ Church University, especially Gabriella Beckles-Raymond, Maria Diemling and Ralph Norman. I am indebted to the organizers and the participants at the F.D. Maurice Lectures at Kings College, University of London. The Lecture Series was an important opportunity to test the ideas of this book.

Introduction

Soulful contemporary gospel music and the soul of the Gospel of Jesus

Black British contemporary gospel songs[1] evade meaningful reflection on social justice. 'Social justice' refers to the fairness in a society and addressing the issues responsible for inequality, impoverishment and indifference to these concerns.[2] Consider for a moment, how many songs have you listened to about social justice performed by a Black British gospel artist or choir? In reality, only a paucity of songs exists in the post-war Black Church gospel music canon. It is incredibly rare to hear songs about socio-economic inequality, gender equality or environmental degradation.[3] Not that the Bible is silent on the pursuit of social justice. Biblical righteousness encompasses social justice. 'Righteousness' is a translation of the Hebrew word *sĕdāqâ*. It describes *the* fulfilling of the obligations of a relationship. Justice (*miš-pāt*) is the pursuit of God's righteousness. The words *sĕdāqâ* and *miš-pāt* are, however, used interchangeably in the Bible (Gen. 18.19, 25). Social justice in the Bible includes numerous concerns such as the pursuit of fairness for the weak and fatherless (Ps. 82.3), gender justice (Gal. 3.28), the opposing of oppression (Isa. 1.17) and equal treatment of all of God's people (Jam 2.1). In the New Testament, social justice is not confined to human species; it extends to all of creation (Rom. 8.19). Christocentrically, many argue that the life of Jesus is the example par excellence of social justice in action. For instance, the teachings of the Sermon on the Mount are foundational for contemporary social justice.[4]

Why is the UK genre mute? Is it excused from contemplating the meaning of God concerning justice in the historical-social world? Are the Black British Christian music *influencers*, the gospel artists, songwriters and worship leaders exempt from the scripture's demand for social justice? If they are *not* pardoned, then, why are these talented, Spirit-filled performers silent? *While there are numerous answers to these questions, this book makes a centrepiece of the colonial legacy in the Black Church and its continued purchase on Black British contemporary gospel music.* The colonial legacy describes the residue of colonial Christian thought in the Caribbean and Caribbean diaspora Christianity.

This book is a practical guide for decolonizing Black British contemporary gospel music. Decolonizing is the overturning of the colonial legacy in the genre, and *this book is decolonizing through praxis* – a description of the motivation and techniques involved in the production of the decolonial contemporary gospel music album, *Jamaican Bible Remix* (2017). Every song on the album includes lyrics informed by a Black British decolonial theological thinking about God.

In this Introduction, I make a distinction between this book's central concerns. These are colonial and decolonial Christian thinking in the genre and the concomitant theomusicological implications. Colonial Christian thinking is discussed in more depth later in this book, but for now a useful way of understanding these categories is thus. Colonial Christian thinking disavows engagement with social justice, and decolonial Christian thinking embraces it. Colonial ideas about God maintain the asymmetric relationships of race, class and gender, while, in contrast, decolonial thinking disrupts these colonial categories with emancipatory Christian thinking. Inscribed in musicality, colonial and decolonial thought impact the content of lyricism, and in the remainder of the Introduction, I will appropriate a Black Church reception theory, to distinguish these lyrical implications as *soulful gospel music and the soul of the Gospel of Jesus*, respectfully.

Black Church reception theory

The reception of gospel music inadvertently demarks the boundaries of colonial and decolonial Christian thinking. As the Jamaican diaspora philosopher Lewis Gordon reminds us, Black British thought often neglects the values developed and framed within Black expressive cultures.[5] To rectify this deficit this book makes as its centrepiece Black expressive cultures, especially those of the Black Church. For instance, concerning reception theory, the Black Church possesses reception practices in the form of responsive verbal metrics. We believe in telling folk who sing in church or concert halls how the song makes us feel – its affect. In regard to African heritage, we might say that in the Black Church we always reply to the 'call' of the music with a 'response' from the congregation. Even silence is pregnant with meaning, but it is the verbal utterances that interest me here. I will reorient two particular audience responses to draw a line between colonial and decolonial Christian thinking in contemporary gospel music.

On the one hand there is the ubiquitous rejoinder 'You all sing so well.' It is made by audiences or congregations in reply to the aesthetic quality or form of the song. On the other hand, there is the response, 'What are you saying?' This second reaction speaks to the lyrical content of a song and has purchase on Black Church music's theological ideas and meanings. Though there are always exceptions to these distinctions, I propose that 'You sing so well' and 'What are you saying?' demark the boundaries of colonial and decolonial Christian thinking in the UK genre. *The former is the preserve of colonial Christian thinking while the latter renders possible decolonial thinking.*

You sing so well

The response 'You sing so well' speaks almost exclusively to the sonic quality of the voices of the singers and music, and equally the 'affective' and sublime dimensions of the song. While a positive affirmation of the *feeling* and beauty in Black music is unproblematic to audiences, a hermeneutic of suspicion nurtures an alternative reading of these prosaic words of praise. Critically thinking, 'You sing so well' is seldom an appraisal of the song's theological content. This omission is telling because the content of lyrics matters – not only for their theological significance but also because of their relationship to the social world of the songwriter. For instance, one cannot fully appreciate the African American spirituals or Jamaican colonial era Revival Choruses without considering the history of racial capitalism (African enslavement in the Americas and Caribbean). 'Go Down Moses' was as much a desire for freedom from slavery as it was a musical recitation of the Exodus story.[6] Similarly, if musicologist Jo-Ann Richards is correct, many of the colonial era 'Revival Choruses' in Jamaica are doublespeak for African retentions submerged beneath a Christian discourse.[7] What I am proposing here is that the verbal response 'You sing so well' is a register for the elevation of the sonic over the thematic, that is, form over content. Though form and content are mostly inseparable in the study of Black Atlantic music(s),[8] the focus on the aesthetic neglects the importance of lyrical content. The latter, lyrical content, is the focus of audience response to the *Jamaican Bible Remix*.

What are you saying?

The response 'What are you saying?' underlines the importance of a song's lyrics and opens a window of opportunity for exploring decolonial Christian thinking around issues of power, 'race' and gender. This causation is not always guaranteed but is definitely accurate regarding the responses to the *Jamaican Bible Remix* album. For example, when I first played the music video of the single 'Incarnation: No Blacks, No Irish, No Dogs' to one of the album's funding bodies, the reception centred on power relationships. In the song the subject of the incarnation is explored in relation to the persistence of post-war racism(s). The first two verses of the song establish a tension between the incarnation and the experience of colonial citizens in the aftermath of the Second World War.

> **Robert** – John 1:14 tells the story of Jesus' incarnation. That the Word becomes flesh and lives amongst us.
>
> It means that God who is fully God and fully man, takes on human form.
>
> The incarnation means that unequivocally, all creation is good and that all flesh, no matter what colour, no matter what tone is good. My parents believed in this meaning of the incarnation, that their flesh was good.
>
> They were immigrants from Jamaica who came to work in Britain after the Second World War.
>
> But they soon came to realise that not everybody thought the same.
>
> When they went to look for places to live, they were greeted with signs that said, 'No Blacks, no Irish and no dogs.'
>
> **Darren** – Sailed 5,000 miles with the sun way off behind me. They said it's gonna be a while till I feel that warm again. Staring at the grey skies as the cold rain starts to soak me. Faces that I recognize but no one I'd call a friend. Just one class above how my fathers sailed before me. Still no wiser 'bout the days that lay ahead. Hands and feet are free but shackled by economy. Just a possibility of a better life instead. Maybe if you give me time just to let me tell my story about how I came to be in the land of hope and glory. Moment that I touched the ground all I see is consternation. You never let me explain that I'm here by invitation.
>
> **Chorus**
>
> Came expecting arms to open wide. No Blacks, no Irish, and no dogs inside. The sign is plain, and you don't try to hide. No Blacks, no Irish, and no dogs inside.

Immediately after the track ended, a Black Church member of the funding team expressed a deep connection with the song's criticism of inequality in Britain. An equally challenging, though confrontational, response came after my presentation of the album as part of the John Collins Lecture at Oriel College, Oxford, in 2018. While this specific response originates from outside of the Black Church context, it had identification with the 'What are you saying?' metric. In reply to the same track, an Oxford University lecturer (racialized as White) responded by asserting that 'there was absolutely no connection between Christianity, British racism, and the negative reception in the British churches experienced by the Windrush generation'. His perspective grates against copious amounts of sociological research[9] but was nonetheless evidence of the song's capacity to solicit discussion about structural racism. Finally, young Black Christian students are equally engaged by the album's lyrics. For instance, after delivering one of the F. D. Maurice Lectures at Kings College London in 2019, a small group of Black women undergrads in theology congregated around the lectern to speak to me. They all agreed that the album's womanist theology-inspired song 'Magnificat' 'opened their eyes' to new intellectual possibilities for Black women in theology (in three years of undergraduate study in London none of them said they had encountered womanist theology). The chorus to the song 'Magnificat' states:

> Oh hear me ladies, oh hear me girls, 'cause God has chosen you to save the world.
> All Black women of the earth, skin like dirt, you need to know your worth.

Finally, in Jamaica in 2018, at the Jamaica Theological Seminary, the Jamaican students attending a lecture I gave as part of a BBC World Service documentary about the album were also intrigued by the shared diasporic politics articulated in the album's lyricism.[10]

Soulful gospel music and the soul of the Gospel of Jesus

The tension between 'You sing so well' and 'What are you saying?' has theomusicological implications, a binary opposition of what I term *soulful gospel music* and *the soul of the Gospel of Jesus*.

Contemporary gospel music in Britain is 'soulful'. It is music that is sung from the heart, communicates deep salvific truths and seeks to move or create *affect* in the souls of the audience. It is *form* motivated. Don't get me wrong here. The music is moving, dynamic and salvific. But it has limitations. In contrast, contemporary gospel rarely articulates the 'soul of the Gospel of Jesus'. The soul of the Gospel of Jesus is the Gospel's radical message. For instance, Jesus begins his ministry in Luke (4.18) proclaiming freedom, justice and liberation for the oppressed:

> The Spirit of the Lord is on me, because he has anointed me to proclaim good news to the poor. He has sent me to proclaim freedom for the prisoners and recovery of sight for the blind, to set the oppressed free. (NIV)

Jesus' message is one of 'good news' to the poor, the weak, the immigrant, the single mother, the climate change refugee and the socially marginalized. The radicality of the message is this: Jesus Christ is an emancipator! The scope of emancipation is significant: Jesus' message does not evade the confrontation of the sins of the social world or social justice concerns. As Luke records Jesus saying (riffing off the Jubilee tradition of Isaiah and Leviticus), the Gospel is 'freedom from oppression' (Lk. 4.18-19).

Contemporary gospel music rarely reflects the 'soul of the Gospel of Jesus'. Based on these metrics and comparisons, it is still predominantly a genre that evokes a 'sing so well' rather than a 'what are you saying' reply. Acknowledging this deficit is not an end in itself but the beginning of a new journey to decolonize contemporary gospel music.

Decolonizing contemporary gospel music

Decolonizing contemporary gospel music is a departure from the legacy of colonial Christian thinking in the Black Church in Britain. The quandary is this: the theological ideas in most Black churches are 'policed' by colonial Christianity. Colonial Christianity refers to ideas about God communicated to enslaved Africans and colonial citizens during the two waves of missionary activity to the West Indies. The first wave is the White colonial era mainstream Protestant denominations, and the second a century of White American Pentecostal and Evangelical mission.[11] With few exceptions, both waves taught beliefs about God which colluded with the prevailing colonial socio-economic subjugation or the hierarchies bases on race, gender and class.[12] Consequently, social justice, especially racial justice, was not integral to the preaching, teaching or songwriting of these missionary churches. Rather than dissipating with time, experience and education, colonial Christianity's justice deficit echoes into the Black Church's theology and musicality. Most Black British churches of African Caribbean heritage cede theological authority to their White American missionary parent denominations and continue to be nourished by White conservative American theologies. For instance, every Sunday members of the Black majority New Testament Church of God defer to a Christian education manual produced by Euro-American theologians and writers. While much of the resource has spiritual value, it does not contend with its own 'whiteness', cultural hegemony, ethnic particularity or histories of anti-blackness, including the failure to support the Civil Rights Movement or condemn the racist politics of 'Make America Great'.¹³ As we shall see in the following chapter, these colonial Christian ideas continue to inform the songs of worship in the same denomination. Without decolonizing, contemporary gospel music evades social justice content. It is a 'You sing so well' genre that is, to quote Frantz Fanon, 'overdetermined from without'.¹⁴

Handsworth revolutions

This book is indebted to Rastafari musicality. The Rastafarians in Britain are the first to decolonize Black sacred music. For over sixty years, Rastafari-inspired reggae music has been at the forefront of the production of a Black emancipatory musicality. While not all Rastafarian reggae music is socially progressive,¹⁵ much of the genre retains a long-standing commitment to resisting racism, blackening interpretation and foregrounding Black experience, especially Black history as a focus for theological reflection.¹⁶ In 1970s Britain, *reggae artists were the Black music organic intellectuals.*¹⁷ For instance, at the time of writing, one of the longest-established Rastafarian-inspired reggae groups, Steel Pulse, is well into their fourth decade of writing and performing songs that address a range of religious and social issues. As we shall see later, the musicality of Steel Pulse, specifically their debut album, *Handsworth Revolution* (1978), is an important epistemological resource for decolonizing contemporary gospel music. That is to say, decolonizing contemporary gospel music through praxis is in part an appropriation of aspects of Steel Pulse musicality or a borrowing, which I term 'Handsworth revolutions'.

Rastafari-inspired reggae was Black religious pedagogy before the advent of religious hip hop. Before the internet or satellite TV, reggae records were the primary form of sociopolitical and religious-cultural communication. I was introduced to Rastafari's instruction by my old school friend from Coventry, the radio presenter and music teacher David Barrett. Back in the late 1970s, during the school holidays we would 'lime' in the bedroom he shared with his brother, Patrick, and play music on Patrick's prized white 'Techniques' turntable, amp and speaker set. Intriguingly, the very first time we engaged in this Black knowledge production technique, David asked me, 'Do you know who Marcus Garvey is?' I replied, 'No'. David continued, 'Then you need to listen to this'. He laid out one of Pat's singles on the turntable and adjusted the playing speed to 45 rpm. He was inducting me in to reggae's resurrection of subjugated Black history and the significance of Marcus Garvey. After a few crackly sounds from the needle kissing the plastic, bellowing out of the matching compact speakers, came Johnny Clarke's recording of the Mighty Diamonds' classic song about political betrayal, 'Them Never Love Poor Marcus'.[18] I remember the song vividly because of its infamous reference to rice and peas: 'Them give weh, them give weh, them give weh fi rice 'n' peas.' In comparison to Rastafari's rich history of sociopolitical and religious-cultural instruction, the arrival of a new decolonial contemporary gospel music (*Jamaican Bible Remix*) is 'playing catch-up'. But we Black Church folk must catch up and provide a new hope and inspiration for the next generation of Christians, so that *all ethnicities* benefit from a musicology that folds Jesus' revolutionary message into contemporary gospel music.

Who is this book for?

This book is for an *outernational* (international) audience. While the social location is the UK, the implications are global. Coloniality and decoloniality are *glocal* issues.[19] In terms of disciplinarity, the book is interdisciplinary with disciplinary concerns within theology, music studies, cultural studies and sociolinguistics. Furthermore, as many of the core themes in this analysis emerge from Black and womanist theology, the book contributes to Black and womanist theology's reach into practical theology, public theology and theomusicology.

Ways of knowing

This book appropriates mixed research methods but is inspired by Black epistemologies.[20] I appropriate ways of knowing from Caribbean and Caribbean diaspora histories and cultures, such as lived experience (auto/ethnography), storytelling (testimony), embodiment, spiritual discernment (extemporaneous prayer) and African Caribbean and Black British cultural theories. These disparate methods are mediated by theological knowledge sourced from 'Duppy Conqueror' theology, that is, a Black radical reading of Black British Pentecostalism.[21]

Read/listen pedagogy

This is a 'read and listen book'. It is a multi-sensory approach to theological learning. In the words of Bourne and Adkins, the book's approach is an example of full-bodied thinking:

> Theology is full-bodied thought. The wordplay in the phrase 'full-bodied' shows both the richness of theology and its nature as a thoroughly embodied discourse regarding God and God's ways with the world. While there is nothing inherently wrong with intense abstract conceptual thinking about theological matters, too often the rigours of theological thinking take place at a remove from the practices of Christians and their embodiment of their faith.[22]

You, the reader, are encouraged to read each of the book's chapters and listen to each chapter's musical illustration from *Jamaican Bible Remix* on Soundcloud.[23] This embodied pedagogy is designed to nurture new ways of doing Black theology in the UK as a *Black body-theology*.

Positionality

I engage with the genre from a location informed by *communal blackness*. Dialogue with Black people and spaces inform my positioning. I am a Caribbean diaspora subject in a relationship with a Black Jamaican woman, and I am the parent of Black British children. I attend a Black Church and am engaged in many Black community organizations and causes both nationally and internationally. One of my academic roles involves teaching the largest cohort of Black students in theology in Western Europe.[24] *Individual blackness*, in contrast, is a positionality where the only condition for blackness is one's personal ethnicity rather than one's commitment to Black people, communities or causes. Communal and individual blackness represent a spectrum of thought and action, and we might debate whether one position or somewhere in-between is superior to the other. Yet we cannot evade the outcomes: their alterity leads to distinctive and sometimes opposing perspectives and insights. I hope my position's communality will provide insights and proposals that are reflective and transformative for the Black Church and its musical influencers.

Outline

Decolonizing Contemporary Gospel Music Through Praxis: Handsworth Revolutions has five parts. Part I (Chapters 1–3) develops the theoretical moorings for the praxis. Part II (Chapters 4–5) is a colonial Christian evaluation of Black Church music in Britain. Part III (Chapters 6–7) articulates the decolonial method and production considerations. Part IV (Chapters 8–10) contours the three songwriting tools for decolonizing gospel music. Part V (Chapter 11) ponders the influence of the album by exploring two impact case studies.

Part I

Chapter 1, 'Groovement', is the first of three theoretical chapters exploring the predicament. The aim of the section is to articulate the book's research questions and provide the theories and methods to answer them. This chapter probes the question, 'Why is there so little music in the Black Church about social justice?' The answer foregrounds Black theologians. Specifically, to transform contemporary gospel music Black theologians must bridge the gap between Black theological knowledge and the musicians, songwriters and worship leaders of the Black Church in Britain. The *Jamaican Bible Remix* album is presented as an example of how to 'bridge' the distance between theologians and the musicians and songwriters and so on. An illustration comes from the introductory track of *Jamaican Bible Remix*, 'The Jamaican Language'. Chapter 2, 'Warrior Charge', turns our attention towards contemporary gospel music's colonial thinking. I seek to answer the question, 'What is the colonial Christian content of contemporary gospel music?' Working with an action-reflection methodology, I identify the theological moorings of this malaise: the colonial Christian thinking within the missionary preaching to enslaved Africans in the West Indies. In response the chapter calls for new action or alternative categories for a decolonial thinking for the Black Church and its music. An illustration of decolonial praxis is the track 'Social Justice' from *Jamaican Bible Remix*. Chapter 3, 'Testimony', identifies the alternative Black Christian decolonial categories stipulated in the previous chapter for decolonial thinking for contemporary gospel music. The new decolonial Christian thought emerges from a narrative theological methodology, that is, Black Church testimony. An illustration of the decolonial thought is the track 'Manifesto' from *Jamaican Bible Remix*.

Part II

This section surveys the influence of colonial Christianity on contemporary gospel music in Britain. After all, it is necessary to demonstrate the reach of colonial Christian thinking. Chapter 4, 'Roots Manuva', argues that the foundational Windrush generation (1948–70) canon is a continuity of colonial

Christian thought. Moreover, this canon 'hails' the post-war Black Church and prevents it from becoming a fully radical Black movement. An illustration is made of the track 'Incarnation: No Blacks, No Irish, No Dogs'. Similarly, Chapter 5, 'Vybz Kartel', examines the evidence for the continuity of colonial Christian thinking in four discrete phases of post-diaspora contemporary gospel music production (1971–2020). An illustration for a counter narrative of colonial Christian thinking is the track 'Work of the Spirit'. I end the analysis of coloniality in contemporary gospel music in 2020 because the death of African American George Floyd in the same year changed the racial climate in Britain. The global outpouring of support for anti-racism in the aftermath has made it easier for everyone, including gospel artists, to discuss social justice issues, including racialised oppression. While I am excited by the prospect of a more socially engaged genre, I am interested in the musical discourse before 2020, when it was less threatening, expedient and commercially disadvantageous for contemporary gospel artists to reflect on the social world in their songs about God.

Part III

Chapter 6, 'Handsworth Revolutions', is the first of two chapters dedicated to identifying the mechanics for decolonizing. This chapter marks the start. It articulates a twofold strategy for delinking from colonial Christianity. The inspiration for this reworking are the pioneers of decolonial epistemes, the Black British reggae band Steel Pulse. Furthermore, to locate decolonial 'options' for decolonizing music, I turn to the musings of former gospel artist Jahaziel at the borders of contemporary gospel music. Musical illustration is provided by three tracks from *Jamaican Bible Remix*. These are 'Magnificat' (again but for different reasons), 'Incarnation' and 'Pay Back', respectively. Chapter 7, 'Black Voices at the Royal Wedding', identifies the practical ways of translating the decolonial options from the previous chapter into everyday songwriting tools. After all, we have to make these complex ideas 'everyday' and doable. The tools are crossover, the Black vernacular and dangerous memories.

Part IV

The penultimate section describes how to use the three production tools for decolonizing contemporary gospel music. Chapter 8, 'Crossover', identifies the first tool for decolonizing contemporary gospel music, 'crossover'. As a resource for decolonial songwriting, crossover practice (the blending of sacred and secular music) has a longer history in the West Indian British heritage. To show how it works, I appropriate a method from the West Indian front room. An illustration is made of the song 'Caesarea Philippi' from *Jamaican Bible Remix*. Chapter 9, 'The Black Vernacular', identifies the second tool, Black language, as a resource for conveying discrete decolonial interests. The practice is relatively simple to deploy, as sampling the Di Jamiekan Nyuu Testament (JNT) version achieves the goal of the second decolonial option. But there is more than one decolonial register for the JNT. This chapter considers an additional theological decoloniality. An illustration comes from the track 'Beatitudes'. Chapter 10, 'Dangerous Memories', identifies the workings of the third tool. Dangerous memories refer to the stories we tell in song. The chapter makes a centrepiece of the memory of slavery as an example of producing dangerous memories in contemporary gospel music. An illustration of remembering slavery's overcoming is the track 'Go and Sin No More'.

Part V

Chapter 11, 'Mercy, Mercy Me', proffers two critical case studies for demonstrating the impact of the *Jamaican Bible Remix*. The first example comes from the 'West Indian Front Room' event of 2018. This collaboration between academics and musicians and songwriters identifies the limited commerciality of decolonial contemporary gospel music. The second example, however, reveals a more fruitful possibility. It is a case study of a partnership, the Kingdom Choir, at the Cop26 United Nations Climate Change conference in Glasgow, Scotland, in 2021. The conclusion, 'Resurrection Revolution', is a call for future collaborations, resistance and contemporary gospel music re-existence.

Part I

Theoretical moorings

1

Groovement

Bridge the gap

Why does contemporary gospel music disavow social justice? In this chapter, I consider the accountability of Black liberation theologians. However, to start to answer the question, I will establish the predicament – the evasion of social justice content in the ordinariness of the worship service. I begin with worship songs because of their proximity to contemporary gospel songs. In modern Black urban worship, worship songs are folded into contemporary gospel music songs.[1] This blurring of genres (coupled with new forms of professionalized, commercialized ministry) makes it challenging for worshippers to decipher where the worship songs end and contemporary gospel songs begin. In the words of African American musicologist Deborah, 'the church has become the party'.[2] Therefore, worship songs are a legitimate place to begin a discussion about the social justice quandary of contemporary gospel songs.

Methodologically, this chapter appropriates 'cut 'n' mix'.[3] Cut 'n' mix is a Caribbean diaspora sensibility. Initially used to describe a technique for producing music, cut 'n' mix has a much longer philosophical history. It also encapsulates a propensity to find connections and entanglements where there seem to be none or for holding disparate ideas, practices or beliefs in tension.[4] Cut 'n' mix can equally apply to ways of knowing, and in this chapter, cut 'n' mix describes the entanglement of research methods. I appropriate methods from ethnography, religious-cultural studies and practical theology. I begin with participant observation, a reflection on the performance of worship songs in the 2016 documentary *The Battle for Christianity* (BBC1). Next, I consider the reasons for the lack of social justice content in the songs. At the end of the chapter, I detail the antidote, the production of the *Jamaican Bible Remix* album. An illustration for social justice content in contemporary gospel music comes from the track 'The Jamaican Language' from *Jamaican Bible Remix*.

Three services, same songs

I attended worship services at three Pentecostal churches over several weeks while making the BBC 1 documentary *The Battle for Christianity*.[5] The programme contoured the ministries of churches challenging the trend of declining congregations, a predicament that Linda Woodhead describes as 'no religion' Britain.[6] I was inspired by aspects of the ministries, including the enthusiasm for evangelism, and the masses of young people at each venue (always a good register in 'television land' for Christian relevance). Yet, for me, what was most telling was the worship songs. *In every context there was a disconnect between the theological content and the sociopolitical context of the worshippers. Even though the songs referred to facets of the being of God, every single one evaded explicit reflection on the meaning of God's justice.*

The first service was in London. A thousand-plus cosmopolitan young people packed into a theatre on Tottenham Court Road. Within this 'sacralization of space',[7] the evening's worship service, led by a multicultural worship team, inadvertently 'detonated' a racialized signifier. Music ministry is one of the few spaces where Black leadership is readily foregrounded in predominantly White or Mixed congregations. Yet, funnelling the Black folks into the musical section of Sunday morning ministry unintentionally reinforces racial stereotypes about an innate Black musicality.[8] Hence, while many evangelical churches claim a new politics of inclusion and diversity,[9] the visual politics presented at worship counter this claim.[10] The worship ministry was dramatic. The service opened in the theatre venue with a smoke machine bellowing out a cloud of white mist onto the stage. A team of singers/dancers ran out like seasoned professionals to take up their positions synchronous with the theatre lights hitting centre stage. Soft rock riffs and mainstream Euro-popular music chic dominated the praise and worship sonics, which were also loud, intense and underpinned by the congregation's collective effervescence. Research indicates that one reason for the success of the songs in this church is a process of refinement and 'quality control'.[11] But, for me, despite the smoke, noise and the aura, the contents of the songs were most revealing. Despite the ethnic diversity of the congregation, and the broader cosmopolitan setting of London, there were neither lyrics in the songs gesturing towards the local social context, nor any sense of songs pertaining to the Spirit and justice. Instead, the songs' contents comprised of generalizations about the love and goodness of God, devotion to God and God's omnipresence.[12] Not to say that these themes do not have an implicit concern with justice or inclusion, but there was no explicit utterance comparable to the words and meaning associated with the prophet Amos in Amos 5:24:

> But let justice roll down like waters,
> and righteousness like an ever-flowing stream. (ESV)

Borrowing from the proposition of the previous chapter, we might say that at this church the songs were *soulful* but lacked the *soul of the Gospel of Jesus*.

The second service was at a New Testament Church of God in Birmingham. Several hundred Black Pentecostals of mainly African Caribbean heritage attended morning worship in the large renovated early twentieth-century red-brick former Anglican Church building. A crew of Black women with superb singing voices led the congregation into worship. Worship leadership in this denomination is also a site of struggle. With restrictions on women's leadership (women cannot become bishops), worship ministry is one of the few places that women can develop their craft without a wholesale capitulation to the denomination's patriarchy. Subsequently, Black women have since the 1950s been at the forefront of the creation of a distinctive, contemporary African Caribbean British music ministry style. Because this worship style has travelled beyond the boundaries of the Black Church, we might surmise that contemporary worship in Britain has Black women's worship ministry in its musical DNA. In comparison to the first London church, the vocal range, harmonies and improvisations were more pronounced here, and the singing underscored by an African musical style which facilitates creative sonic and lyrical processes of 'continuity and change'.[13] The worship service began with a series of up-tempo choruses. After which, the style altered. A collection of slower, melodic praise songs ushered in a powerful sense of the Spirit of God, evidenced by the congregation's response: a sense of awe in the presence of the *numinous*, embellished by a solo gospel song performance before the sermon. The lyrical content was also restricted to the subjects of the love and goodness of God, and devotion to God. There were no songs about social justice issues related to what Black British scholars Ackah and Reddie term the 'contested multiculturalism' of Black British experience.[14] Given the griotic role of Black music in Britain (a voice for expressing social realities), the omission of social justice themes here is noteworthy.[15]

The third service was at a Nigerian diaspora denominational church also in London. An auditorium constructed out of a shell of a former modern telesales complex was filled with African British Christian families. West African migration to Britain runs concurrent with its African Caribbean counterpart, but the number of African settlers dramatically increased in the 1980s. Both peoples were colonized by the British, their economies underdeveloped by colonial capitalism and, subsequently, their peoples are a reserve pool of cheap labour for the post-colonial British economy. African churches as *Black* churches are in the ascendency. The decline in African Caribbean migration and the rise of Mixed Caribbean heritage ethnicities have contributed to a numerical waning of African Caribbean British citizens. With its younger and more populous demographic, West African Christianity is the new powerhouse of Black British Christianity. According to Andrew Rogers, 'Southwark in London has the greatest concentration of African Christianity in the world, outside of Africa'.[16] Indeed, most of the largest churches in Britain are West African, including the bulk of London's mega churches.[17] At Brent Cross, the believers were led into worship by a youthful, dress-coordinated, energetic ministry team on the front stage. An immediate sense of welcome and embrace emanated from the persistent outbreak of smiles, and expressions of joy among the singers in the choir, stationed centre-right of the stage. The soundscape was similar to their African Caribbean diaspora counterparts – a mix of well-known popular praise and worship songs and a few of the famous 'back home' choruses from Nigeria. The worship choreography – the singing, preaching and announcements – was perfectly timed to synchronize with the live broadcast and the church's television ministry. All the music was performed on the syncopated beat which kept in time the worshippers' expressive physicality (the moving of bodies, clapping of hands and other physical expressions registering the experience of the Spirit of God). The embodiment of worship in African diaspora worship cultures communicates a mixed message. On the one hand, it is an affirmation and celebration of the publicly maligned yet secretly desired corporeal Black body. On the other hand, the prioritizing of Black flesh in worship indirectly militates against the culturally diverse forms of worship and liturgy that some propose is necessary for attracting a culturally diverse congregation.[18] The songs were characterized by themes of confidence in God's providence and the abiding power of the Spirit in the life of the believer. Again, there was an omission of songs with subjects about the meaning of God in the social world, and there were no songs theologically reflecting on this community's sociopolitical location, concerns or aspirations.

Why are there no songs about social justice?

Why did the songs omit social justice consideration? Why was the content of the songs in various locations the same? There are three possible explanations.

The first explanation for the lack of social justice content is liturgical. All the songs were performed in a worship context where their function is to usher believers into a sacramental experience.[19] The ecclesiastical requirement, therein, is that the songs create a spiritual climate for sensitivity to the presence of the Holy Spirit and preparation for the preaching of the Word of God.[20] While this explanation accounts for what Woods and Walrath term the *leitourgia*[21] or the service, ministry and worship roles of the songs, it does not escape the possibility of worship songs engaging with social justice. For instance, as Lisa Allen-McLaurin argues in her study of worship and justice, Black people in the United States have always incorporated justice issues into worship, and therefore justice themes in songs are not an anathema for the worship service.[22]

The second explanation is commercial. Similarities in the content of the songs reflect the business ecology of contemporary church music. A paucity of new musical material emerges from the British Christian music industry, and most churches draw from a limited pool of popular writers and composers. Most of the songwriters in Britain are racialized as White and outside of Black experience and history.[23] Furthermore, borrowing from John Drane's analysis, a 'McDonaldization' of worship music, that is, a process of rationalization and regulation, leads to the promotion of fixed sonic and lyrical aesthetics for the sake of guaranteeing spiritual satisfaction.[24] Taking this second explanation seriously clarifies the common themes and styles of the songs, and equally the lack of variation. Worship leaders are sticking to what 'works' well for their congregations and choosing not to venture beyond the safety net of commercially proven styles.

A third explanation is theological: a failure of Black liberation theological influence. The case is this; there are no songs exploring social justice because Black liberation theology has failed to effectively communicate its ideas about social justice to the songwriters, musicians and worship leaders of the Black Church. There is no regular cojoining of ideas, peoples or ministries among these two church communities. The outcome is ignorance in gospel music circles of the broader soteriological dimensions of the Gospel, and conversely, indifference among theologians towards the importance of church music. *All three explanations have merit, but it is the third one which is the focus of this chapter. My concern is, what must Black liberation theology do to address the lack of social justice within contemporary gospel music? What practices are necessary?*

Black theologians in Britain cannot 'write off' or disengage from the musicality of the Black Church; Black Church music is too important. We must learn from the emerging school of Black British Womanist musicology. Dulcie McKenzie and Pauline Muir have broken new ground in their respective studies of music and spirituality.[25] Whether congregational or commercial, Black Church music matters. It is a source of theological thought with extensive reach into the interiority of Black spirituality.[26] Theology in music has consequence. As Melvin L. Butler notes in his study of Pentecostal music in Jamaica:

> Pentecostals use music to declare what they believe and where they stand in relation to religious and cultural outsiders.[27]

Church music has didactic power.[28] It can shape the Christian imagination of both performers and congregations.[29] It communicates a range of theological possibilities from Christian social criticism[30] to spiritual escapism.[31] For instance, studies of the impact of contemporary gospel music in diverse global contexts reveal a wide-ranging pedagogic field including evidence of songs as subversive conduits against political authoritarianism,[32] and conversely, an echo chamber for Western neoliberal world views.[33] The question of impact is a tricontinental one.[34] Black Church music circulates transnationally, crisscrossing the Americas, West Africa and Europe. Therefore, the theology of songs is a concern for theologians in the global majority South as much as the overdeveloped North. The failure of Black liberation theologians to engage has consequence. Without dialogue from Black liberation theology, Black Church music's soundscapes evade theological reflection on some of the most pressing issues of the day such as racism, sexism, environmentalism and militarism.

Grenfell

The aftermath of the Grenfell Tower tragedy of 2017 is one such example of the consequence of the failure of Black liberation theology's engagement with contemporary gospel music. The Grenfell Tower tragedy rocked the nation. The country was in collective shock over the loss of life and its apocalyptic unveiling of the social and racial inequality in housing in 'austerity Britain'.[35] The disaster made visible the overrepresentation of Black and Brown migrant workers and working poor in London's cramped, dated and potentially unsafe accommodation. A comparative analysis of two musical responses to the tragedy makes evident the lack of Black liberation theological influence.

On the one hand, the 'grime rap' artist Stormzy directly confronted the failure of government policies in the fire's aftermath, during his iconic Brit Awards performance of 2018.[36] In his song, Stormzy included a criticism of the then prime minister and leader of the Conservative Party, Theresa May:

Yo, Theresa May where's the money for Grenfell? What, you thought we just forgot about Grenfell? You criminals, and you got the cheek to call us savages? You should do some jail time; you should pay some damages.[37]

On the other hand, aside from church choirs and a few gospel artists supporting fundraising events in the wake of the tragedy, the most significant post-Grenfell contemporary gospel music release was the Kingdom Choir's debut album, *Stand by Me*.[38] This high-powered collection of gospel and secular anthems of love and inspiration, while a commercial masterstroke, has no direct, explicit lyrical engagement with the tragic events of the year. As Obery Hendricks warns, when commercialization and commodification are foregrounded in the production of contemporary gospel music, the genre disavows concern for the 'psycho-emotional and socio-political edification of the communities that spawned them'.[39] We may equally add that when Black liberation theology fails to engage with contemporary gospel music, the songs are less likely to address the concrete social issues in the communities that spawned them.

The gap

Why is there a communicative distance between Black theologians and the songwriter, musicians and worship leaders? What factors have prevented meaningful dialogue? What forms of communication are best suited to fostering communion and exchange of ideas? To answer these questions, and with a focus on the British context, the remainder of this chapter explores some of the barriers or 'gaps' preventing a meaningful dialogue. However, the chapter does not end there: it articulates a solution by describing the mechanics that made possible the production of the *Jamaican Bible Remix* album. The album is a 'bridge' in the sense that it is a communicative strategy for exploring the decolonization of contemporary gospel music.

Why has Black liberation theology in Britain failed to impress change on the contemporary gospel music genre? What are the barriers separating the discipline's prophetic mandate from one of its core constituencies? I suggest that there are at least four basic reasons for the failure. These are chronology, mission, academia and method. Yet, in this study, I contend that the last category, 'method', is the most significant reason for the limited impact of Black liberation theology.

Black liberation theology fails to engage with songwriters and song leaders, and so forth, because it is a relatively new discipline. Like all academic discourse, it requires generations of development to become 'ordinary' in the Black Church. The mission of Black liberation theology is also prohibitive. As Gayraud Wilmore noted some time ago, Black theology is fundamentally a prophetic discipline, and 'speaking truth to power' from the context of the theological academy is neither popular nor welcome.[40] It is a 'narrow path' and therefore even if it is accepted by the church, Black liberation theology will remain a minority pursuit; its primary goal is to disrupt and disentangle unjust power relations through cogent and critical analyses rather than becoming a mass movement.[41] But a prophetic role should not dissuade engagement with all departments of Christian ministry in the Black Church. Finally, in the UK at least, the number of active Black theologians is a crucial variable. *Despite the multitudes of Black Christians swelling the ranks of churchgoers in Britain's cities, the British theological academy remains a 'Whites-only' guild.* At the time of writing, only two-and-a-half Black theologians are in service in related departments in the whole of the Theological and Religious Studies university sector.[42] This means, again, at the time of writing, there are a larger number of Black sociologists working in one university department (Birmingham City University). There are also more Black geographers working nationwide in British universities than Black theologians. With such small numbers of Black theologians, we may sympathetically decline to burden this minuscule percentage working in the university sector with the mission of transforming the theology of song. But we should encourage them to at least think critically about what they write about and also how they communicate their ideas. These explanations are relevant, but they do not fully account for what is at the heart of the quandary. I propose *the primary reason is a methodological divide*, and this explanation is central to this study.

The primary reason for the failure of engagement is methodological. The predicament is this: the dominant discourse on Sunday mornings is music. No matter how great the preacher may be, Black Church folks still identify music ministry as a key component of the church's liturgy. As C. Eric Lincoln and Lawrence Mamiya state, 'In the Black Church, good preaching and good singing are almost invariably the minimum conditions for a successful ministry.'[43] In contrast, British Black theologies with few exceptions are logocentric disciplines, and their ideas are disseminated in books, journals and conference papers. Between the pulpit and lecture theatre exists a communicative mismatch. With so few Black theologians teaching in the academy, and conversely an overrepresentation of Black people in the pews, the discipline's devotion to the

Western logocentric rationalist hegemony risks both isolation from the church and a self-inflicted epistemicide.⁴⁴

Bridging the gap

How can we bridge the distance between Black liberation theologians and the songwriters and musicians? While there is no *precise* precedent in the UK to follow, I propose that we move beyond logocentricity and broaden the modalities for doing theology. This is not a completely new idea. In *Documentary as Exorcism: Resisting the Bewitchment of Colonial Christianity* (2014), as a documentary filmmaker, I make a case for documentary film practice as a decolonial theological praxis.⁴⁵ Likewise, my fellow countryperson Anthony Reddie has appropriated drama theory and practice to develop new epistemes for Christian theology.⁴⁶ In a similar fashion, I am suggesting that to have an impact Black liberation theology must be multimodal. Here the preferred medium for engagement is contemporary gospel music. After all, if music is the currency of the Black Church, then it makes sense to exchange ideas in this style. The remainder of this chapter describes the mechanics that made possible the production of a musical 'bridge' between the two discourses – the production of the *Jamaican Bible Remix* album.

Jamaican Bible Remix

The album is an example of how to bridge the gap. The album was made possible by uniting two disparate Christian ministries in the Midlands area of Britain: biblical translation and contemporary gospel music production.

The Bible Society partly financially supported the album. Their assistance was born of a common interest. The Bible Society wanted to promote Di Jamiekan Nyuu Testiment translation of the New Testament, and I desired to produce contemporary gospel music to engage with the Black Church. Promotion was an issue because despite the JNT's accuracy, creativity and cultural significance, like all new translations from a spoken to a written form, audiences struggled to read their own language. Without an understanding of the grammar and phonetic structure of the written Jamaican patwa (patois), it was difficult to parse even well-known texts. Take, for instance, Jn 1.14:

> 14. Nou, di wan we a di Wod ton man, im kom kom liv mongks wi,
> an wi si ou im big an powaful.
> Im a Faada Gad wan an onggl dege-dege Bwai Pikni.
> Faada Gad sen im kom an a di Faada mek im so big an powaful.
> Di Bwai Pikni shuo wi nof nof lov iivn duo wi no dizorv it, an a
> bier chuu sitn im shuo wi bout Gad. (JNT)

> (The Word became flesh and made his dwelling among us.
> We have seen his glory, the glory of the one and only Son,
> who came from the Father, full of grace and truth). (NIV)

My first encounter with the JNT version was overwhelming – an unveiling of the decolonial linguistic possibilities. I thought to myself, 'If we can decolonize the biblical language, surely, this text can also become the basis for a decolonizing of the songs.' Inspired, I approached the Bible Society with a proposal to produce an album that would broaden the appeal of the JNT.

My proposal to the Bible Society detailed my musical intentions – to sample from the audio version of the JNT translation and layer tracks inspired by Black liberation theology and Black music. The written proposal to the Bible Society made mention of three levels of mixology or 'groovement':

> The core idea is to remix the JNT audio. Remixing is a complex process of layering sound and developing an accessible, compelling, and entertaining narrative. Hence, in this project there will be at least three layers or 'texts' on each track:

- First is the remixing of the JNT. We will sample key passages that will function as the central and defining narrative of each track. For example, John 1:14, the Incarnation of Jesus, will be sampled to explore contemporary meanings.
- The second layer is vocal accompaniment, and this has two parts. First, there are the 'music' vocals – voices of singers/rappers to embellish the Bible story and make it compelling. Second, there is the narrative/comment of Dr Beckford.
- Finally, the Bible passage will be mixed with contemporary music (grime, dub, reggae-dancehall etc.)

Combined, these elements will seek to retell a biblical story or event.

The Bible Society agreed. Their initial decision was courageous; it moved them out of their 'comfort zone' of judiciously promoting the reading of the Bible and towards the relative insecurity of critical contextual interpretation. But this new position was unsustainable. After much 'soul searching', the Bible Society retreated to a background role, to not deviate from their historic mandate.

Tracks

I made use of technological and professional resources to produce the album. The technical resource was the digital recording software. It was the most convenient music-making method for composition. Musicking this way works by tracking or layering tracks in a digital workstation such as the *Protools* or the *Cubase* software programmes. Tracking, however, is much more than a technical, mechanical process; it is also experimental. As John McClure notes in *Mashup Religion*, tracking is also an improvised process, a trial-and-error experimentation to find the right sound, mood or feel by combining instruments and samples and ordering them to produce a compelling narrative. As such, rather than working within a set tradition or way of knowing, this approach is transgressive.[47] Similarly, as Michael Fishbane indicates, improvisation is not merely a rehash of the tradition or what was presented before. It is an interruption of the piece to produce a difference within the work. 'Improvisation is awareness of both the contingency of experience and the fissures that make existence contingent.'[48] Hence, each song is an experiment: a quest to integrate or juxtapose theological meaning. The tracking technology structured the music-making.

The three essential tracks identified in the pitch to the Bible Society govern each recording. The tracks are (1) audio samples from the JNT or scripture track, (2) the message or verbal narratives track and (3) the music or instrumental track. The scripture track describes the samples from the JNT that are cut and mixed into every song. The use of scriptures in the mix is varied. Samples from the JNT are looped and positioned in the mix as stand-alone reference points or as choruses or verses. For example, on the pro-reparations track 'Pay Back', the sample comes from Paul's letter to Faliiman (Philemon) v.18. We sample the verse and loop it as a chorus:

> Ef im did du notn rang tu yu ar im uo yu, . . . wi pie yu bak , pie yu bak. (x2)
>
> (If he has done you any wrong or owes you anything, charge it to Me). (NIV)

By contrast, in the song 'The Beatitudes', the whole of St Matyu (Matthew) 5.3-12 is sampled and cut into sections or verses and a chorus:

> Aal a unu we nuo se unu niid Gad iina evri wie, Gad bles unu, kaa di gud sitn dem we Gad gi wen im ruul piipl laif iina evri wie, a unu a-go get dem.
>
> (Blessed are the poor in spirit,
> for theirs is the kingdom of heaven). (NIV)
>
> Chorus
> Gad bles unu. (X6)
>
> Aal a uu a baal nou, Gad bles dem, kaaz di taim a-go kom wen Gad a-go osh dem an mek dem api agen. Aal a uu ombl demself, Gad bles dem, kaa yu si di ort, a dem piipl de a-go kom get it.
>
> (Blessed are those who mourn,
> for they will be comforted.
> Blessed are the meek,
> for they will inherit the earth). (NIV)

Next is the message track. It is the theological narrative of the song. The delivery comprises various performance styles, including spoken word, singing or rapping. The theological orientation of the message track (decolonial theological thinking) is detailed in Chapter 3. Finally, the music track describes the musical genres appropriated to surround the scripture and message tracks. The music(s) of choice are genres from the Black British music canon, such as reggae, drum 'n' bass, UK soul, UK jazz, Black opera and grime. However, while comprising of unique aesthetic qualities, these traditions are never outside of political consideration. As Ifeona Fulani notes, within the particularity of 'enslavement and colonialism musicianship incorporated guardianship of historical and cultural memory and social commentary'.[49] Black music's function is always pedagogic: part griot and part organic intellectual.[50] Layering and combining these three tracks produce the meaning.

Tony Bean provided the professional resource. Locating a skilled musician and producer within the Black Church context was not difficult. Artistry is a function of the Black Church in Britain, and the church is fecund with musicians.[51] However, to facilitate a range of musical and production needs, including awareness of the history, culture and politics of the Black Church, it was essential to work with an open-minded Pentecostal musician-producer. Fortunately, the main gospel label in Birmingham, 5 AM Records, had one such individual. Tony Bean has been on the contemporary music scene for decades and has won numerous national and international awards. He was raised in the Black Church and is a competent musician (guitar, drums, keyboards) and songwriter. As Tony states in his biography:

> I was blessed to have a great 'mom' who was a very gifted musician. She read music and played guitar and piano. I was more interested in football until I realised a growing passion watching the musicians at church. It was then that I took an interest in what my mom wanted to teach me. She was my first music teacher. From age 11, I was playing guitar in the church band every Sunday, a great opportunity to learn and develop.[52]

Tony and I made use of a specific music-making process. First, I identified a social justice issue and how it might be reflected on in scripture. For example, the second track on the album, 'Social Justice', foregrounds social justice in society and scripture. 'Luuk' (Luke) 4.18 is the sample on this track. Next, we discussed some musical ideas based on styles of music I thought appropriate. I have spent an inordinate amount of time in my life listening to music and had some idea of the genres that constitute the Black British music canon. Finally, Tony 'worked his magic' by developing a soundtrack based on the original idea. For instance, on the track 'Social Justice', I wrote and performed the verses, Tony wrote and performed the chorus, and after accepting my invitation, the gospel reggae-dancehall artist Witness Dis makes a guest performance. The music of the British rap artist Roots Manuva inspired the sonic texture.[53]

The ambition for the album, that is, mixing the JNT with social justice themes and Black music, is articulated in the introductory track 'The Jamaican Language'.

Illustration: The Jamaican Language

Robert – Welcome to the Jamaican Bible Remix.
It's a remix of the Jamaican New Testament, published in 2012.
We mix audio from the Jamaican New Testament with black urban music from Britain, and we provide a social and political-theological commentary on the audio.

So, when you mix it all together you end up with a powerful sonic fiction. You hear the Jamaican Bible come alive in the black urban context and you hear the Bible relate to real-life, social, political, historical and cultural concerns.

On another level, we are trying to demonstrate that translation is much more than grammar and syntax; it's also about communicating a peoples' worldview, their history, their hopes and their aspirations.

I guess you could say that we see language as being redemptive.
To say the Jamaican language is redemptive is to affirm the way in which Africans who were captured found ways of keeping their language and their culture alive in the way that they spoke.

But not everybody holds this view of the Jamaican language. For some, the Jamaican language is problematic:

David Starkey – This language, which is wholly false, which is a Jamaican patois.

Robert – But for others it's a legitimate language: a carefully retained expression of the history of the Africans on the island:

Rev. Courtney Stewart – It is patois, our language, and the critical part of this translation is that our language is what makes us who we are.

Robert – Now we're mixing this up from the location of the diaspora, the Jamaican diaspora in Britain.
And as a diaspora we have the gift of second sight: we live in two worlds.
So, we draw on ideas from the Caribbean, and we mix them with information, concerns and experiences that we have here in Britain.

This is a collaboration between 5AM Records (Tony Bean), The Bible Society and me, Robert Beckford.

On this album, we cover a variety of themes, all of them bound together by social justice.

Conclusion

Black liberation theologians must take responsibility for the social justice deficit in contemporary gospel music. They cannot evade meaningful dialogue with the musical influencers in the Black Church. Appropriating the medium of music as the preferred platform for conversation provides a crucial modality for sharing theological thought. However, music as the source for a Black theological pedagogy does not presuppose that the songwriters and worship leaders of the church do not read or are not scholarly. Instead, this communicative strategy points to a deeper, historic malaise – that the mainstream academic logocentric platforms which disseminate theological ideas are limited in their capability to reach, impact and *move* everyday ordinary Black Church folk including those writing songs or leading worship.

2

Warrior charge

Confronting the coloniality within contemporary gospel music

What is the colonial Christian content of contemporary gospel music? What specific themes and issues must theologians engage with, and subsequently, what are the decolonial alternatives for contemporary gospel music? To answer these questions, I will appropriate the pastoral spiral as an interpretive method.[1] *The method is suitable because it facilitates an interpretation of a predicament (contemporary gospel music) in relation to the historical social world (colonial Christianity), before contemplating a theological response and meaningful action (decolonization).* Central is the method's commitment to action, or what Elaine Graham and Heather Walton term 'performative knowledge':

> This method of reflection characterizes theology as performative knowledge, that is, a way of knowing that is inseparable from doing. The fundamental assumption here is that theory and practice are inextricably joined. This conviction is often expressed in the use of the terminology of praxis, denoting a dialectic of theory and practice, a synthesis of committed and critical action, and reflecting the insistence that proper theological understanding cannot be formed independently of practical engagement. Theology-in-action, therefore, places primacy on orthopraxis (right action) over orthodoxy (right belief). This is more than simply another form of 'applied theology', however, in which systematic and historical theology provide norms for pastoral care or ethics. Rather, for this method, practice is both the origin and the end of theological reflection, and 'talk about God' cannot take place independent of a commitment to a struggle for human flourishing. Doctrinal statements or propositions of belief are inadequate unless they can be incarnated into the particular, immediate, and concrete world of action. To proclaim God as love-in-action is not an abstract existential exercise but an event in which God's promise of justice, healing and reconciliation erupts into history, something that cannot be

viewed dispassionately but that demands a corresponding participation in the renewal of social reality.[2]

There are psychological difficulties associated with beginning all human experience and theological reflection with a 'problem'. However, conscientized Black people do not have the luxury of ignoring injustice and, moreover, confronting these difficulties head-on has produced long-standing traditions of resistance and re-existence.[3]

The pastoral spiral has four basic stages. These are experience, analysis, biblical reflection and action, and these generic stages are adopted for my reflection here.[4] This chapter begins with a concrete experience, my personal experience of participation in singing a contemporary gospel song in a moment of crisis. I have chosen this experience because it raises relevant social and theological questions. Next, *this* experience is the subject of analysis, specifically the passive and active-radical tropes developed by Black British womanist theologian Valentina Alexander. Alexander's measures are germane for the social evaluation of all Black Church activities. A historical-theological investigation follows, to make sense of the social analysis produced by Alexander's scheme. Finally, we will explore new action based on the findings of the previous stages; specifically, I will identify new categories of thought and action required for a new approach for contemporary gospel music. These new categories are sketched out here but explored in more detail in the following chapter.

Experience: 'Soon and Very Soon'

Experience is the first stage, and I will begin by recalling a personal experience. We were surrounded by right-wing sympathizers. It was a spring Sunday morning in the early 1980s in Birmingham, England. Our packed-out, rickety Ford transit van was stationary at traffic lights in the district of Digbeth when we found ourselves in the middle of a protest march by the National Front and a counter demonstration by the anti-racist Anti-Nazi League. Surrounded by a sea of animosity, time went into slow motion. Yet, we Black Christian folk did what we do in moments of uncertainty: we defaulted to the crisis management of African Caribbean diaspora Christianity – we raised a chorus. One of the church sisters, with a soft voice, instinctively started singing a song. It was Andrae Crouch's 'Soon and Very Soon'. She began with the first two lines of the song and then we all joined in and completed the first verse.[5] At the second repeat of the song (the tradition was to sing till we sensed the time was right to stop), the crowd dispersed. Like the church members in the van, the neo-Nazis had a schedule to keep! The anxiety passed, and shortly afterwards, we arrived at our venue. On reflection the church van experience was a particular 'pedagogy of crossing': an epistemic awakening leading to new ways of knowing and doing. That is, it was a time when

> subordinated knowledges that are produced in the context of practices of marginalization in order that we might destabilize existing practices of knowing and thus, cross the fictive boundaries of exclusion and marginalization.[6]

The experience was both *constructive* and *problematic*. Constructively speaking, singing 'Soon and Very Soon' was empowering and an experience of *liminality* and *communitas*.[7] In real time, we were *transformed* from being early morning Christian commuters to persecuted pilgrims.[8] The experience was also problematic. While there is nothing theologically improper with looking to God for hope in moments of trial, within the superstructure of Black Pentecostalism 'raising a chorus' with lyrical content celebrating eschatological hope evades the possibility of ever 'speaking truth to power'. The content of our song propelled us heavenward and did not contest the racial terror of late 1970s Britain.

Analysis: Passive radicalism

The next stage is analysis. What does social analysis of the experience unearth? To answer this question, I appropriate the analytic framework of the first Black British scholar to frame Black Christian experience, the womanist scholar Valentina Alexander. Alexander's study of African Caribbean Christian spirituality proposes two basic interpretations. These are 'passive radicalism' and 'active radicalism'.[9] Both emerge from what Alexander refers to as a general liberational spirituality of the Black Church.

Liberational spirituality produces these two distinct modes of operation, and both have implications for how Black Christians engage with the social world. The first analytic mode, 'passive radicalism', describes a social-political understanding confined to the personal sphere, omitting social consideration.

> Liberational spirituality is, therefore, the key epistemological tool . . . it has most often been, however, essentially an *implicit* tool enabling believers to identify, challenge and overcome the various levels of their ideological and material oppression *without necessarily seeking out its socio-historical source and without*

> *making an explicit theological alignment with that liberational process*. To the extent that this manifestation of social analysis . . . it has been identified in this study as *passive radicalism* (italics mine).[10]

Applied to a song's meaning, passive radicalism makes personal empowerment the focus of concern. In this mode, these songs unwittingly mediate Black faith by reducing its locus to the transformation of the Black body and, thus, a negation of the social world. The second mode, or 'active radicalism', engages with the structures of the social world and makes explicit an experiential and cognitive liberation spirituality. Applied to a song's meaning, active radicalism is the folding of the gospel message into questions of social injustice. This is because active radicalism seeks to

> broaden the scope of social analysis, providing it with a multi-dimensional insight into social transformation and allowing for the possibility of an historical-analytical element to be added to its method of interpreting the social world . . . it is now able to more effectively undermine the oppressive hegemonic practices of society which in its latent state it could only attempt to *cope with* and *survive* under. Believers can recognise therefore that liberation must address structures of oppression as well as provide personal empowerment for individual advancement.[11]

Liberational spirituality renders legible the theological parameters of our performance of 'Soon and Very Soon'. Our musicking was passive radicalism. Even though the performance was designed to comfort us, and we were consoled, the song's lyrics had no connection to a wider consideration of racism in Britain, and subsequently, we made no attempt to reflect on our predicament as Black British people. Hence, at best the performance was a spiritual catharsis, and at worst an annulment of social consideration.

The analysis reveals a protest song deficit.[12] Protest songs are derived from a commitment to social justice and therefore protest songs are social justice songs. We had no songs in our canon that spoke to the hostile social world. This deficit does not characterize all Black Atlantic cultures. In comparison, in Black Christian America there exists a rich tradition of protest songs. Protest songs provided hope in the struggle against slavery, resistance to 'Jim Crow' and a psychological support for the Civil Rights Movement in late modernity.[13] In Black Britain, the only context where we find a history and plethora of songs of protest is the secular music canon.[14] For instance, while we in the church van were singing choruses of eschatological hope, a few blocks away in the then predominantly African Caribbean and South Asian district of Handsworth, the reggae band Steel Pulse had recently released a Black protest album, *Handsworth Revolution*. One of the songs on the album is entitled 'Ku Klux Klan' and makes legible a more direct confrontation with the National Front and other forms of racial terror. The song calls for retribution.[15] Emerging from the same Black social context, our sacred and secular music are estranged. I am not suggesting that we should have responded to the neo-Nazis with verses from Steel Pulse's song (I don't think us bellowing out the song's chorus would have been particularly helpful). However, I am pointing out that an absence of protest songs leads to a failure of church songs to engage directly with all of Black experience. *I can only wonder what might have been the outcome in the short term if at that time we had access to church songs that inspired us to practically resist the experiences of racism.*

The pandemic

The neglect of protest songs is evident in the Black Christian contemporary gospel music responses to the Covid-19 pandemic in Britain in 2020. There are two mainstream Christian musical rejoinders, and both have the same outcome; they fail to critically reflect on protest or outrage concerning the broader social context of the crisis in which Black and Brown people were disproportionately negatively impacted.

The first example of the failure to reflect on the social context during the pandemic is the a capella version of the powerful church hymn 'Great Is Thy Faithfulness'. Performed by a talented group of Black Church musicians and singers, the song tells of divine providence to all people, at all times.[16] The motivation of the musical collective was to inspire National Health Service (NHS) workers. There is no doubt on my part that the song was recorded with the best of intentions, and my analysis here is not to disparage the work and commitment of my Black Christian brothers and sisters. However, I was struck by the choice of song because it is hard to comprehend how conveying a tone of praise, gratitude and celebrating God's abundant provision is appropriate given the dire predicament faced by many NHS and other frontline workers. For instance, during the pandemic, Black workers complained of racialized discrimination in health services, which led to their increased vulnerability.[17] Sadly, like the church members in the van, these musicians also looked heavenward for empowerment rather than proffering a worldly oriented Black Christian protest in song.

The second example of the failure of Black Christian gospel music to reflect on the social context during the pandemic is the musical responses from outside of the denominational Black churches. Although Black Christians originated the first musical response to the pandemic, through the lenses of racial bias in the British media,[18] it was the second, White-led, mainstream contemporary gospel music project which made the headlines and gained public praise from the prime minister, Boris Johnson.[19] The song of choice was 'The Blessing Song'[20] and unlike the first song this one was released concurrent with a public statement. The statement acknowledged the importance of practical support for people during the pandemic. The YouTube write-up underlines the necessity of Christians also providing material support during the pandemic:

> At this unique and challenging time in the United Kingdom over 65 churches and movements, representing hundreds of others, have come together online to sing a blessing over our land. Standing together as one, our desire is that this song will fill you with hope and encourage you. But the church is not simply singing a blessing, each day *we're looking to practically be a blessing*. Many of the churches included in this song have assisted with supplying over 400,000 meals to the most vulnerable and isolated in our nation since COVID-19 lockdown began. This alongside phone calls to the isolated, pharmacy delivery drops and hot meals to the NHS frontline hospital staff (italics mine).[21]

Yet, the song is nonetheless devoid of a lyricism replete with social consideration. Even where one artist was afforded the opportunity to improvise on the problem of Black suffering, the lyrics were mute. In the rap improvisation at the end of the track, a Black British artist from Hillsong, Bermondsey Church, *unwittingly* disavows any awareness of Black people's propensity for premature death. Instead, the rap claims otherwise. The rapper repeats the mantra for blessing from heaven[22] and thus retreats into the personal empowerment of passive radicalism. Clifford Hill gets to the heart of the failure of the second song, arguing that calling for 'blessing' during a global crisis reflects a spiritual immaturity that is incapable of calling for lament, protest or social justice.[23]

Reflection: Colonial Christianity

The third stage is theological reflection. Here, I explore the theological foundations or moorings of the passive radicalism as identified in the analytic phase. I consider the questions: Where in the origins of African Caribbean religious history is individual empowerment foregrounded and social consideration disavowed? What role does scripture play? Also, what theological components or attributes are integral to this theological politics? *I propose that the origin of passive radicalism lies in colonial Christianity.* Colonial Christianity has its roots in political decision-making in the violent settler colonization of the West Indies. European missionary activity is complicit with colonial Christianity, and this collusion is expressed in and through the practice of 'Christian slavery'. Colonial Christianity has its own distinct theological components: a soteriology, a hermeneutic and an ontology.

Mission to the 'New World'

Colonial Christianity is the historical-theological background for understanding the origins of passive radicalism. Colonial Christianity originates in the discovery of the so-called New World in the late fifteenth century. It is concomitant with the Western invasion and subjugation of the indigenous peoples, the trafficking of thousands of enslaved Africans and the creation of racial capitalism. Caribbean slavery is distinguished by the introduction of 'racial hierarchy' as a marker of ability, potential and spirituality. While other forms of enslavement existed in African and Mediterranean societies, none were underpinned by 'race' theories validated by religion or 'science'.[24] Diverse missionary organizations conversed on the colonial West Indies, representing a range of perspectives on the Caribbean's racial capitalism. Not all missionary groups and colonial churches condoned slavery: while the Anglican Church was with a few exceptions allied to the colonial regime, dissenting traditions such as the Quakers, Baptists and Methodists were anti-slavery.[25] However, *none* of the missionary organizations sought to overthrow the slave regime actively, directly or rigorously dismantle the foundations of racial capitalism. In the heat of the West Indies, dissenting groups were willing to swallow their Christian pride and exploit slave labour in their missionary efforts. If James Perkinson's analysis of supremacy in religion is correct, European Christianity was in one way or another inside of empire and its hierarchical, racialized cosmology.[26] That is to say, whether pro or anti-slavery, all European Christian traditions were negatively predisposed in their expectations and assessment of the capacity of Blacks.[27]

Colonial Christianity is the product of *statecraft* and rendered legible in the governmental decision to facilitate Christian conversion without manumission. This decision is made legible in the instruction by Governor Willoughby of Barbados/Leeward in the mid-seventeenth century:

> And for the propagation, and Increase of ye Christian's faith and Religion, you shall make it your special care, that all Negro Slaves, and servants remaining in the said colonies be instructed in the Principle of the same Religion (Church of England). And that such who shall arrive at a competent knowledge therein, be admitted to the Sacrament of Baptism. And that it be declared by Law in the respective Colonies that such Baptism shall not at all be extended to their Enfranchisement or Manumission.[28]

Christian mission colludes with colonial Christianity. The collusion is the practice of 'Christian slavery'. First articulated by Morgan Godwyn (1640–85), the Anglican clergyman and missionary to the Americas,[29] Christian slavery promoted conversion without manumission. In other words, a slave's conversion should not relinquish the asymmetrical master-slave relationship. Yet, for the planter class Christian slavery was a 'win-win' position. They could claim to be promoting the Gospel of Jesus, and moreover, Christian slaves were likely to be more hardworking and docile and, therefore, more profitable. While the meaning of Godwyn's views remains the subject of academic debate,[30] for enslaved Africans, who were the real victims, Christian slavery was still slavery by another name. Not all theologians today view Christian slavery as unscrupulous. For instance, in a debate in 2022 on the BBC's flagship ethics programme *Beyond Belief*, Nigel Biggar, the Anglican priest and Oxford professor of ethics, called Christian West Indian slavery 'humane'.[31] While it is hard to ascertain if a form of racial terror/racial capitalism is ever 'humane', the suggestion by Biggar reflects a highbrow challenge to the orthodox view that British slavery was racial terrorism and therefore a crime against humanity.

The Bible was appropriated to support Christian slavery. While the Bible has little to say about what we understand today as pseudo-scientific ideas about race, scripture was sufficiently fecund with images of division of peoples and unequal power relations that were easily manipulated to project domination and subordination onto White and Black bodies respectively:

> Yet while it would be inaccurate and anachronistic to project a politics of racial difference on to the Bible, both the Hebrew Bible and the New Testament are preoccupied with questions of genealogy, exile, migration, conquest, empire, and 'nation'. As 'a source book of evidence for the dispersion of races and the beginnings of racial divisions and patterns', the Bible's silence on the physiological manifestations of ethnicity was an opportunity rather than an obstacle for exegetical ideologues.[32]

Key scriptures to support the colonial Christian agenda were the 'Curse of Ham' narrative (Gen. 9.24-27) and Paul's letter to the Colossians (3.22). Both were presented as justifications for chattel slavery.[33] The Curse of Ham narrative tells of a curse of slavery by Noah on his son's descendants (Canaan), which was subsequently (mis)interpreted to support the enslavement of Africans. Noah, after awakening from a naked drunken stupor, curses Canaan for covering him up while he was drunk:

> When Noah awoke from his wine and found out what his youngest son had done to him, he said,
>
> 'Cursed be Canaan!
>   The lowest of slaves
> will he be to his brothers.'
> He also said,
>
> 'Praise be to the Lord, the God of Shem!
> May Canaan be the slave of Shem.
> May God extend Japheth's[a] territory;
> may Japheth live in the tents of Shem,
> and may Canaan be the slave of Japheth.' (NIV)

The Colossians text was also read literally to command obedience.

> Slaves, obey your earthly masters in everything; and do it, not only when their eye is on you and to curry their favor, but with sincerity of heart and reverence for the Lord. (NIV)

This text was read literally despite Paul, on another occasion, seeking freedom for an enslaved servant named Onesimus (Philemon). These racist reading strategies legitimated White rule and Black subjugation. Concomitantly, resistance to this interpretation was to also resist the will of God. As Nathaniel Samuel Murrell states:

> During slavery in the English-speaking Caribbean, slaves were instructed. Preachers insisted, based on their colonial reading of the Bible, that slaves must obey their masters and servants be submissive to their lords. Disobedience and resistance were viewed as anti-Christ and Anti-Christian and warranted severe punishments in the slave society even for simple infractions.[34]

Colonial Christianity operates as a 'coloniality of power'. The 'coloniality of power' is an expression coined by Anibal Quijano to name 'the hegemony of control over bodies, sexuality and subjectivity – an entire system congruous with the modern/colonial era'.[35] Colonial Christianity, which operated in and through Christian slavery, was a totality, a regulation of Black bodies as part of the colonial Christian mission. *Colonial Christianity is therefore inherently politico-epistemic; that is, knowledge production about God as a source of control.* But what I want to propose here is that we think of colonial Christianity as a discrete form of *control*. To identify its categories, I turn to a part of an early eighteenth-century sermon to enslaved people from a leader of the Moravian Church, Count Ludwig von Zinzendorf.

Colonial Christianity's coloniality of power is articulated in sermons to the enslaved in the West Indies. For instance, in a sermon in 1739, a hundred years into Caribbean chattel slavery, and at the birth of meaningful mission, he states:

> Be true to your husbands and wives, and obedient to your masters and bombas. The Lord has made all ranks – kings, masters, servants, and slaves. God has punished the first Negroes by making them slaves, and your conversion will make you free, not from the control of your masters, but simply from your wicked habits and thoughts, and all that makes you dissatisfied with your lot.[36]

There are three central components of Colonial Christianity's coloniality of power. The categories are broadly located in the fields of soteriology, hermeneutics and ontology. *Soteriology is the most dominant category as it dictates the structure and trajectory of interpretation and ontology.* Collectively, the coloniality of power reduces salvation to the body and maintains this reductivism through the interpretation of scripture and the concomitant meaning of Black bodies.

The first component is soteriological. It is parsed from the statement, 'Your conversion will make you free, not from the control of your masters.' Here, salvation/conversion is folded into obedience to slavery's racial hierarchy and control. Moreover, the boundaries of salvation do not extend to equating blackness with whiteness or freedom in Christ with freedom from slavery. In other words, salvation has no social justice consideration. This part of the sermon also echoes Morgan Godwyn's justification of Christian slavery in the 1680 publication *The Negro's & Indian's advocate*.[37] As Katharine Gerbner notes in her evaluation of Christian slavery, before the advent of the abolition movement, the goal of Christian mission was always 'conversion' without manumission:

> Protestant theologians and missionaries drew on biblical descriptions of slavery as well as the idea of the godly household to encourage slave owners to assume responsibility for the spiritual lives of their enslaved labourers.... As missionaries faced opposition from slave owners, however, the meaning of Christian slavery shifted. Missionaries increasingly emphasised the beneficial aspects of slave

conversation.... They also sought to pass legislation that confirmed the legality of owning enslaved Christians. Over time, they integrated race into their argument for Christian slavery.[38]

The second component is interpretive. Specifically, a negative interpretation of Black presence in the Bible. It is parsed from 'God has punished the first Negroes by making them slaves.' Zinzendorf's hermeneutical strategy alludes to a racialized reading of the Curse of Ham narrative in Gen. 9.25-27. While having a contested history,[39] the text is deployed, here, as unequivocal legitimation for chattel slavery. As Wongi Park shows, a pro-slavery reading is made possible by four interpretive moves. First, the idea of the Bible's history of the division of 'races' into three groups (Gen. 9.18-19). Second, that Ham is inferior because he is Black (though this link is linguistically ludicrous). Third, that Japheth and his descendants (White Europeans) are superior. Fourth, that 'race' and racism are divinely decreed.[40] Marcus W. Shield proposes that the colonial thinking that produces the racialized interpretation of the Curse of Ham yields terror: violence and death to Black bodies. The death is experienced in reality and in literary interpretive terms.[41]

The final component of colonial Christianity concerns ontology, specifically the meaning of blackness. At no point in the statement is there an affirmation of blackness. Instead, we are told of their 'wicked habits and thoughts'. Also, that salvation will not free them from their unhealthy lust for freedom. Overall, the vision of blackness, even saved Black bodies, is inferior. In other words, Blacks experience a 'double fall'. It is the notion that Blacks are estranged from God by consequence of both their blackness and sinfulness.[42] The third category renders everything Black problematic. Anti-blackness is normalized. Furthermore, gender oppression exacerbates the 'double fall'. In addition to the demonization of their blackness and 'sinfulness', enslaved women were also subject to gendered subjugation. As Stella Dadzie demonstrates in her study of Black women during Caribbean slavery, sexual coercion and exploitation represent an additional structure of dehumanization.[43] Hence, in real terms, in the Christian imagination, Black women experienced a 'triple fall' – dehumanization in regard to race, gender and Christian thought.

Collectively, these components make legible the theological moorings of passive radicalism. The coloniality of power of colonial Christianity (soteriology, interpretation and ontology) restricts salvation to the locus of the Black body and discredits blackness in interpretation and being. All of which seeks to render impossible social justice consideration.

Action: Decolonial praxis

The final stage of the spiral is action or praxis. What new action is required? Well, if we accept that colonial Christianity is a coloniality of power, a meaningful response is decolonial thought and action. Decolonial thought or decoloniality describes the production of subjugated Black Christian knowledge in response to the coloniality or continued colonial suppression and destruction of colonized people's ways of knowing and being. It is an politico-epistemic project to reconstruct ways of knowing in the context of formerly colonized people.[44]

> Disrupt the logic of violent settler colonialism by foregrounding the colonial subaltern's different ideas, histories, identities, and beliefs in the production of knowledge out of lived experience.[45]

Decoloniality does not replace one hegemony with another. Instead, it seeks to identify 'multiple knowledges emerging from a re-linking with subjugated knowledge', which collectively constitute a pluriverse of thinking.[46]

Within the particularity of this study, decolonial thinking must yield an alternative soteriology, hermeneutic and Black ontology. A useful way for Black Pentecostals to conceive of this process is as a form of healing. Ultimately, decolonial thinking must repair the damage caused by colonial Christian thought. New decolonial categories of thought are identified in Chapter 3. These are social soteriology, contextual interpretation and loving blackness.

Illustration: Social Justice

An illustration of decolonial thinking is the track 'Social Justice' from the *Jamaican Bible Remix* album. The track's message promotes social justice from the location of the Black Church – in other words, an active-radical approach which sees salvation as both personal and social. In terms of tracking, the scripture track is taken from Luuk (Luke) 4 – Jesus' introduction to his ministry in his hometown of Nazareth. The message track is an exploration of the meaning of Jesus' appropriation of Isaiah 61 and the tradition of the Jubilee for Jesus' ministry. In short, the message track suggests that Jesus' interpretation signals the continuity and realization of the revolutionary social-economic practice of the Jubilee in his life and mission. The song continues by projecting the meaning of the Jubilee onto today's Black Church. As the chorus states, 'we don't have a faith if we don't have social justice.' At the end of the song, the reggae-dancehall gospel artist Witness performs a rap which contextualizes social justice in the life setting of everyday, ordinary Christians. The music track is inspired by the Bristol hip-hop sounds of the recording artist Roots Manuva.[47]

Robert– Witness, good to see you.
Witness – And you too, Robert.
Robert – This is a project about social justice.
Witness– OK.
Robert – I've been going to church for 40 years, and I've not heard one decent sermon about social justice.
Witness – Wow!
Robert – Yet, social justice is at the heart of the gospel. Jesus begins His ministry talking about social justice.
Witness – Well it's funny that you should say that, you know Robert, because I don't believe that the church don't know it. I just think that they ignore it, 'cause Luke 4 declares it.

JNT – Luuk 4
'Di Spirit a di Laad de pan mi,

kaaz im pik mi out

fi kyari gud nyuuz go gi puo piipl.

Im sen mi fi mek di prizna dem nuo se dem a-go frii, fi mek blain piipl nuo se dem a-go si agen,

fi mek piipl we a sofa nuo se dem naa go sofa fi eva.

An im pik mi out fi mek piipl nuo se dis a di taim wen di Laad a-go siev im piipl dem.'

Robert – This is one of the most important passages in the whole of the New Testament. Jesus begins his ministry, and what he says will determine how people understand him: what his life is about, what he is going to do. So, he needs to make an important impression on the people. He begins by using the language of Jubilee. For the people who were listening, the language of Jubilee was the language of revolution, revolution.

Chorus

We've got to know if we never touch this.
We don't have a faith if we don't have social justice. We've got to know if we never touch this.
We don't have a faith if we don't have social justice. (x2)

Robert – Jesus is drawing on a long tradition that goes all the way back to the book of Leviticus. In Leviticus 25, there is a tradition called the Sabbatical. Every seven years, slaves were supposed to be set free, debts were cancelled, and poor people could go and feed off the land. It was a revolutionary statement by God that was intended to ensure that there was social justice. That people wouldn't want, that all people would be able to share in the blessings of the Promised Land.

Then every seven, seven years, or every 49 years, there was the Jubilee. All the land that had been taken from your ancestors was given back to you. It was a revolutionary statement by God, suggesting that all people are equal, and in the sight of God, all the resources of the land should be shared out equally amongst the people. Nobody should want, nobody should be poor, and nobody should be oppressed.

But the people couldn't do it, and they are still not doing it today.

Chorus

We've got to know if we never touch this.
We don't have a faith if we don't have social justice. We've got to know if we never touch this.
We don't have a faith if we don't have social justice.

Witness – Ah ha, ok then, you tell me you're preaching the gospel, but is it the gospel or a good-spell? Binding the people making them unwell. Some of you need go and spell, as you're theologically unstable and still unable to meet the needs of the people. Some of you are so feeble. Kingsley (Burrell) died under police brutality, and only a few marched with me, church community, still sitting in their ivory singing their song, 'Close to Thee'. Hypocrisy, He came to set the captives free, those that are blind and cannot see. But what you see is not real to me. You need to be relevant to the point of people's needs, not your own needs. More social justice is what we need. So many mouths to feed. This empire building with egos to please, oh please! It's time to release, true social justice chorus please.

Chorus

We've got to know if we never touch this.
We don't have a faith if we don't have social justice. We've got to know if we never touch this.
We don't have a faith if we don't have social justice.

Robert – Many of us within the church were taught to ignore social justice. But it was bad advice. The Jubilee means social justice. To serve God means being involved in making a difference in this world, a difference in your country, a difference in your community.

Chorus

We've got to know if we never touch this.
We don't have a faith if we don't have social justice. We've got to know if we never touch this. We don't have a faith if we don't have social justice. (x4)

Conclusion

We church folk never mentioned the singing in the van again. After the event we made the return journey home. Once the street cleaners did their work, the roads were clear, there was no evidence of the earlier protest march and counter demonstration. At the forefront of our minds was the wonderful worship and fellowship we enjoyed that day, especially the quality of the preaching and the spiritual gifting of the worship team. For many in the van, the residual Christian coloniality had accomplished its additional work of devaluing the social experience of Black Christians. However, for me, the earlier event was an awakening of the limitations of the Black Church music and the necessity of a social justice tradition. A social justice tradition built on decoloniality requires a new Black Christian decolonial thinking, and this concern is the focus of the next chapter.

3

Testimony
Categories for Black Christian decolonial thinking

So far in this study, I have argued that Black liberation theologians appropriate musicality to communicate with the songwriters and worship leaders in the Black Church. Also, I have argued that the predicament for Black liberation theologians to address in song is the coloniality of Black Christian thought. Colonial Christianity 'colonized' Christian soteriology, interpretation and Black ontology. Conversely, the decolonization of contemporary gospel music requires decolonial thinking concerning the categories of soteriology, interpretation and Black ontology. This last concern, decolonial categories for thinking, is the focus of this chapter.

Decolonial turn

This chapter takes a theological 'decolonial turn'.[1] That is to say, it develops new ways of thinking from outside of the traditional Western theological-epistemological method. Rather than beginning the theological enterprise with propositional truth, Eurocentric Christian historiography or whiteness positionalities dressed up as a mythic universality,[2] the starting point is the Windrush generation Black Church 'testimony'. This way of knowing is the first move towards departing from colonial Christianity, as later, in Chapter 6, I will define 'delinking' and decolonial 'options' to complete the process.

I will begin by describing Black Church testimony as a source of knowledge production and outline the testimony's basic characteristics. Afterwards, I will defer to the testimony episteme, specifically, my personal testimony, to parse new decolonial ways of thinking about soteriology, interpretation and Black ontology. I conclude the chapter with an illustration from the *Jamaican Bible Remix* album. The track 'Manifesto' is proffered as an example of decolonial thinking in contemporary gospel music.

Testimony

Black Church testimonies emerge from 'testimony time.' It is the segment of the liturgy, often before the sermon, where the preacher invites believers to share their personal experiences of God in their lives with the congregation. Testimonies are gendered and dialogic ways of knowing, which produce alternative ideas for reflecting on the meaning of God. In churches dominated by male leadership, testimony time is one space where women in the church can speak freely about their faith journey. Female members of the congregation appropriate personal stories and experiences as hermeneutical templates for the meaning of God in their lives and also the community of faith. Testimonies are sometimes coded and, like the Anancy tradition of stories in Jamaica, gestures towards wider social realities marked by power relationships and the struggle to survive and thrive.[3] Hence, while deeply personal, testimonies are never outside of political consideration. Testimony time is not an echo chamber – it is not 'group think' about God: it is inherently dialogic. Through antiphonal communicative strategies (African diaspora call-and-response) ideas about God are explored, accepted and sometimes rejected. For instance, great testimonies are met with worlds of approval ('Amen', 'Glory' and 'Hallelujah') and questionable ones with silence. Testimonies about spectacular miracles, healings, amazing financial transformations and the visceral experience of the restoration of broken relationships all underline what K. A. Smith describes as Pentecostalism's 'affective narrative epistemology'.[4] As Keri Day reminds us, testimony also has prophetic potential. It is an opportunity for believers to articulate stories of faith that challenge structural forces and present an alternative vision of what God demands in the lives of believers and the community outside.[5] Testimony time also gestures towards an African past. Within the storytelling histories and cultures of the diverse African ethnicities trafficked to the Caribbean as enslaved peoples, testimony time is also a window into an older 'griot' tradition.[6] Sadly, though, today testimony time is under threat. New liturgies in Black churches, inspired by televangelism and megachurch performativity, have inadvertently reduced the opportunity for spontaneous congregational participation, which has long defined, empowered and distinguished the Black Church experience.[7]

Characteristics

Testimony as episteme has distinctive features. These are narrative theology, Christocentric and pastoral concern.

Narrative theology is a good way of contemplating testimony. It describes the telling of the story to produce knowledge about God.[8] While associated with the analysis of scripture in academic theology, narrative methods equally apply to the interpretation of all religious 'texts' including *the text of life* – personal experiences. Narrative theology has many purposes, but it is the epistemic role that is of interest here:

> The category of narrative has been used, among other purposes, to explain human action, to articulate the structures of human consciousness, to depict the identity of agents (whether human or divine), to explain strategies of reading (whether specifically for biblical texts or as a more general hermeneutic), to justify a view of the importance of 'story-telling' (often in religious studies through the language of 'fables' and 'myths'), to account for the historical development of traditions, *to provide an alternative to foundationalist and/or other scientific epistemologies,* and to develop a means for imposing order on what is otherwise (italics mine).[9]

Narrative theology has resonance with the Black Church. As Delroy Hall notes in his seminal work on Black British pastoral theology, texts of the Black experience, such as personal testimony, are integral to the Caribbean diaspora's discerning God's meaning in the world. [10]

Scripture

Christian scripture legitimates narrative as ways of knowing. Whether the story of the Exodus from Egypt or Jesus' engagement with what womanist theologian Jacquelyn Grant calls 'the little people',[11] scripture's narratives are the source of knowledge about God. As American theologian H. Richard Niebuhr reminds us, for the early church, the storytelling was integral to its preaching and mission:

> The preaching of the early Christian Church was not an argument for the existence of God nor admonition to follow the dictates of some common human conscience, unhistorical and super-social in character. It was primarily a simple recital of the great events connected with the historical appearance of Jesus Christ and a confession of what had happened to the community of disciples. Whatever it was that the church meant to say, whatever was revealed or manifested to it could be indicated only in connection with an historical person and events in the life of his community. The confession referred to history and was consciously made in history.[12]

The revelation of Jesus as Christ elucidates the Christian story. However, how we interpret the story of Jesus, that is, the reading strategy and its attendant sociopolitical and religious-cultural values, has practical and ministerial consequences. For instance, elsewhere, I propose an emancipatory reading strategy.[13] Emancipation has deep resonance in African Caribbean history and experience. Emancipation is an ongoing project from physical bondage to address the mental and discursive forms in the contemporary postcolonial context in Britain. Applied to scripture, emancipation is the norm or filter for theological sources. Emancipatory readings are those that pronounce God's liberation from all forms of bondage. Emancipatory reading strategies, however, do not disregard the 'texts of terror' or oppressive narratives within the Christian scriptures but choose to wrestle with them.[14]

Pastoral care

Finally, testimony as theological knowledge production is inherently pastoral. Testimony has the capacity to empower and encourage by 'telling what the Lord has done'.[15] For this reason, great testimonies go viral as a pastoral resource to be shared, discussed and debated as part of a more comprehensive communal pastoral care. Thus, testimony has the potential to extend knowledge and repair to the whole of the community.

Testimony epistemology delivers a discrete resource for forging a decolonial Christian thinking. Here, testimony is stories about experience with God, evaluated within a wider cultural context, to underline the emancipating significance of the life of Jesus. Furthermore, the testimony episteme has agency. As a pastoral resource, they enable believers to take stock of their lives, communities and the issues they face and consider prophetic actions.

Testify

I want to testify! That is to say, I will parse experiences to identify decolonial theological components. Three narratives are rehearsed because of their significance in my personal biography. I have told them often, in church, in the university classroom, during prison ministry, and on radio and television programmes. Their repetition underlines their heuristic importance for interpreting my life's unfolding. Yet, as is the case with all personal experiences, their interpretation is subjective and constantly open to critique and challenge from others.

The first testimony takes place in 1976. It occurs in the context of Black education in the state education system in the post-war years.[16] I recall one of my earliest experiences of intervention by my father, which, I suggest, signifies a social soteriology.[17] The second encounter is a dialogue with adherents of the Rastafari faith: an early 1980s experience of engaging in debates with 'dreads' about contextual interpretation. This revelation 'opened my eyes' to my inherited colonial hermeneutic and the necessity for a contextual interpretation. The final encounter is cultural, the empowering experience of meeting the African American scholars Randall Bailey and Jacquelyn Grant. Bailey and Grant were pioneers of trans-Atlantic Black theological dialogue in the early 1990s; both significantly contributed to the discipline's development in Europe. But in this retelling, I focus on their pedagogy of Black love, that is, the necessity of 'loving blackness'.

Social soteriology

'I will put you on a banana boat back to Jamaica!', snapped my design technology (DT) teacher, Mr Brady. The background to this encounter is unspectacular. I was struggling to prepare the design for a metal candleholder made from an aluminium square and screw to hold the candle aloft – most children are introduced to DT with this task. I could not make precise the 45-degree angles for each corner of the squared paper we were using for practice. When I asked the teacher for help, Mr Brady responded, 'If you don't get its design right, I will put you on a banana boat back to Jamaica!' As shocking as this might sound today, it was not a novel experience. As the educational scholarship of that period reveals, Mr Brady's behaviour is one of the numerous components of a racist educational system which, among other things, contributed to the educational sub-normalizing of vast swathes of African Caribbean pupils. As one qualitative study notes, Black pupils felt oppressed from the beginning:

> When discussing how they were perceived, many Black former students felt that teachers judged their academic potential based on their home address; whether they were from a single parent family; their parents' employment history and educational background, and, shockingly, even the colour of their skin.[18]

My classmates' responses to Mr Brady's outburst were mixed. Some children reacted with nervous laughter. Others, particularly the Black and Brown children, were embarrassed, afraid and fixed their gaze on their gridded design paper and were silent. The story does not end here, as I also recalled the encounter with Mr Brady to my parents at home in the afternoon.

My parents were disappointed by what I recalled but not surprised. I saw in their eyes a transgenerational pain born out of the weight of everyday racism. But neither was dismayed or disheartened. They were working-class first-generation colonial citizens. They did not possess the Black middle-class 'moral capital' that Black British academic Nicola Rollock would expose several decades later as a resource for Black parents to leverage power in the educational system. Instead, they relied on 'old school' first-generation tactics.[19] My mother doubled up on her protective prayers over me. As a devout woman her prayers were protest. In the words of the German theologian Dorothee Sölle, Mum partook in the creative disobedience tradition of prayer.[20] Her prayers were not passive or ethereal but proactive and dynamic. She frequently embellished their efficacy with the spiritual discipline of fasting. My father's response was dissimilar. His reading of scripture identified with the Caribbean Christian resistance tradition. Within this frame, 'faith without works' (Jas 2.17) is instrumental. With the calm of the Yoruba spirituality that gave birth to the 'cool' that Joel Dinerstein talks about, he informed me that the next time I was in Mr Brady's class, he would 'talk' with him.[21] 'Talk' did not mean having a casual conversation, but instead resolving a problem. My father's *praxis* was unusual. Not every Black Christian parent dared confront the school system or schoolteachers. Colonial deference taught him submission to White authority figures, but trade union activism rehabilitated him; he was emboldened. Organizing strikes, negotiating with bosses and representing the views of disgruntled workers transformed his outlook; he welcomed confrontation rather than seeking to suppress it. A physical presence underscored his politicking. He was a builder by trade, and his natural muscularity and athleticism were enhanced by years of physical labour and nourished by 'Ital' Jamaican food. Yet he did not need to overpower with his physicality. He knew how to 'chat bad'. As a 'Westmoreland man', schooled in the slave/post-slave country-folks oratory and wisdom traditions, he had the capacity to speak with a level of intensity and criticality to 'frighten the devil'. Despite their differences, my parents' approach found homeostasis. While my mother thought in terms of categories of prayer and fasting, Dad's faith was comfortable with an embodied confrontation with injustice.

My father confronted Mr Brady the next time I was in DT class. While I was busy trying to fix my model, my father knocked on the classroom door and asked in the most respectful way possible if he could have a 'talk' with Mr Brady. There were no security gates at schools in the 1970s, and it was not unusual for parents of children to seek out their progeny for legitimate reasons for leaving the school grounds during the day. The design technology block was at the front of the school, and access was unencumbered. Mr Brady left the class and returned a few minutes later. Upon his return, I noticed his face was red from blushing and his demeanour shaken. I discovered later from my father that the 'talk' was short and straightforward:

> My father: (In a calm voice) Did you tell my boy that you were going to put him on a banana boat back to Jamaica because he could not fix his project?
>
> Mr Brady: Yes, I did.
>
> My father: Are you going to put *me* on that boat too?
>
> Mr Brady: [Silence.]
>
> My father: Put me on that boat.
>
> Mr Brady: [Silence.]

My mother's prayers and my father's confrontation had a long-term structural impact: they literally 'saved' a class at that school from the viciousness of an individual who could educationally do what pan-Africanist Toyin Agbetu terms 'kill the dreams' of Black students.[22] Neither my classmates nor I received any more negative racialized comments from Mr Brady. Yet my father's physical presence (he physically outsized Mr Brady) leads to a potential reading of this incident as consent for a stereotypical aggressive Black masculinity. History matters. As I noted earlier, he was raised in colonial Jamaica, and therefore understood very well the nuances in deportment which distinguish physical intimidation from a strategic non-violence. In his mind, the latter informed his action.

The first story isolates a social soteriology. Social soteriology has identification with Jesus' mission, where the inbreaking of salvation takes place in concrete historical experience.[23] Social soteriology presupposes that salvation is never solely an individualistic enterprise. Jesus brings salvation to individuals to share it with others (Luke 19). Social soteriology is counter hegemonic. It is a challenge to those in authority (Lk. 17.14). In conversation with colonial Christianity, social soteriology refuses colonial Christianity's reduction of divine activity to the private spheres of the Black body, a cartography of salvific action that I term in the previous chapter as 'passive radicalism'. Social soteriology is not a new idea: it has roots in the social gospel tradition of Western Christianity and the radical nineteenth-century African Caribbean Christianity.[24] Underlining social soteriology is the recognition that God's emancipating power in scripture engages with peoples, nations and communities. Later in this study, I will elaborate on social soteriology to articulate womanist soteriology as the primary resource for decolonizing contemporary gospel music.

Contextual interpretation

'Do not talk to him "I-dren," do not talk to him!' said the Rasta at the top corner, on the top of the 21-route bus. I remember the moment distinctly because, as the Jamaicans say, 'Mi did shame' (I was embarrassed). The other Rastas, about four or five seated adjacent and ahead of him, obliged: they withdrew their goodwill, and the atmosphere changed from engaged to divorced – there was a 'dead silence' only broken by the hum of the diesel engine two decks below where we sat. It was the early 1980s; I was fifteen and travelling to the district of Alderman's Green from the city centre. For a part of the summer term, I caught the same bus home daily, like clockwork. The precision timing facilitated a coordinated 'reasoning session', or 'grounding', with a group of early twenties-aged 'dreads'. The Rastas and I sat on the top tier at the back of the bus because we thought it was the peak location and, therefore, the symbolic place for 'higher learning'.

It was a critical time for Rastafari in post-diaspora history just before the mainstream commercialization of their aesthetics and the diminishing of the religious moorings of their attire. The Rastas' tams (hats), beards and wrist bracelets distinguished them from the other Black workers in the same industry (dressed only in regulation dark-blue overalls and black steel-toe boots).[25] Like most Black men of their generation, structural racism and classism in the school system afforded them few opportunities for meaningful post-sixteen education, such as winning a university place. In recent years, the 'Small Axe' series of BBC films by the film-maker Steve McQueen identifies this educational 'segregation' in the documentary *Subnormal*.[26] All the Rastas alighted in Wood End, a notorious working-class council estate. In contrast, I wasn't living in the suburbs. My family resided in an upper working-class area, 'one notch up' the property ladder and three roads away from the borders of Wood End.

The Rastas and I compared the reading strategies of Rastafari and Christianity. The Rastas articulated a 'dread hermeneutic'.[27] Dread hermeneutics describes an interpretive lens which correlates scripture with Black experience. It is a reader-response strategy prioritizing Black identity, history and culture.[28] It is a highly reflexive approach which refused to separate interpreter from their social and historical context. Unlike colonial Christianity, it does not seek to represent its particularity as universal but instead engages in dialogue or reasoning with others to test the validity and truthfulness of the interpretation. In opposition, I appealed to two Black Church interpretive practices. Neither had any space for the exploration nor foregrounding of identity. These were *concordism* and *spiritual interpretation*. I was taught to only read the surface of the Bible and look for parallels and correlations with my own life, but only as a universal, disembodied reader. Likewise, a spiritual hermeneutic taught me to view interpretation as mystical and transcendent with few, if any, concrete or immanent implications. The combined effect was that I did not consider the contextuality of scripture or my social location as unnegotiable features of biblical interpretation.[29]

But this conviviality did not last long. After a few months of taking advantage of their 'coming-down time' from the 'hard graft' of manual labour, the conversation channels abruptly closed. The Rastas presumed that I would not change my viewpoint, not even for the sake of compromise (I was young), and therefore they suspended their participation. Eventually, one of the Rastas said to the group, 'Do not talk to him I-dren, do not talk to him!'

The second category is contextual interpretation. The conversation with the Rastas ceased, but the impact was enduring. The long-term benefit was an introduction to new reading strategies, precisely, consideration of the broader sociopolitical and religious-cultural contexts in the life of the text and interpreter. In opposition to the interpretive schemes of colonial Christianity, my introduction to 'dread' hermeneutics underlined the role of the reader in interpretation. Race, class, gender and social history all contribute to how we read the text; there is no neutral reader. We must also consider how social and historical factors inform the construction of biblical texts. As Mitzi Smith notes, this di-unital focus is the practice of reading the text inter(con)textually.[30] A helpful way of understanding Smith's hermeneutic is as a contextual theological interpretive method:

> Contextual theology takes two things seriously: the experience of the *past* (recorded in Scripture and preserved and defended in tradition) and the experience of the *present,* that is, *context* (individual and social experience, secular or religious culture, social location, and social change. . . . Contextual theology is done when the experience of the past engages the present context.[31]

Later in this study, Black language, specifically the JNT version, is presented as the fulfilment of contextual interpretation.

Loving blackness

I quit the PhD on Friday but reversed the decision the following Monday. The catalyst for the change of mind was a chance meeting with Professors Randall Bailey and Jacquelyn Grant. I met these distinguished scholars at a conference in Sheffield, England during the summer of 1992. The Methodist minister Inderjit Bhogal organized the conference as part of his work with what was then a dedicated contextual theology unit associated with the University of Sheffield called the Urban Theology Unit. The purpose of the meeting was a trans-Atlantic theological dialogue to exchange ideas between African American and Black British ministers and theologians. At that time, Jacquelyn and Randall worked as academics at the Interdenominational Theological Seminary in Atlanta, Georgia, United States. Within the history of Black theology in Britain, both were 'pioneers' for extending the reach of Black theology into the UK. Grant was a missionary for womanist theology. She was the first womanist theologian to travel to Britain and converse with the first generation of Black theological students. In response to our 'Macedonian call', she would return, unselfishly, after Sheffield to the UK to present papers at the Queen's Foundation in Birmingham. Bailey would also return on many occasions to support our developing Black theological project. As a Hebrew Bible scholar and ideological critic, his exploration of power dynamics in the text resonated with fragments of the left-leaning undercurrents in our African Caribbean working-class political culture.

Randall Bailey made me reverse my decision. After I read my paper at the conference, Randall began by asking if the fragment I read was the core of my PhD. I explained that it was but also that I had decided not to pursue the research. He pressed me further to find out why I had made the decision. I rehearsed my reasoning. I withdrew out of frustration. As a Black research student, I felt a great sense of loneliness and isolation. And I was struggling to convince myself and others of the viability of my thesis – a correlation of Rastafari and Pentecostal Christianity in pursuit of political theology (I had taken to heart the Rastas' criticism on the 21 bus). I started to think it was better to quit than to stay the course. Randall called Jacquelyn over to our conversation at that point. I think his pastoral intuition called for a witness. His response was emphatic, endearing – and slightly problematic from the perspective of Pentecostal piety. 'Your supervisors don't know shit', he retorted. 'You get back on that programme, and I/we will supervise you.' Now, I didn't think Randall was disparaging the academic ability of my supervisor(s), or their commitment to supporting Black students, but instead articulating the importance of insider knowledge and lived experience for the research process; that is, an affirmation of Black research, Black people and blackness in general. What he said caught me off-guard, but I was nonetheless overwhelmed, grateful and humbled at the show of support for my work and its potential. Bailey and Grant were true to their word. Not only did they maintain contact after the conference to monitor my studies, but they also became mentors and friends.

Bailey's intervention was an example of 'loving blackness'. Loving blackness speaks to the value of Black people's experience. In the particularity of this case, Bailey was valuing my experience and encouraging me to love it too. Loving blackness has resonance for Black ontology because loving blackness places love at the centre of Black life in the post-slave world.[32] This is a resistance. As J. Kameron Carter notes, theological anthropology in Europe, upon encountering Black bodies in the so-called age of discovery, was racialized to secure a superior place for White bodies and the demeaning of Black bodies.[33] Black bodies were relegated to a second tier of human development and blackness the subject of scorn, belittlement and non-being. As mentioned in the previous chapter, this form of anti-blackness is represented in a colonial Christian negative Black ontology. The consequence of this negative colonial history is still with us. Caribbean theologian Carlton Turner identifies the immediate impact as 'self-negation', a refusal and repudiation of all things Black – such as valuing Black history, culture and politics.[34] Loving blackness, therefore, is the antidote to colonial Christianity's anti-blackness.

> Loving Blackness as political resistance transforms our ways of looking and being, and thus creates the conditions necessary for us to move against the forces of domination and death and reclaim Black life.[35]

Loving blackness has diverse social modes of operation. On the one hand, it is defined as a radical commitment by Black people to affirm the histories, cultures and politics of Black people, and a commitment to Black business, and producing Black families, including choosing to love other Black people romantically.[36] On the other hand, loving blackness is a personal internal transformation, which does not require external verification such as promoting lateral Black romantic relationships or supporting Black communities, businesses or students.[37] Furthermore, for some, loving blackness is not exclusive to people racialized as 'Black'. It is a political orientation committed to working intersectionally against oppression.

Loving blackness is the third decolonial category. It is the affirmation of Black life and Black being. Loving blackness has theological moorings. It is not outside of the Christian tradition because loving blackness is an affirmation of the inclusivity of divine creation (Gen. 1.1). Furthermore, if the incarnation is also an affirmation of all bodies in the plan of salvation, then loving blackness is also inside the incarnation (Jn 1.14). Loving blackness, therefore, is not essentialist or exclusive. It is simply a decolonial theological corrective. Later in this study, I will focus on history, specifically the history of slavery as the tool for expressing this third decolonial resource in contemporary gospel music.

Decolonial theological thinking

I coalesce these three testimonies, that is, social soteriology, contextual interpretation and loving blackness, as decolonial theological thinking.[38] A useful way of discerning their operation is as frames. Frames are predetermined explanations of the world that allow us to make sense of current events. While frames are often linguistic and metaphorical in structure, they are also distinctively theological in their form. All theological categories, in one way or another, operate as frames. My strategy here is not to present frames as universal but instead as subjective and inherently dialogic. Concerning this last point, and borrowing from Hans-Georg Gadamer's theory of ideas, we might say that a frame is always in the pursuit of greater understanding:

> a single idea in by itself is not knowable at all. . . . In any insight an entire nexus or we of ideas is involved.[39]

Colonial frames exist in Christian music.[40] For instance, Becca Whitla's study of congregational music in Canada demonstrates the contingency of empire's thinking with the theology of songs. In the postcolonial metropole, singing, she suggests, is always inside of empire.[41] Conversely, this project seeks the opposite, to 'out' empire in song. This task is discussed in greater depth in the two following chapters, which explore the presence of colonial Christian thinking in contemporary gospel music in Britain.

Illustration: Manifesto

A useful example of the decolonial categories at work in contemporary gospel music is the song 'Manifesto'. The song styles the Lord's Prayer as a political manifesto. Viewed this way, Jesus' teachings represent a social soteriology entangled in the sociopolitical world of the first century. The song makes contemporaneous the Lord's Prayer with discrete struggles for social justice today – an inter(con)textual interpretation. Finally, the track gestures towards loving blackness but loosely. The fifth 'manifesto' commitment mentioned in the song is to be part of an ongoing social justice in Britain that naturally includes loving blackness. The scripture track is a sample from the JNT Lord's Prayer in 'Luuk' (Luke). The message track is a sociopolitical reading of the Lord's Prayer inspired by the scholarship of Obery Hendricks.[42] Roni Size's drum and bass style is the inspiration for the music. [43]

Robert – And now, a party-political broadcast on behalf of the Jesus Party from Luke Chapter 11. Chorus
Marlene Kerr – Manifesto, need you to know. (x2)
JNT – Luuk 11

Wan die Jiizas did de somwe a prie. Afta im don, wan a im speshal falara dem se tu im se, 'Laad, shuo wi ou fi prie.'

Robert – This isn't really an issue of prayer.
Every Jew knew how to pray.
They were taught how to pray three times a day.
Instead, what's at stake here is what they are meant to pray for? What are Jesus' disciples meant to stand for?

Jesus obliges them and introduces *five* commitments that form to make up his manifesto. Chorus

Marlene Kerr – Manifesto, need you to know.
If there is hope, then we got to show it in the way that we live today. More than words let the hungry know it, we got to wipe all the debt away. Manifesto, need you to know.

Commitment number 1

JNT – "Laad, shuo wi ou fi prie, laik ou Jan shuo fi im falara dem ou fi prie." Jiizas tel dem se, 'Wen unu prie, unu fi se:"Faada, Faada, Faada."'

Robert – This is a god for all, a god for all.
A god who is not partial and a god who is inclusive.

Commitment number 2

JNT – mek piipl av nof rispek fi yu an yu niem, Mek di taim kom wen yu ruul iina evri wie.

Robert – Respect God's name, you do God's business here on earth. But what is that business?

Commitment number 3

JNT – Evridie gi wi di fuud we wi niid. **Robert** – Feed the poor.

Commitment number 4

JNT – Aadn wi fi aal a di rang we wi du, kaa wi paadn piipl we du wi rang tu. **Robert** – Cancel the debts.

And finally, commitment number 5

JNT – An no mek wi fies notn we wi kaaz wi fi sin. **Robert** – Never ever give up on the struggle! Chorus

Marlene Kerr – Manifesto, need you to know.
If there is hope, then we got to show it in the way that we live today. More than words let the hungry know it, we got wipe all the debt away. Manifesto, need you to know.

Robert – Could it be that this is much more than just a simple prayer?
For the people who were listening to Jesus, who were experiencing hunger.
Who found themselves in debt to the Roman administration. Who found themselves in debt to the Temple authorities. That this was a manifesto: a proposal for change in their lives introduced by God *herself*.

Chorus

Marlene Kerr – Manifesto, need you to know. (x2)
If there is hope, then we got to show it in the we live today.
More than words let the hungry know it, we got wipe all the debts away. (x6)

Conclusion

In Part I, I have identified the reasons for the failure of Black liberation theology to engage with the songwriters and worship leaders of the Black Church and proffered a communicative strategy, a contemporary gospel album. The album seeks to address a coloniality of power, that is, the continued influence of colonial Christianity. To develop a decolonial response, I appropriate the testimony tradition of African Caribbean Christianity as a way of knowing to produce new decolonial categories for thinking about the doing of contemporary gospel music. My personal testimonies give rise to a new thinking and doing, that is, a social soteriology, contextual interpretation and loving blackness.

Part II contours the residue of colonial Christianity in contemporary gospel music. First, Chapter 4 develops a theory for its presence in the Windrush generation churches (1948–70), then Chapter 5 examines how it is reconfigured in the post-diaspora contemporary gospel music context (1971–2020).

Part II

Colonial thought in Black British gospel music

4

Roots Manuva

Colonial Christianity in the songs of the Windrush generation

Previously, I identified colonial Christianity as the root cause of the failure of Black Church music to produce songs of social justice (see Chapter 2). However, the next question to consider going forward is this: 'How pervasive is colonial Christianity in contemporary gospel music?' What evidence do we have for a colonial Christian continuity in the songs? That is to say, are there any echoes of the colonial Christian categories at play in contemporary gospel music? These questions are foregrounded in the chapters in Part II, and to answer them, I will contour a history of contemporary gospel music in Britain. There are two parts to this appraisal. First, I will reflect on the origins of contemporary gospel music in the aftermath of the arrival of West Indian colonial citizens in Britain (late 1940s to 1960s). Further, in Chapter 5, I will turn my attention to the second and third generations or post-diaspora Black Church experience (1970s to 2020).

This chapter explores the continuity of colonial Christian thought in post-war contemporary gospel music. To make legible colonial Christian thought, the chapter folds the emergence of Black Church music into the hostile social world of post-war Britain. The hostile social world refers to domestic secular and religious racisms, mediated through discourses of immigration, racialization and discrimination. As ethnomusicology asserts, music and song are inextricably entangled with the machinations of a social context and its cultures,[1] and therefore, it is legitimate to place these songs in conversation with the social predicament as a means of parsing the significance of the former – specifically, the theological ideas that the songs project within the social situation and also the *ideological* role which the songs perform. The first Black Church music canon is varied. Many of the songs are a carry-over from the Caribbean; others are imported from the gospel music recording industry, and some new songs are created by the first gospel bands from the Black churches. Combined, these sources convey a distinct musical response to the hostile social world.

The historiography employed herewith departs from previous studies of music in Black churches in three distinct ways. First, I do not seek to engage in a customary comparative analysis with African American contemporary gospel music.[2] While possessing an appreciation for African American gospel music, as this is a contextual study, I foreground the performance of Black British Church music(s). Second, this study departs from the emerging theomusicology school of Pauline Muir and Monique Charles. My interest in songs is textual rather than sonic.[3] Finally, as mentioned earlier, I am concerned with the entanglement of a song's themes and words and the prevailing social context. Precisely, I am concerned with how ideas about God in song relate to the West Indian predicament in Britain.[4] The illustration at the end of the chapter is a critical reflection on the Windrush generation experience in Britain: the track 'Incarnation: No Blacks, No Irish, No Dogs'.

Hostile social world

West Indian Christians arrived in Britain in the post-war years as British colonial citizens – a right bestowed upon them as subjects of the British Empire.[5] However, the government challenged their suitability to settle soon after the arrival of the *Empire Windrush* and the first cohort of several hundred colonial citizens in 1948. Contrary to popular belief, West Indians were not the largest group of immigrants to arrive between 1948 and 1962 (before immigration controls). About 115,000[6] people from the West Indies arrived in Britain. They were outnumbered by around 200,000 from South Asia, 345,000 continental Europeans and hundreds of thousands of Irish-born people across Britain.[7] Most West Indians settled in areas thirsty for manual labour, such as London, the West Midlands, Manchester, the East Midlands and West Yorkshire.

The British government was caught unawares by the arrival of the first cohort of West Indians onboard the *Empire Windrush*. The ship's docking at Tilbury on 21 June was neither planned nor expected. In fact, efforts were made previous to their arrival to keep them out. A series of laws made during the inter-war and post-war years were designed to ensure that Black workers left Britain: they were not supposed to be returning. With little room for manoeuvre (forced removal was not an option), the government articulated a contradictory message which placed sufficient doubt in the public sphere to stoke negative feelings towards the Black settlers. But what was the view of the host churches, the mainstream congregations in the regions where the colonial citizens settled? Rather than radically opposing the emerging racialized discourse, these churches are tainted by it.[8]

Problematizing

The government proceeded to problematize the arrival of West Indians in Britain – they were a crisis to be resolved.[9] There was little attempt by the political leadership to win a battle of 'hearts and minds' to ensure that the settlers had a smooth entry and undoubted welcome in Britain. Instead, the government's response was contradictory. On the one hand, the government acknowledged that the West Indians had a right to settle in Britain, but on the other, they did not want them to stay or others to follow. The prime minister, Clement Attlee, exemplified this fudge when he stated, duplicitously, that the immigrants had a right of settlement but implored them not to do so.[10] The problematizing of the West Indians is instantaneous with their arrival and echoes long-standing racialized tropes. For instance, on the same day the *Empire Windrush* docked in Tilbury, a group of eleven Labour MPs wrote to the prime minister to voice their concerns over the 'discord and unhappiness' the arrival would cause. The letter reads:

> Dear Prime Minister,
> May we bring to your notice the fact that several hundreds of West Indians have arrived in this country trusting that our government will provide them with food, shelter, employment and social services, and enable them to become domiciled here. . . . Their success may encourage other British subjects to imitate their example, and this country may become an open reception centre for immigrants not selected in respect to health, education, training, character, customs. . . . The British people fortunately enjoy a profound unity without uniformity in their way of life and are blest by the absence of a colour racial problem. An influx of coloured people domiciled here is likely to impair the harmony, strength and cohesion of our public and social life and to cause discord and unhappiness among all concerned.[11]

Little seems to have been learnt from the recent history. A debt was owed to these citizens. Many of those aboard *Empire Windrush* were ex-service people. West Indian servicemen and women had answered the 'motherland's call' to lay down their lives for Britain and her allies during the Second World War.[12] Hence, as the activist and author Akala notes, after the war, in practical legal terms, it became easier for former enemies of Britain from Europe to enter and settle in Britain than it was for the Black West Indians who had fought alongside the British armed forces.[13]

The West Indians' arrival was furnished with an official government inquiry. The administration tasked the Colonial Secretary, Arthur Creech Jones, to ascertain why the colonial citizens had arrived and what could be done to prevent another such occurrence.[14] However, the inquiry's scope for redress was limited. There was no turning back the tide. The government was constrained by its political priorities. Efforts to unite the old empire under a new Commonwealth of nations inadvertently created a legal framework for authorizing all colonial citizens' settlement in the mother country.[15] It would take the passing of a decade before the political and social environment was conducive to 'racialized' immigration controls. But from the outset, the government firmly established a narrative of the Black arrivals as a 'problem'. This narrative was reproduced in the popular press, and the new racialized *representation* did not go unnoticed. Stuart Hall, in his exploration of images of Black post-war settlement, shows how colonial citizens as 'problem' is concretized in the British press and public imagination. He identifies several articles and headlines to reveal their discriminatory content. For example, a headline in the *Picture Post* from 1956, 'Thirty thousand colour problems', portrayed the colonial citizens as a social timebomb.[16]

What was the response from Britain's White churches? How did they cope with the problematization of colonial citizens? On the one hand, as Christians, they had to speak out against racism, but on the other, these churches had no awareness of their historic racial prejudice.[17] The consequence of this contradiction was that while believing in a gospel of equality and inclusion, they did not have the Christian imagination to furnish an unreserved welcome. This failure is identified by David Muir's study of the White Christian response to the 'Windrush generation'.[18] Muir unearths articles in the *Church Times* that reflect a complex response. White Christians acknowledged the racial hostility faced by the West Indians. Headlines such as 'Coloured outcasts of Stepney' (9 June 1950) and 'Stranger in our midst' (18 March 1955) gave voice to Black alienation. Yet Muir also provides evidence of an inconsistent welcome. An early study of the church's response to the colonial citizens' presence acknowledges the experience of West Indians in the face of the Church of England. It notes how for many the response was 'like discovering that one's mother is a liar and a hypocrite'.[19]

Racialization

Racialization is also a feature of the government's response to the *Empire Windrush*'s arrival.[20] The racialization of African peoples has a long history.[21] Rather than declining with the post-Holocaust international consensus against racialism, racial reasoning evolves from biological determination to new cryptic cultural forms in mid-twentieth-century Britain.[22] Cultural racism denotes where culture is infused with the fixity of 'race', so that discourse on Black cultures maintains the pernicious pseudo-science thinking of biological racism. Cultural racism is evident in the post-war debate over the suitability of West Indian labour.

There are several examples of governmental *cultural racism*. It appears in the interdepartmental working party established in autumn 1948 to 'enquire into the possibility of employing in the United Kingdom surplus manpower of certain Colonial territories in order to assist the manpower situation in this country and to relieve unemployment in those Colonial territories'. As Kennetta Perry shows in her study of immigration, records from the correspondence between government departments reveal the presence of a cultural-racial logic underlying a spurious case for denying Blacks entry to Britain.[23] For instance, considering West Indian labour's suitability in the textile industry, an argument was made by employers that Black women lacked the intellectual ability to sustain the rigours of work in Lancashire. Similarly, in another government paper, West Indian labour's suitability is questioned on an alleged dubious morality.[24] Referring to West Indian women, it was noted, 'the moral standards of the young women in the Isles are quite different from those that prevail in this country'.[25] The question of public safety was also raised and racialized. In another branch of government, cultural racism emerged in a discussion in a working party on the 'Employment in the U.K. of Surplus Colonial Labour', convened in early 1949 to address the problem of West Indian labour. The report acknowledges that the West Indies provides a viable source of work for the British economy but cautions against the recruitment of Black men as they are perceived as troublesome:

> The worst troubles concern men who settle in unsatisfactory districts and get into street fights owing to quarrels about coloured men associating with White women, etc.[26]

Racialization also features in the reception of West Indians in Britain's host churches. It is founded on a presupposition that Blacks would be better served by going to the emerging Black churches. This Christianized 'sociobiological' racism (Blacks with Blacks and Whites with Whites in worship) is evident in stories told by founding members of the Black churches – for instance, in a documentary I originated and developed with BBC Bristol in 2001 on the history of Black churches in Britain ('Black Messiah', BBC 4). The founders of independent Black churches we interviewed speak openly about a discrete 'push factor': a gentle Christian racialized discourse which implied that they were better off worshipping with their own 'kind'.[27] In sum, one of the drivers for the emergence of Black majority churches in Britain is the gentile hostility of White churches that drove many colonial citizens away. Not all Black people left. A determined cohort of Black Anglicans, Methodists and United Reformed Church members stayed put and fought to be accepted within their respective denominations.

Discrimination

The government's problematizing and racialization are accompanied by broader anti-Black discrimination. Anti-blackness is particularly evident in the essential areas of social necessities of employment and housing. The first wave of West Indians was the most qualified and accomplished – less than 20 per cent were unskilled – yet ability and talent were no protection for underemployment and poor housing.[28]

Discrimination in employment is captured in a classic Pathé News report on Caribbean migration in 1955. Awkwardly entitled 'Our Jamaican Problem', the news piece narrates a set of contradictions in a West Indian settlement.[29] The new Black presence, while 'a national controversy', is no reason for West Indians *not* to have the right of settlement. Britain is no 'Eldorado', but the film depicts one family living comfortably in a flat in Lambeth. This carefully worded statement hints at the limited employment opportunities.[30] The narrator notes that one of the men featured (Samuel David) 'is a machinist, though he is a qualified commercial teacher'. These contradictions disguise a more sinister force at play. A forensic analysis of discrimination in the post-war years by Clive Harris and Winston James unearthed an official government policy to restrict West Indian labour. Government agents spread misinformation in the Caribbean that jobs were unavailable in Britain. For the West Indians who did arrive, they influenced the labour exchanges to assign them to the least attractive job roles despite their previous work experience or qualifications.[31]

Housing was another arena for discrimination. In London and other major industrial cities, an unofficial 'colour bar' (racial discrimination) restricted the areas where West Indians might reside and inadvertently left them vulnerable to exploitation by unscrupulous landlords.[32] A critical study by Ruth Glass lifts the veil on housing and immigration to reveal unofficial segregation in the 1950s. Glass discovered over 300 housing adverts discriminating against West Indian tenants in a weekly West London paper between November 1958 and January 1959. Some of the adverts were unambiguous. They read 'Europeans only' or 'No Coloured Applicants'.[33] The Pathé News report 'Our Jamaican Problem' also confirms the housing predicament. It states that many West Indians face crowded conditions, some living 'six or seven to a room'. One can assume that this journalistic language is code for restricted housing opportunities and poor sanitary conditions. Segments of the British press seized upon the image of housing deprivation to stereotype Black settlement. In 1955 in Birmingham, one of the local papers began to refer to Black settlement in the Handsworth suburb of the city as 'little Harlem'[34] and stoked fears of age-old racist anxieties expressed in the discourse of miscegenation:

> How many coloured men are there in Birmingham. . . . Where will it all end? Marrying White girls? Is Birmingham going to become a coffee-coloured town?[35]

Finally, racial discrimination also features in church life. Racialization led to open discrimination. *Only now is this shameful past being acknowledged.*[36] For example, in December 2020, St Paul's Church in Clapham, London, one of the churches famous for eighteenth-century anti-slavery campaigning, held a service of apology for its history of racial discrimination. The focus of the service was the act of discrimination in 1955 against a Mr Carmel Jones, a seventeen-year-old who had recently arrived from Jamaica. *His rejection did not, however, limit his aspiration.* He went on to resist and re-exist and founded one of the largest credit unions in Britain, the Pentecostal Credit Union. The review of the apology in the press notes:

> Yesterday the current vicar of St Paul's Rev Jonathan Boardman presided over a moving and heartfelt service of Absolution for the despicable act of racial exclusion perpetrated in that place in 1955. Rev Jones attended the service by Zoom and his address was read to the church by his daughter Elaine Bowes. In accepting the apology Rev Jones said that he had forgiven that act of humiliation many years ago and viewed the event as positively life altering and no less than The Holy Spirit working in his life as it had led him to The Pentecostal Church, to him meeting the woman that would be his wife of 63 years and had provided the inspiration for him founding The Pentecostal Credit Union 25 years later. He said that reflecting he was happy, and deeply grateful for the experience and concluded with a verse of scripture from

Proverbs 17 v 9 'Love prospers when a fault is forgiven but dwelling on it separates close friends'.[37]

Resistance

West Indian colonial citizens in Britain resisted the oppressions they encountered. They were not passive; they constructively responded to the hostile social world. A significant milestone in West Indian activism's history was the disturbing summer in 1958. A series of racial attacks on Black communities in Nottingham in the East Midlands and Notting Hill in London was a catalyst for action. The racial attacks underscored the necessity for Black self-help, organization and collective action by *all* of the Commonwealth citizens. West Indians organized in diverse ways. They mobilized cultural traditions to counter the state's problematization. For example, to extend the hand of interracial friendship in London they established the forerunner to the Notting Hill Carnival that took place early in 1959.[38] In response to the racialization they encountered, West Indians promoted solidarity to accompany their interracial friendship. They formed anti-racism bodies and organizations such as the West Indian Standing Conference (WISC).[39] Mobilization was not just exclusive to members of the Caribbean community.[40] For instance, in 1961, Birmingham Blacks and Asians, inspired by a visit by Martin Luther King in 1964, allied and marched together under the banner of the Co-ordinating Committee Against Racial Discrimination (CARD).[41] Finally, in response to discrimination in the labour and housing markets, West Indians challenged the legality of the colour-bar and organized finance to buy their own homes, respectively. A significant employment victory was secured in 1963 in Bristol when a group of Black citizens, inspired by the tactics of the African American Civil Rights Movement, organized a bus boycott. Their actions shamed the bus company into lifting its unofficial colour bar and provided a successful template for Black political action.[42] To resist housing abuse by securing their own properties, many formed financial cooperatives ('pardner hand')[43] to purchase houses.

Black women

Especially pertinent were the efforts of Black women. For instance, the pan-Africanist Amy Ashwood Garvey, the first wife of the Jamaican Black Nationalist

Marcus Garvey, contributed to numerous campaigns in Britain, the Caribbean, and the United States. Garvey was an influential figure in the Pan African Congress in Manchester in 1945, organized demonstrations in response to the shocking racist murder of Kelso Cochrane in London in 1959 and collaborated with the Caribbean activist Claudia Jones in a myriad of campaigns against racism. Jones, who is best known for establishing the Notting Hill Carnival's forerunner, also helped to found one of Britain's first Black newspapers, *The West Indian Gazette*, in 1958.[44] Black women's leadership was also evident in the fledgling Black Church movement. Almost every African Caribbean denomination had a plethora of 'church mothers' who opened their homes, evangelized on the streets and raised money to buy the first church buildings. As Elaine Foster wrote in the 1980s, women's leadership was an inverted pyramid: beneath the apex of male leadership, an army of women were leading congregations from the base.[45]

Black Church

The founding of the Black Church is Black resistance. The motivations of the pioneering 1950s founders were complex. Missionary aspirations and cultural differences in worship were important factors, *but I propose that the primary driver was resistance to the racism they experienced from established churches.* If there was no racism in the Christian religion in Britain, then the vast majority of the first generation of colonial citizens would have readily blended into White churches and, similarly, even the Black churches with designs on establishing new multicultural denominations would have more resembled the multi-ethnic communities in which they were originated. The first generation of Christians were not Black Nationalists or cultural essentialists; on the contrary, they were colonial subjects, Christians who believed in inclusivity and also a dose of deference to Whites. Nevertheless, by rejecting them, the host churches lost opportunity for an injection of diversity, energy and a renewed passion for Christ. There is a certain irony at work here. Dogged by centuries of racialized Christian discourse, White Christians who had prayed for a Christian revival in post-war Britain did not see God's gift of renewal in the arrival of their Black brothers and sisters.

Many West Indian Christians chose to resist Christian racism from *within* the host White churches. Their politics was intricate. As I noted some time ago in 'What Kind of Freed Slaves Worship in the Slavemaster's Church When Slavery Is Over?', many West Indians remained in White churches for various reasons.

Some believed they could negotiate with the church to produce an anti-racist theology.[46] Others felt at home despite the oppression(s) and were not perturbed. In other words, at best, they are a holy remnant or, at worst, a group who were prepared to legitimate their own oppression. Intriguingly, as the BBC Panorama documentary 'Is the Church Racist' (2021), a programme I contributed to, demonstrates, the battle for racial justice in the mainstream churches is yet to be won. Seventy-plus years on from the arrival of the *Empire Windrush*, the Anglican Church has only just acknowledged its failure to welcome the colonial citizens. Speaking at Synod in February 2020, Justin Welby, the Archbishop of Canterbury, responded to stories of unwelcome towards West Indians and offered an apology: 'Personally, I am sorry and ashamed. I'm ashamed of our history, and I'm ashamed of our failure. I'm ashamed of our lack of witness to Christ.'[47] Ben Lindsay's study of Black experience in contemporary evangelical churches further underlines the persistence of racialized oppression in Britain's mainstream churches and also the willingness of Black people to *confront* it.[48] In contrast, the West Indians who established their own places of worship were 'cut from a different cloth'. These pioneers were unprepared to settle for the unreformed colonial Christianity of the White churches. While they were not learned people, in an academic sense, they possessed a *spiritual intelligence* sensitive to the presence of spiritual malevolence and a strategy for resisting it.

Black Church resistance is not realized in political action or social justice campaigns. Even at the height of African American civil rights campaigning in the 1960s, these congregations had no desire to become British affiliates. Instead, these churches looked inwards (passive radicalism) for their adherents' welfare, support and psychological empowerment. Appropriating the neologism originated by Todne Thomas, these fledgling congregations reinvented Christian resistance as diaspora 'Kincraft': a process of extended familial support, mental health and community formation.[49]

Hailed

There are several reasons for the Black Church's passive resistance. Denominational constraints limited them. After all, many are affiliated with Euro-American parent denominations with an aversion to political participation.[50] Yet, the African American-led denominations such as the Church of God in Christ, even without the Euro-American parent church's constraints, also declined direct political contribution and engagement. Educational attainment is another possible cause, as many first-generation preachers and church leaders had a rudimentary education. However, they were no different in educational status from the swaths of men and women who organized for change in the nascent Black British political movements outside of the church. The final reason is discursive. The church was constrained by a dominant source of theological knowledge – its canon of songs. It is this factor that I want to explore further.

I propose that a key reason is the influence of its songs. The songs have an ideological role – to maintain the colonial Christian presence. My argument here is that the canon of songs *interpolates* the Black Church. Interpellation describes the way that a person is 'hailed' or recruited as one would flag down a taxi driver by sticking out an arm to get a lift.

> I shall then suggest that ideology 'acts' or 'functions' in such a way that it 'recruits' subjects among the individuals (it recruits them all), or 'transforms' the individuals into subjects (it transforms them all) by that very precise operation which I have called *interpellation* or hailing, and which can be imagined along the lines of the most commonplace every day police (or other) hailing: 'Hey, you there!'.[51]

Black Christians are 'tractor-beamed' by colonial Christianity away from social engagement, and the songs' lyrics are of paramount significance. The evidence is laid bare in the lyrics of the canon of songs listened to and sung by the Windrush generation of Black Christians.

The colonial influence in church songs

The Black Church canon of music consists of several sources. Arriving in Britain, West Indian Christians are positioned on a unique nodal point for transnational Black music and the interchange of ideas between the Caribbean, Britain and North America. As Dulcie McKenzie shows in her study of Black Church music in Britain, three types of music(s) flowed into homes and churches.[52] First, there are the back-home songs from the Caribbean. These were primarily indigenous Christian songs with possible origins in the Caribbean Revival of the mid-nineteenth century.[53] Some songs were edited versions of evangelical hymns and songs from US hymnals. Second, there are the Euro-American-inspired hymnal compilations such as the 'Sankey' and the *Redemption Hymnal*.[54] These collections are comprised exclusively of nineteenth- and early twentieth-century White American evangelical hymns. The final source is the emerging trans-Atlantic contemporary gospel music market – Christian gospel artists from primarily, but not exclusively, the Euro-American scene. White Christian music was welcomed. With few qualms about the history of the White American evangelical entanglement with segregation and racism in America, many songs were appropriated for their theological content despite their social origins. A few Caribbean gospel artists are also present in this third category, such as Joseph Niles and the Consolers and Jackie Edwards. But these singers were not dissimilar in their theological approach to the Euro-American scene that I set out further.

The first group of songs in the canon are the Caribbean choruses, the beloved, snappy 'warm-up' songs. Some have no identifiable origins, and recently were appropriated, repackaged and resold back to Black Britain as 'Caribbean Melodies' by African American gospel artist Donne McClurkin.[55] Three dominant themes or 'a canon within the canon' characterize these songs. These are personal salvation, spiritual empowerment and eschatological hope. An excellent example of the personal salvation motif is the chorus 'Born Born, Born Again'. The chorus tells of Spirit baptism, in water, blood and Spirit. The locus of salvation, however, is the individual. Next, an example of a song emphasizing the Pentecostal doctrine of the Holy Spirit is the chorus 'Fire, Fire, Fire'. In Pentecostalism, the infilling of the Spirit is a spiritual experience consistent with the spiritual occurrences in the book of Acts; believers are blessed for a second time.[56] Yet, reading the book of Acts the arrival of the Spirit for personal empowerment does not negate the social dimensions of the Spirit's work.[57] The final theme in this first collection of songs is eschatological hope. One example is the shortening of the hymn 'Will Soon Be Done' by Cleavant Derricks. The chorus for the song tells a story of heavenly longing and the desire to be reunited with the saints of God and Jesus.[58] Yet, Pentecostal eschatology, even as a *realized* modality, is not a revolutionary offering. This is because the future's breaking into the present in West Indian churches is modified by personal salvation and spiritual empowerment. In other words, the locus of the realized eschaton is confined to passive radicalism (Chapter 2).

The second group of songs are from the imported Euro-American hymn books, either the *Sacred Songs and Solos by Ira D. Sankey* (c. 1907) or the *Redemption Hymnal* published by Elim Pentecostal Church in 1951.[59] The 'Sankey' holds great affection. It was the first and arguably most enduring hymnal among the first generation, and many of its songs are incorporated into other collections, including the *Redemption Hymnal*. As it was colloquially known, the 'Sankey' was the product of evangelist and songwriter Ira David Sankey, who, along with his missionary companion Dwight Lyman Moody, became a stalwart of authoritative evangelical songwriting. For the first generation of Black worshippers, it was as important a church accessory as the Bible. The collection of songs, however, had no structured theological pattern but 'followed the salvific model of Armenian or free will theology of evangelical Christianity'.[60] As Stanley Grundy puts it, the 'three Rs' of gospel hymnody were: 'Ruined by the Fall, Redeemed by the Blood, and Regenerated by the Spirit'.[61] In other words, the songbook projected a personal salvific experience and heavenly hope with no sociopolitical interest in the world.

The third group of songs are the Euro-American Christian 'pop songs'. For instance, Euro-American singers Pat Boone and Jim Reeves produced gospel albums that became extremely popular with West Indian Christians in the 1950s and 1960s. Boone's first major gospel album, *A Closer Walk with Thee* (1957), recorded a selection of songs that underlined personal faith ('Just a Closer Walk with Thee') and heavenly hope ('He'll Understand and Say Well Done'). A similar narrative emerges from Reeves' popular album *We Thank Thee* (1962). The album contains songs emphasizing personal salvation ('I'd Rather Have Jesus') and heavenly hope ('I'll Fly Away', 'This World Is Not My Home', 'Where We'll Never Grow Old'). Therefore, the theological content of both albums resonates with the limited personal soteriological imperatives of the 'back-home' songs and hymnals.

The three Black Church music(s) have resonance with colonial Christianity. The repetitive categories of personal salvation, the individualization of the Spirit's work and the emphasis on the other-worldly hope, inadvertently convey a disavowal of a social soteriology and by extension a negation of blackness in interpretation and being.

The first Black British gospel bands reproduce colonial Christianity in songwriting. With few exceptions, the first bands comprised of young people from the Black churches. Some travelled to England with their parents or were born in Britain soon after. These young people were also *hailed* as they were exposed to the church's musical canon. But this is not how the young people who formed the first bands understood what they were undertaking. For many, the opportunity to develop musical skills was the main attraction of the church experience. With no meaningful children's church or youth ministries, singing or leading worship was the only ministry young people could get involved with. However, the church context was not the only influence on the emerging Christian musicality. The first Black gospel bands were also induced by the emerging youth culture of the 1960s. This was a time of rapid social change, spurred on by a new consumer culture. The church did not embrace the new mood; instead, within its conservative world view, youth culture was a temptation and represented the things of the 'the world'.[62] However, the young people in the Black Church discovered a compromise. The arrangement was to borrow secular musical styles and sonics and mix them with the traditional religious themes of the Black Church. Yet this negotiation did not detach the first bands from the colonial influence; the arrangement reproduced it.

The Singing Stewarts exemplify the colonial influence on the first gospel bands. A family of gospel singers, the Singing Stewarts were originally from Trinidad and settled in Handsworth, Birmingham. They were members of the Seventh-day Adventist Church, a conservative Christian denomination with strong roots in the Caribbean. The Singing Stewarts' first appearance on British television underlines the group's interpellation. 'The Colony' (1964)[63] was a snapshot of the African Caribbean experience in post-war Britain, especially the racial hostility and identity politics in a postcolonial city. Inadvertently, the film captures a tension between the church's *radicalism* and the Singing Stewarts songs' colonial Christianity. In the documentary, the first appearance of a Black Church positions it as a resistance movement. An African Caribbean Apostolic Church in Handsworth appears after a sequence on resistance to slavery, which gestures towards continuity of struggle from slavery to the hostile environment of post-war Britain. Then, the first entrance of a gospel group, the Singing Stewarts, has them performing a song, 'I Want to be Ready'. Beautifully performed, the song tells of personal piety and eschatological hope, both underlined by an interpretive neutrality.[64]

The Overcomers are a second example of the reproduction of coloniality in song. This trailblazing gospel band were a collection of singers and musicians from the African Caribbean-dominated Church of God in Christ in London. Again, while this denomination has Black leadership in America and is relatively free to express a broader range of concerns in their doctrinal constitution, their British musicians chose not to do so. Their first live EP, *The Overcomers* (1969), contains four tracks: 'By the Door', 'All Good Gifts Around Us', 'Lord Bring Me Down', and 'If You're Saved and You Know It'. Thematically, the album's lyrics affirm the personal salvation tradition of the first generation ('By the Door', 'If You're Saved and You Know It'). 'All Good Gifts Around Us' mixes a traditional hymn with a church chorus, and 'Bring Me Down' concerns the subject of personal piety and humility. Crafted in arguably one of the most tumultuous periods of Black history, The Overcomers' songs are thus rooted in colonial Christianity.

In sum, the first canon of songs reproduces colonial Christian discourse, despite the radicality of the formation of the Black Church movement in Britain. The songs *hail* the church, and the influence spreads to the first gospel bands. Not even the agency of youth or contact with the new trends in secular music prevented the first bands from being captivated by colonial Christianity.

Illustration: Incarnation: No Blacks, No Irish, No Dogs

By way of contrast, a critical engagement with the Windrush period appears in the song 'Incarnation: No Blacks, No Irish, No Dogs' from *Jamaican Bible Remix*. The song seeks to reflect on the social world of post-war Britain by correlating the meaning of the incarnation of Jesus with the arrival of West Indian colonial citizens. On the single, the scripture track is Jan (John) 1.14, a key verse for the meaning of the incarnation of Jesus. The message track explores the meaning of the incarnation in relation to the hostile social environment. West Indian experience is navigated through a fictional account of a West Indian colonial citizen, sung by Birmingham-based soul artist Darren Ellison. Finally, the 'music track' is inspired by the UK soul musicality of the 1980s soul artist Junior Giscomb.

> **BBC News** – In 1954 about 10,000 West Indians came to Britain. In 1955, it is believed another 15,000 will make the long journey. Already their coming has caused a national controversy.
> But one point must always be borne in mind. Whatever our feelings, we cannot deny them entry, for all are British citizens, and as such, are entitled to the identical rights of any member of the (British) Empire.
>
> **JNT** – Jan 1
> Nou, di wan we a di Wod ton man, im kom kom liv mongks wi, kom liv mongks wi. (x2)
>
> **Robert** – John 1:14 tells the story of Jesus' incarnation. That the Word becomes flesh and lives amongst us.
> It means that God who is fully God and fully man, takes on human form.
> The incarnation means that unequivocally, all creation is good and that all flesh, no matter what colour, no matter what tone is good. My parents believed in this meaning of the incarnation, that their flesh was good.
> They were immigrants from Jamaica who came to work in Britain after the Second World War.
> But they soon came to realise that not everybody thought the same.

When they went to look for places to live, they were greeted with signs that said, 'No Blacks, no Irish and no dogs.'

Darren – Sailed 5000 miles with the sun way off behind me. They said it's gonna be a while till I feel that warm again. Staring at the grey skies as the cold rain starts to soak me. Faces that I recognize but no one I'd call a friend. Just one class above how my fathers sailed before me. Still no wiser 'bout the days that lay ahead. Hands and feet are free but shackled by economy. Just a possibility of a better life instead. Maybe if you give me time just to let me tell my story. 'Bout how I came to be in the land of hope and glory. Moment that I touched the ground all I see is consternation. You never let me explain that I'm here by invitation.

Chorus

Came expecting arms to open wide. No Blacks, no Irish, and no dogs inside. The sign is plain, and you don't try to hide. No Blacks, no Irish, and no dogs inside.

BBC News – Much of the outcry against the immigrants arises from the Colour-Bar, which legally does not exist in Britain, does not exist in Britain.

JNT – im kom kom liv mongks wi, kom iiv mongks wi.

Darren – 5 years 3 days to go till I get back to my family. Got to find a place to stay with a people playing games. There's a lot of empty rooms and I know I've got the money. Funny how my currency doesn't seem to be the same. Working from 5-to-5 and the guys are always on me. Now the fight to stay alive, never figured in my plans. Tried to find the house of God, only made the people angry. Sadly, realised that I'm seen as less than just a man. Maybe if you give me time just to let me tell my story. 'Bout how I came to be in the land of hope and glory. Moment that I touched the ground all I see is consternation. You never let me explain that I'm here by invitation.

Robert – The strange thing is that in church history the brilliant minds of the church have spent a great deal of time trying to explain the doctrine of the incarnation, that Jesus had to be fully God and had to be fully man and use that as a way of countering heresy. But less time has been spent on the *meaning* of the incarnation, what it means to *practice* the equality of all humanity. If the church had spent more time on the meaning and the practice of the incarnation, we wouldn't have this terrible Post-War story: No Blacks, no Irish and no dogs.

Chorus

Came expecting arms to open wide. No Blacks, no Irish, and no dogs inside. The sign is plain, and you don't try to hide. No Blacks, no Irish, and no dogs inside.

Darren – God is not dead, He's still alive. (x2)
I can feel him in my hands,

I can feel him in my feet,
I can feel him all over,
Feel him all over me. (x3)

Conclusion

If the Windrush generation were incapable of moving beyond colonial Christianity, what about their progeny? Can the children of Windrush, the post-diaspora Black British subjects, fare any better? Would their British nationality, complex postcolonial context and social aspiration rupture the continuity of colonial Christianity? Can their songs register interests beyond the Black body? The next chapter considers the evidence for colonial Christianity in second- and third-generation Black British contemporary gospel music.

5

Vybz Kartel

Coloniality in the golden age of contemporary gospel music

Is there evidence for a continuity of colonial Christian thought in Black Church music among post-diaspora Black Christians? Or has the second and third generations confronted the influence of colonial Christianity? If the answer is yes, then to what extent? Is the engagement indirect or direct? What is the prognosis? Is it decolonial? These questions inform this second historical chapter. Methodologically, I persist with the previous chapter's dialogic approach between songs and context in order to isolate a song's meaning. In terms of context here, I consider four discrete phases of post-diaspora experience. The phases are 'holiness music', 'the golden age', 'crossover' and 're-inscription'. 'Holiness music' describes the music emerging from the newly established African Caribbean churches of the late 1960s to early 1970s. I have covered some of this ground in the previous chapter and so will only consider new information. The second phase, 'the golden age', is the most prolific period for African Caribbean gospel music and is defined by Thatcherism's political economy of the 1980s. Here we discover evidence of *indirect* social engagement but with a colonial Christian prognosis.[1] The 1990s is the 'crossover phase' where, again, despite a factious social environment contemporary gospel music consumes itself with crossover soundscapes. The halt of the third period is 're-inscription'. This phase is marked by a paradox. In the face of new social conflicts, some songs register a *direct* social awareness, though, as was also the case with 'the golden age', their social prognosis is still constrained by colonial Christianity's limited soteriology.

Holiness music

Holiness music is produced in the new racialized context of late 1960s Britain.[2] Arguably, the touchstone for the emergence of a new racism in Britain is the infamous 'Rivers of Blood' speech delivered in April 1968 by the Conservative minister Enoch Powell:

> As I look ahead, I am filled with foreboding. Like the Roman, I seem to see 'the River Tiber foaming with much blood'. That tragic and intractable phenomenon which we watch with horror on the other side of the Atlantic but which there is interwoven with the history and existence of the States itself, is coming upon us here by our own volition and our own neglect. Indeed, it has all but come. In numerical terms, it will be of American proportions long before the end of the century. Only resolute and urgent action will avert it even now. Whether there will be the public will to demand and obtain that action, I do not know. All I know is that to see, and not to speak, would be the great betrayal.[3]

Enoch Powell's speech collapsed the notion of a White 'race' into nation, which inadvertently positioned Black and Brown bodies as an enemy within:

> The doctrine of 'Powellise' – a combination of demand for national sovereignty and anti-immigration plus residual beliefs in an Empire – surfaced regularly over the years, although it should be noted that Powell's anti-immigrant stance was reserved for those he perceived as 'not White'. Powell had a respect for working-class opinion and regarded the marches in support of his speeches by dockers and market traders as patriotic out-pouring, defending a (White) nation state which had been at the apex.[4]

The 'Rivers of Blood' speech had social agency. Thousands of White workers across the country held pro-Powell strikes and marches shortly after. The speech also impacted Black people.[5] The name 'Enoch Powell' became synonymous with racial abuse and the call to repatriate Blacks. For example, I remember seeing racist graffiti sprayed across walls of derelict buildings, playgrounds and over advertising hoardings which read 'Powell was right! Niggers Out' in Coventry in the early 1970s.

Powell's *racecraft* impacted music. It was a catalyst for both anti-racist and anti-immigrant views.[6] Coincidently, three months after Powell's address, the multi-ethnic pop group The Equals had a smash hit with their single 'Baby, Come Back'. The band were not protesting Powell, but their mixed ethnic line-up signified an alternative vision for Britain: a more diverse, convivial society rather than Powellism's White volk. A more direct lyrical critique of Powell in music emerges from the decade's global superstars, The Beatles. According to Jon Stratton, Paul McCartney's 'Ob-La-Di, Ob-La-Da' (1968) from *The White Album* gestures towards 'a hoped-for multiculturalism'.[7] A year later, a more provocative pro-inclusion song topped the UK charts. Blue Mink, a six-piece group with an African American lead singer, unapologetically agitate for racial harmony in their smash hit 'Melting Pot' (1969).[8]

Prominent White musicians supported Powell. For instance, in the mid-1970s the White British R&B singer Eric Clapton parroted Enoch Powell's sentiment in a concert in Birmingham. He told the audience: 'I think Enoch is right, I think we should send them all back, stop Britain from becoming a Black colony.'[9] Rod Stewart, another British artist famous for appropriating African American music(s), supported Clapton. He said, 'I think Powell is the man. . . . This country is overcrowded. The immigrants should be sent home.'[10] Clapton went on to express remorse over what he said, describing it as a drunken, ignorant and uninformed tirade. But that was not the last of it. In response to Clapton, left-wing artists agitated for a more strident anti-racism in music.

A large number of White and Black artists opposed Powell. Many decided to organize against the rising tide of racism and to show the world that in British music Clapton and Stewart were aberrations. Under the banner of 'Rock against Racism', a diverse collection of bands and genres united to perform concerts.[11] Joe Strummer, the lead singer of *The Clash*, said in support of 'Rock against Racism':

> People ought to know we're anti-fascist, we're anti-violence, we're anti-racism and we're pro-creativity. We're against ignorance.[12]

In contrast, the fledgling contemporary gospel music was silent on racism. Though Black Christians faced discrimination at work, on the streets and even in the pews of mainstream churches, none of these concerns registered in the lyrics of the songs they wrote and performed. As noted in the previous chapter, the songs of the nascent Black Church evade explicit mention of engagement with the social world. They were *hailed* by their canon of songs. But not all Black Christian musicians were mute. The only evidence we have for engagement with the social world to appeal for racial equality appears in Christian music *outside the boundaries of the Black Church context*. In 1972, the mixed ethnic rock gospel group Out of Darkness produced a cryptic racial inclusion song on their *The Celebration Club Sessions* album.[13] While some of the members of the band were raised and 'cut their musical teeth' in the Black Church, the only place to perform and perpetuate these ideas was outside the Black Church. As we shall see later (Chapter 6), the 'borderlands' of church music proffer an opportunity to resist colonial Christianity.

The golden age

The next phase is 'the golden age of gospel'. It is termed thus because it is viewed as its most prolific period. During this 'age', a post-diaspora second-generation

Black British take centre stage in the emerging gospel music marketplace. However, they perform in a sociopolitical context, which is marked by a distinctive brand of political economy, Thatcherism. The differences between the music and politics are resolved with a novel synthesis.

Thatcherism

The sociopolitical context for the 'golden age' of gospel is Thatcherism. The election victory of Margaret Thatcher in 1979 led to profound transformations. Thatcherism's introduction of neoliberal economics inspired by the Milton Friedman Chicago School of Economics promoted the 'market' as the best regulator of prosperity. Neoliberal economics was presumed to be the medicine for a British economy stifled by a bloated welfare state, low productivity and overbearing trade unions. In this brave new economic world, individualism trumped collectivism; as Thatcher would state, 'there is no such thing as society'. Thatcher's implementation of her new right ideology led to seismic socio-economic changes.[14] The economy's focus shifted away from manufacturing to the service sector, the financial industry was deregulated and the trade unions curtailed. However, despite the economic upheaval racial discrimination remained a 'changing-same'. As one left-wing commentator states unapologetically about Thatcher and race:

> Thatcher's attitude to foreigners can be summed up in two phases: 'people are really rather afraid that this country might be rather swamped by people with a different culture' (January 1978) and the war cry 'Sink the Belgrano' (May 1983) over the Malvinas. She was, without doubt, a xenophobe, an unapologetic imperialist with a natural penchant towards the far Right. She hosted and defended the former Chilean dictator Pinochet in London, supported the apartheid regime for many years (till uneconomic) and denounced as terrorist Mandela and the ANC.[15]

Compounded by long-standing social disadvantages, the new economic changes left most Black people particularly vulnerable to the rising unemployment caused by the decimation of Britain's manufacturing base.[16] Thus, a second generation of Black youths born to African Caribbean parents inherited an environment exacerbated by the changing economic times and continued racial hostility.[17] Economic disadvantage and racial hostility colluded in the racialized policing of Black youth. Oppressive policing was in part due to a 'manufactured' crisis over youth crime, which represented Black youth as a social problem (enemy within).[18] In *Policing the Crisis*, Stuart Hall demonstrates how policing Blacks in London had little to do with confronting crime and was an attempt to suppress dissent. For instance, in the months leading up to the 'Brixton Riots' of 1981 in London, of 1,000 Black people arrested by the police, only 100 were charged.[19] It took the 'uprisings' of the Brixton Riots, and the Lord Scarman Report (1981) into the causes of the disturbances, for the country to 'wake up' to the racial discrimination in society and the harmful practices that were responsible.[20] Repeated disturbances in 1985 in London and Birmingham underlined the frustrations of a new generation disenfranchised by the toxic mix of monetary policy, racialized policies and the indifference of policymakers.

Black Christian Protestant work ethic

Aspects of Thatcherism found resonance in the Black Church. Thatcher's emphasis on hard work and discipline chimed with Black Christian values of spiritual discipline and Christian duty and responsibility. But it was Thatcher's commitment to the market as the arbiter of human worth that made legible a Black Christian conservatism and Black Christian protestant work ethic.

> The politics of Thatcherism emphasised those values – hard work, thrift, ambition, and so on – which would find reward in the market, and it was the market which would now determine the worth of each citizen.[21]

Thatcherism exposed a deep-seated Black Christian conservativism rather than creating it. Black conservativism precedes Thatcher. It has a long history in Black Atlantic cultures.[22] In this discrete version of Conservativism, Black people do not believe in relying overbearingly on government or social intervention for their flourishing – they can achieve success individually through communal efforts, industry and ingenuity.[23] Black African Caribbean Christian conservatism, however, nuances the meaning of enterprise and political affiliation associated with Conservative ideology. African Caribbean people have historically gravitated towards educational attainment rather than capitalist entrepreneurialism and its celebration of excessive wealth accumulation.[24] For this reason, the African Caribbean churches in Britain have never flaunted the necessary capitalist credentials for them to be effectively courted by the British Conservative Party and have remained overwhelmingly left-leaning at the polling station.[25] But Thatcherism's marketplace politics and emphasis on reward made legible and otherwise obscured discrete Black Christian Protestant work ethic.

The Black Christian Protestant work ethic is Black British Christian conservatism. Similar to Max Weber's origination,[26] the Black Christian version comprises folding religious asceticism or personal piety into personal aspiration for the sake of societal advancement.[27] The African Caribbean *ethic*, however, has its genesis in the post-slave, colonial world. Out of slavery Caribbean Blacks with no social welfare or security developed practices of hard work, thrift, economic development and entrepreneurialism. However, if C. L. R. James is correct, these endeavours were structured by colonial thought, especially Victorian values, and sporting ideas.[28] Yet, while it has much to be credited for, *all* Black conservativism, secular and Christian, *neglects a critique of the social and economic system that causes the damage in the first place.*

Contemporary gospel music of 'the golden age' signifies on the Black Christian protestant work ethic. That is to say, some of the songs of the period affirm the Black Christian Protestant work ethic and thereby unwittingly supported Thatcher's work-reward paradigm. 'The golden age' gave rise to a plethora of new bands, choirs and solo singers. Concerts, albums and new music emerged coterminous with a second generation of Black British Christians hungry for Christian *edutainment*. Sifting through the songs of the period distils 'echoes' of the *ethic*, rather than explicit pronouncements. Two musical examples are noteworthy.

Success

The first example of the *ethic* was the contemporary gospel, soul/funk band Paradise – arguably, the most successful contemporary gospel band of the period. Their importance cannot be underestimated. As a young contemporary group, bursting with the energy of second-generation Christian enthusiasm, they provided a vital voice for young Black Christians coming of age in the late 1970s and early 1980s. Their brand of gospel rendered possible a positive and dynamic Black British Christian outlook. Their song 'Success' from their *World's Midnight* album (1982) gestured towards the Black Christian Protestant work ethic. The social context is instrumental. In a period where Black youth were feeling the harsh effects of youth employment and increased police surveillance, a gospel band produced a song entitled 'Success'.

The title and lyrics of the song *indirectly* engage with the social predicament but proffer an age-old colonial Christian solution. The track begins by signifying Black unemployment by calling out to a fictional character 'doing nothing'. The song continues by offering the person advice on how to 'make something of your life' especially if they are seeking 'fame and glory'. The chorus provides the last piece of transformational knowledge. The song claims that success comes with righteousness: 'There is one thing that you should know . . . Ahh don't you know success comes with righteousness.'[29] The chorus is more than a throwaway line, as the words resonate with Thatcher's emphasis on personal responsibility rather than challenging unjust structures or practices. The song not only fails to challenge the broader social factors contributing to the period's Black distress but also underlines the personal piety and personal salvation myopia of the previous generation.

Abundance

A second example of the Black Christian Protestant ethic is found in the work of the most successful gospel choir of the period, the London Community Gospel Choir (LCGC). Their chart hit 'Fill My Cup' (1984) was released after a tumultuous period in Black communities. In 1981, rioting in Brixton, London, and similar disturbances in other Black communities caused a rethink in Conservative Party politics towards the inner cities. The government decided the solution for deprivation and low aspiration was to promote individual enterprise and entrepreneurship in Black communities. In short, they invited young Black people into British neoliberal capitalism. Several emerging Black businesspeople were profiled as success stories and role models for others to follow. But Conservative Party dogma was not the only discourse prodding second-generation Blacks to embrace the enterprise culture. Running concurrent with the government initiative was a distinctive imported Christian capitalist discourse – the arrival of North American prosperity doctrine through the introduction of sermon tapes and books by devotees of the Word of Faith Movement in America such as Kenneth Copeland and Kenneth E. Hagin. Combined, Thatcherite individualism and World of Faith doctrine solidified in quadrants of the Black Church a positive embrace of the new doctrine of material abundance. Having 'more' became a good, and one song reflects this mantra. 'Fill My Cup' rehearses the Pentecostal doctrine of the infilling of the Holy Spirit and calls for spiritual direction. But the Spirit's purpose is muddied when the song is placed within the context of Thatcher and Word of Faith; the listener is left wondering if the 'cup' to be filled is spiritual or material.[30]

In sum, the 'golden age' set a new trend. It *indirectly* engaged with the social context. Yet this discrete form of Black conservatism, rooted in missionary Christianity, offered no counter to colonial Christianity.

Crossover

Racial violence and collective Black trauma dominated the 1990s social context. The racist attack on the Black teenager Stephen Lawrence in 1993 in Eltham, London, was arguably the most significant event in Black communities in the 1990s. Stephen was murdered in an unprovoked confrontation with several White youths. From the outset, the investigation failed to scrutinize all the potential perpetrators.[31] With racism in the foreground of the investigation, the police criminalized the victim, Stephen, and later deployed police surveillance officers to monitor and undermine the family's protestations.[32] The botched investigation sent shock waves through Britain: a Black collective trauma. The murder and failed investigation confirmed the Black pessimism school's evaluation of the stark reality of enduring racism in postcolonial Britain.[33] The failure to convict the primary suspects and the continued protests by the family and their supporters culminated in a public inquiry led by Lord Macpherson in 1999.[34] The report into the investigation identified evidence of 'institutional racism' in the police and also the legal failings in the trial of the suspects. Its recommendations included legislative change in the criminal justice system and policy modification in policing.

Black Church musicians were *not* ignorant of the 1990s racial climate. On the contrary, individual Black Christians, such as the contemporary gospel music entrepreneur Del White, participated in the family's campaign, and collectives of gospel artists supported events to raise finance for the campaign for justice. But the songs of the church tell a different story.

Crossover genre was the dominant style of the period. Crossover is the capacity to craft music that appeals to both gospel and secular audiences.[35] As a multidirectional art form, Christian artists can crossover into the mainstream, and conversely, secular artists reach out to the contemporary gospel music marketplace. Built on the performance of dual meanings and lyrical ambiguity, artists doublespeak in their songs to engage Christian and non-Christian audiences alike. Subsequently, crossover seeks to convey the Gospel of Jesus while not necessarily making explicit reference to the Christian experience. Artists trust the audience will 'read between the lines'. Crossover in the 1990s was inspired by a mixture of factors. These are mission, money and role models. The missional imperative is the desire to reach a wider non-Christian audience and therefore fulfil the dictates of the Great Commission (Mt. 28.16-20). The economic aspect pertains to commercialism, specifically a downturn in the mainstream record companies' interest in contemporary gospel music and the need to find new routes into popular music audiences.[36] British crossover's role model or inspiration was the commercial success of African American artists BeBe and CeCe Winans. BeBe and CeCe's *Different Lifestyles* album of 1991 was an elixir for the post 'golden age' gospel industry performers.

> More than any other act of the late 1980s and early 1990s, BeBe and CeCe Winans demonstrated the massive crossover potential of Black contemporary gospel music. Their two best-selling records, *Heaven* and *Different Lifestyles*, were monumental achievements. With Its three radio hits, *Heaven* became the first Black gospel album to sell 500,000 units since Aretha Frankin's 1972 classic *Amazing Grace*.[37]

Nu Colours exemplifies the Black British crossover dynamic. These singers 'cut their contemporary gospel music teeth' on the gospel scene before being courted by the secular music market and signing to mainstream commercial labels in the 1990s. The band produced several albums,[38] which exhibit the significatory scheme underlining crossover. For instance, their hit single 'Power' from the early 1990s is lyrically ambiguous. The music video is equally opaque. The subject of the song and video is either spiritual power or possibly the ecstatic experience of the nightclub.[39] Does crossover fulfil its missiological aims? Speaking of this lyrical doublespeak practice about another one of their crossover songs, 'Greater Love', band member Fazay is adamant that this subliminal method is effective:

> Take the song *Greater Love* for instance. A lot of people used to go, 'Is that gospel?', but sit and listen to the lyrics. To me they're so simple: the man [sic] that's not a Christian can understand them. And it's so refreshing when after your shows that one person comes up to you and says, 'You've helped readjust my life.' For us, we feel the victory in that.[40]

Not all crossover was socially quiet. In the American context, the African American gospel choir Sounds of Blackness proffered a more nuanced approach which included direct engagement with the history of racism. Their debut album, *The Evolution of Gospel* (1991), contained the song 'Optimistic'. In the video of the song, the choir members are seen wearing slavery chains that seem to represent the middle passage, for the initial thirty seconds. It is out of this historical experience that the crossover song 'Optimistic' emerged. The song/video is a powerful memory of racial capitalism and the empowering place of Black music within it. Later, I will reprise a different type of crossover gospel as a tool for producing decolonial gospel music (Chapter 8).

In sum, British crossover also failed to overturn the stranglehold of the colonial Christian influence in contemporary gospel music. The lyrical ambiguity and evangelical motivation failed to signify on the social context, especially the spectre of racial attack and Black collective trauma. *Arguably, this was the greatest missed opportunity by the songwriters. The lyrical flexibility was a precious opportunity to engage with the social world and issues of social justice.*

Re-inscription

At the turn of the twenty-first century, a third generation of songwriters, musicians and singers reinscribed colonial Christianity. However, rather than ignoring social crises, they were *directly* acknowledged. But this rise in awareness was not all that it seemed: their theological *prognosis* refused to disavow the colonial Christianity.

A systemic failure characterized Black working-class life in the early part of the twenty-first century. Despite the emergence of a small Black middle-class and increased Black representation in government and the media, a noticeable breakdown of family structures, community cohesion and stagnated education attainment ran concurrently with new levels of criminality, deprivation and inter-communal violence. The new social environment gave rise to an 'outlaw culture' among sections of young people cut adrift from the social mobility culture of the New Labour project of Tony Blair and Gordon Brown.[41] The systemic failure was compounded by the global economic crash of 2008 and the introduction of austerity policies by the Conservative-led government in 2010.[42] Arguably, the most talked about social issue in Black communities emerging during this final period was the scourge of gun crime and gang violence. While not a new phenomenon in Britain, gang violence re-emerged as a racialized 'Black issue' in the national consciousness after a series of tragic shootings linked to gang rivalries. For instance, in Birmingham, UK, the spectre of gang violence and its brutal outcomes came to national attention in 2003. The shooting of two teenage girls, Charlene Ellis (18) and Letisha Shakespeare (17), outside the back entrance to a Black hair salon in the Aston district brought to light the prevalence of systemic failure.[43]

African Caribbean gospel artists acknowledged the new social crisis (gun crime issue), but their prognosis, however, was personal salvation rather than a structural critique. Arguably, the Birmingham-based gospel reggae-dancehall artist Witness was one of the first artists to engage with social issues in the Black community. In the song 'Ghetto Cry' (1999), he explores the tragic consequences of urban violence. The song begins with a rehearsal of the familial cost of the serious youth violence,[44] though the causes of the predicament are the personal failings of morally and socially inadequate individuals.[45] Redemption comes from personal salvation and through turning to Christ, a process described using classic Pentecostal visions of future judgement.[46] Following suit is the former London-based gospel rapper Jahaziel's anti-gun/gang violence song 'In My Neighbourhood' from his debut album, *Ready to Live* (2007). The song samples John Holt and the Paragons' 'I've Got to Get Away' (1968). Whereas Holt's song speaks of a quarrel between love rivals, the Christian rap remake expresses the community's struggle against gun crime: 'Everyday another gun gets manufactured, another man's blasted.'[47] Though the song expresses awareness of the power relationships contributing to the crisis (criminalization of Black youth, underemployment and regressive tax systems), personal salvation remains integral to achieving change: 'I thought that it was much too late.... But God's love was just too great.'[48]

African British gospel artists reproduced the approach of their African Caribbean peers. The emergence of West African British contemporary gospel music and its forays into gospel hip-hop provided a much-needed boost to the contemporary gospel music scene. However, with few exceptions, African British artists followed the footsteps of their African Caribbean predecessors. Migration from West Africa in the 1980s and 1990s transformed Christianity's landscape in Britain and across Europe.[49] A 'reverse mission' to Britain produced a proliferation of new denominations and churches, including the emergence of West African 'mega' churches. The swelling of British Pentecostalism's ranks led to significant demographic and theological shifts. First, a younger and more populous West African Christianity moved to the epicentre of the Black faith, displacing the older African Caribbean tradition in size and influence.[50] Second, they superseded the (African Caribbean) Black Christian Protestant ethic with a West African *neo-Pentecostal prosperity doctrine* – that is, a foregrounding of wealth creation.[51] Whereas the Black Christian Protestant ethic's material success was built on righteous living, in neo-Pentecostal prosperity, the equation was turned on its head – monetary gain became a sign of spiritual success.[52] This new approach to betterment has complex historical, cultural and sociological entanglements in African congregations. It is amiss to reduce its attraction to a single story, such as capitulation to capitalism.[53] Less opaque, however, is the music production.

The change in the epicentre of the Black Church did not lead to widespread engagement with the social world or calls for social justice. A focal point for renewed concern over the persistence of inequality was the national riots of 2011. The riots took place in the wake of protests in London against the police shooting of the 29-year-old Mark Duggan:[54]

> It was estimated that 13,000 to 15,000 people 'rioted/looted' across English cities from 6th to 10th August 2011. Numerous people lost their businesses, family homes, had property damaged and, sadly, five people died. There were also financial costs. The disorder cost £50 million to police and £43.5 million to clean up. There was £300 million worth of damage to property and £80 million lost in business and sales. Insurance claims were estimated to reach £300 million, and the figure thought to be lost in tourism revenue stood at £250 million. This amounts to around half a billion pounds. . . . However, many people didn't seem to know where to start when considering 'why' this all happened and the 'insanity' of the events raised complex causal questions that most of the media, the police and prominent politicians failed to address.[55]

West African artists responded with a message of personal salvation. For instance, the Nigerian British-based rapper Triple O addressed gun crime in the song 'I'm Not About That' (2017) and asserted in response to the crisis, 'Jah rules, clap back . . .'[56]

Ben Okafor was the only West African Christian artist to offer an alternative. But his craft and audience were outside of the Black Church. Okafor's experience of injustice and inhumanity as a child soldier in the Nigerian Civil War shaped his interpretation of the Christian message as a source of social justice.[57] In addition, his appropriation of reggae music's protest tradition created a potent sonic expression for a Christian protest music.[58] Again, as was the case with Out of Darkness in the 1970s, physical distance from the borders of the Black Church provided a creative political space for an alternative theology of music. S.O., the African British rap artist, also experienced greater lyrical freedom upon relocating to North America. For instance, S.O.'s third studio album, *Augustine's Legacy* (2019), contains a critique of White Christology[59] and affirms the Jewishness of Jesus. This was radical thinking for African British Christianity, but still, the prognosis is a retreat into personal piety. He retreats into an affirmation of the Holy Trinity.[60]

What can we surmise from this historical review? It is clear that in the post-diaspora, despite the differing alterity of contexts and experiences, the stranglehold of colonial Christian thought dominates the genre. Continued colonial Christian influence reduces the capacity among artists and songwriters for thinking about faith beyond the confines of a limited soteriology, and even when direct consideration is given to the Black condition the prognosis is consistent with colonial Christian thinking. The killing of George Floyd in 2020 sparked a significant change within the Black Church and contemporary gospel music. With the global shift in attitudes towards racism, church leaders and gospel artists were motivated to openly condemn it. It is important to note that this change occurred at a particular time and arguably was driven more by expediency than the dictates of a social interventionist tradition.

Illustration: Work of the Spirit

The illustration for this chapter is another example of the folding of the Christian message into a sociopolitical consideration. The example comes from the track 'Work of the Spirit'. As shown in the last two chapters, pneumatology is a major feature of the Black Pentecostal songwriting, yet very little is said in song about the *social dimensions* of the Spirit's work. This track addresses this omission by exploring the Spirit as a social force in the world, confronting evil. To reimage the work of the Spirit, the track appropriates socially meaningful images of the Spirit from scripture. The scripture track takes samples from the JNT, II Tesiluoniyan (II Thessalonians) 2 and Jan (John) 14. The message track is inspired by a reading of Hispanic theologian Eldin Villafañe's New Testament pneumatology.[61] Subversively, the message track is also layered with a sample from traditional songs about the Holy Spirit (Ron Kenoly's *Anointing Fall on Me*[62]) to signal a departure from the traditional locus of the work of the Spirit – the Black body. Finally, the music track is a mixture of samples from the Black British opera singer Abigail Kelly and UK grime music.

> **Abigail Kelly** – What is the work, what's the work of the Spirit?
>
> **JNT** – II Tesiluoniyan 2
>
> Nou, unu don nuo aredi di wan we a uol im bak, an im a-go gwaan uol im bak so im kyan kom wen a fi im taim fi kom. Kaaz wan wikid sitn de bout we a wok anda di kwaiyat fi kaaz piipl fi go gens Gad Laa. Bot sumadi a uol it bak. An di wan we a uol it bak a-go gwaan uol it til im get muuv outa di wie.
>
> **Robert** – In church people sing many songs about the Holy Spirit. None of them more evocative than '*Anointing Fall on Me.*'

In this song, the Holy Spirit is presented as a personal empowerment for people.
Something they can call upon to strengthen them.
It is very personal and very individual.
But this isn't the only image of the Spirit.
II Thessalonians paints a picture of the Spirit as a defensive force,
restraining the evil within the world, and keeping it in check.

Chorus
What's the work of the Spirit? Bot sumadi a uol it bak. (x4)

Robert – The work of the Spirit isn't just about individual empowerment. It's also about holding back the terror within this world.

The Spirit is a dam against a tide of wickedness.

Chorus
What's the work of the Spirit? Bot sumadi a uol it bak. (x4)

Robert – But the Spirit's work isn't just about defence; it's also about attack. We need to take this in a different direction.

JNT – Jan 14
An mi a-go aks mi Faada fi sen wan neda sumadi fi elp unu an de wid unu aal di taim.

fi elp unu. (x2)

Robert – Before Jesus goes back to heaven, he says to the disciples, he is not going to leave them alone. He will send the comforter; the comforter is going to be there to help them.
And be there to drive them forward.

Chorus
Work of the Spirit. (x5)

Robert – The work of the Spirit is an offensive force in this world, puts people who believe in God on the attack. To 'mash up' the forces of wickedness in this world.

Chorus
Work of the Spirit. (x4)

Robert – So what's the work of the Spirit within this world? Within this world. (x2) Defence and attack. (x 24)

Conclusion

If the music of the Black Church is incapable of explicating itself from the reach of colonial Christianity, where can we locate a resource for disentangling it? Neither the Windrush nor post-Windrush generations have succeeded in moving beyond the boundaries of colonial Christian thought. Hence, the next task in this book is to delink contemporary gospel music from the colonial moorings and specifically to engage with decolonial Christian thinking. To begin, I turn to reggae music and the borders of contemporary gospel music, after which we will consider production techniques for translating the new thinking into music practice.

Part III

Decolonial methods

6

Handsworth revolutions

Delinking contemporary gospel music from colonial Christianity

This chapter and the one that follows develop the practical steps necessary for decolonizing contemporary gospel music. The direction is somewhat predictable, as the basic theological components for decolonization (social soteriology, contextual interpretation and loving blackness) were identified in Chapter 3. However, less evident is the mechanism for decolonization, the considerations we must undertake to depart from or delink from the influence of colonial Christianity. What strategic thinking or epistemes are necessary to re-envision contemporary gospel music as a decolonial genre? Furthermore, how *do* we do decolonization in music-making – what tools do we need to make it happen in the production process? To answer these questions, this chapter considers epistemes or ways of decolonial knowing, and the following chapter identifies the production tools for making decolonial contemporary gospel music.

Several decolonial resources are integral to decolonial knowing. The first is 'decoloniality'. Decoloniality presupposes that modernity is founded on colonial ways of knowing (coloniality/modernity) and therefore, decolonization requires decoloniality or ways of knowing from formerly colonized peoples who have been subjugated or hidden. While a broad category of thought and action, here, as noted previously (Chapter 2), decoloniality is reconfigured to contest colonial Christian knowledge (its coloniality of power) with new ways of knowing.[1] While not a completely new concept in Caribbean culture (ways of knowing are contingent to the decolonization of Caribbean/diaspora theologies),[2] decoloniality proffers several additional resources helpful to this study. The next is 'border thinking'. Border thinking describes a strategic location for decoloniality – at the borders of the colonial matrix of power. Emerging from studies in the sociology and anthropology of the Mexican/American border, border thinking is the way of perceiving borders as spaces of in-between or new consciousness.[3] As noted previously, the borders or borderlands of contemporary gospel music are fecund with social justice potential. In Chapter 4, we identified *Out of Darkness* and, in Chapter 5, Ben Okafor and S.O. as examples of a relative challenge to colonial Christian normativity in the history of contemporary gospel music in Britain. Border thinking is appropriated here to provide options for decolonizing.

The next resource, 'delinking', is essential for this chapter. Delinking is a process for separating from Western ways of knowing.[4] It is a two-stage procedure for producing knowledge from other locations and experiences. Delinking creates 'decolonial' options, and options are the resource for new thinking and being or re-existence.[5] All of these resources assist with the process of separating contemporary gospel music from colonial Christianity.

The first part of this chapter contextualizes 'delinking' within Black musicality. I want to show that the practice has deep roots in Black British music and is not an imposition. To identify a contextual delinking, I contour a distinctive approach within Rastafari reggae music. As noted in the Introduction, Rastafari reggae music has a long history of decolonial thought and is arguably the most appropriate genre in Britain to work with.[6] Central to this is the pioneering work of the reggae band Steel Pulse. Their debut album, *Handsworth Revolution*, is the epitome of decoloniality, or what I term 'Handsworth revolutions'.

In the second part of this chapter, I travel to the borderlands of contemporary gospel music to locate decolonial options. I focus on the music craft of the former Christian rap artist Jahaziel. Between the Black Church and Afrocentric thought, he makes a statement and music that gesture towards three decolonial options. Three songs from *Jamaican Bible Remix* are provided as illustrations for each option. These are 'Magnificat', 'Incarnation: No Blacks, No Irish, No Dogs' and 'Pay Back'. 'Incarnation' is appropriated for a second time in this study to illustrate another aspect of decolonizing.

Delinking

To separate contemporary gospel music from colonial Christianity, we must 'delink' it. Delinking is epistemic disobedience, a rebellion against colonial Christianity's coloniality of power and a move towards thinking and action from the contexts and experiences of formerly oppressed and colonized peoples. As Walter Mignolo notes:

> If delinking means to change the terms of the conversation, and above all, of the hegemonic ideas of what knowledge and understanding are and, consequently, what economy and politics, ethics and philosophy, technology and the organization of society are and should be, it is necessary to fracture the hegemony of knowledge and understanding that have been ruled, since the fifteenth century and through the modern/colonial world by what I conceive here as the theo-logical and the ego-logical politics of knowledge and understanding.[7]

Delinking takes place at the borders of colonial thinking, where there is a confrontation and departure from Western ways of knowing:

> 'Border thinking' (or border epistemology) emerges primarily from the people's anti-imperial epistemic responses to the colonial difference – the difference that hegemonic discourse endowed to 'other' people, classifying them as inferior and at the same time asserting its geo-historical and body-social configurations as superior and the models to be followed.[8]

We must delink from the *theo- and ego-logics,*[9] the dominant theological and rationalist thought. The alternatives for these two colonial categories are what Mignolo terms 'geo and body-politics'. These are

> a politics of knowledge that is ingrained both in the body and in local histories. That is, thinking geo- and body-politically.[10]

The (delinked) inversion of theo- and ego-politics of knowledge is 'geo- and body-politics' of knowledge.[11] Geo-politics describes the source of epistemology in geography, that is, 'epistemology has to be geographical in its historicity.'[12] Additionally, 'body-politics' refers to Black subjectivities, as a source of knowledge or 'the biographical sensing of the Black body'.[13] *To summarize and simplify delinking, I propose we consider delinking as the mining of contextual knowledge from Black social contexts and experience at the borders of the colonial Christian matrix of power.* To contextualize a musicological example of the geo- and body-politics of knowledge, I turn to the Rastafari musicality of Black British reggae band Steel Pulse.

Rastafari theomusicology

Delinking is integral to Rastafari-inspired reggae music. Embedded in Rastafari doctrine is a rejection of aspects of European Christianity and concomitantly its epistemes.[14] However, Rastafari's delinking is not a total severing or de-Westernization.[15] Instead, it is a departure from the hegemony of Christian coloniality, its trafficking of White supremacy dressed up as theological normativity. As such, Rastafari epistemology is best viewed as a contribution to the pluri-verse of thought, the realization that there is more than one epistemic tradition to follow:

> De-linking then shall be understood as a de-colonial epistemic shift leading to other-universality, that is, to pluri-versality as a universal project.[16]

Babylon

'Babylon' signifies delinking in Rastafari reggae. In Rastafari biblical hermeneutics, the Babylonian captivity of the Jews (586 to about 516 BCE) is recontextualized to connote Black suffering in the West – the African diaspora experience of slavery, colonialism and neo-colonialism. But Babylon is a floating signifier. As Anita Waters shows, 'Babylon' has come to imply a range of meanings beyond Rastafari theology, including malevolent statecraft.[17] However, my interest is with Babylon as a sign for decolonial activity. Its appearance signals a delinking from the oppressive system and its way of knowing. Thus, Rastafari-inspired reggae songs which reference Babylon inadvertently gesture towards epistemic challenge and alternative knowledge production. Following this rationale, classic Rastafari-inspired reggae songs such as 'Move Out of Babylon' (Johnny Clarke), 'Chant Down Babylon' (Bob Marley), 'Babylon the Bandit' (Steel Pulse) and 'Moving Out a Babylon' (Luciano) all, in one way or another, express epistemic rebellion against colonial Christianity's coloniality.

Handsworth revolutions

Steel Pulse's first album's lyrics exemplify 'Babylon' delinking. Steel Pulse were founded in the early 1970s. By the end of the decade, the group had achieved international fame upon the release of their first two studio albums, *Handsworth Revolution* (1978) and *Tribute to the Martyrs* (1979). While the line-up has changed over their four decades of music, the lead singer, David Hinds, remains the driving force behind the band's studio albums. The thematic range of the band's discography traverses various subjects, including history, pan-African politics, Rastafari religion, anti-racism, environmental degradation, human trafficking and social media manipulation.

'Babylon' as a sign for delinking is established at the outset of the band's studio career.

The signature track from their debut album ('Handsworth Revolution') makes a centrepiece of 'Babylon': it is the 'fallen' UK in which Black people (in Handsworth) are a 'holy remnant'.[18] Two moves later in the song signal delinking. The first move is a new geopolitical or contextual knowledge sourced from the social context of the Caribbean diaspora peoples of Handsworth. As noted previously (Chapter 4), Handsworth is the district in Birmingham where the vast majority of the post-war Windrush generation settled in the West Midlands. By the 1960s, the working-class area was synonymous with Black and Asian people. Intriguingly, the contextual knowledge identified by the band in the song emerges from a Jamaican diaspora appropriation of Caribbean philosophy. The singers defer to the Jamaican proverb 'one hand wash the other'.[19] Jamaican proverbs are traditional wisdom or domestic philosophies[20] and echoes of ancient African philosophy.[21] In the Caribbean context, these proverbs communicate resistance. As Hugh Hodges notes, 'Jamaica proverbs as a genre, reflect the people's struggle with oppression.'[22] This proverb is also oriented towards resistance but concerns the postcolonial context of Handsworth. In this locale, the proverb underlines resistance as Black solidarity, reciprocity and community. Contextualized, the proverb militates against the postcolonial history of 'divide and rule' for Black peoples in Britain. The second move is a learning from Black bodies: a positive affirmation of blackness. This affirmation is denoted in a description of emerging self-consciousness. The song tells of a psychic conversion of Blacks from 'beggars' to 'choosers'. This is important thinking. It reverses the external negative racialized characterization of the people of Handsworth. Their embodied experience communicates a new trajectory; that is, 'striving forward with ambition'.

Delinking produces decolonial options. To source options relevant to contemporary gospel music, I turn to the former gospel artist Jahaziel. His delinking from colonial Christianity takes place at the borders of the genre and provides three discrete options for contemporary gospel music.

Jahaziel

I now turn to the borders of contemporary gospel music to process options for decolonizing contemporary gospel music by critically engaging with the thought of the former Christian gospel artist Jahaziel. As Mignolo and Tlostanova remind us, it is at the border that epistemic challenge emerges from formerly colonized peoples.[23]

The first two options emerge from his new context as an ex-Christian rapper. Specifically, Jahaziel's 'leaving statement' identifies issues within Christian music which, through deductive reasoning, I reconstitute as decolonial options. The third option arises in his new embodied experience as a post Christian artist. His first post-Christian single release gives voice to another option.

Jahaziel's leaving statement is this:

> Now, after 20 years of being vocal about the positives of the Christian faith, I would like to take some time to be equally vocal about the negatives I have found. i.e. Christianity and its controlling dictatorship, its historic blood trail, its plagiarized Bible stories, characters and concepts, the many human errors of the Bible and its contradictions, the brutal nature of its God, its involvement in the slave trade, the crusades, the inquisition, the witch hunts, its second-class view of women, its masculinization of God, its emasculation of men, its financial corruption . . . you get the drift.[24]

This leaving statement was a shock to his fans. Nothing in his award-winning albums prepared for this. No sign of his Black consciousness in the song titles such as 'I Said Yes' and 'Jesus'. Yet, amid the rubble of the disappointment, this new context and experience proffer an epistemic opportunity.

Option 1: Womanist soteriology

The first option is womanist soteriology. Unwittingly, Jahaziel underscores the basic components of womanist thought; that is, 'race' and gender oppression. Racialized oppression is registered in his critique of Christian collusion with racism: 'Christianity and its controlling dictatorship, its historic blood trail . . . its God, its involvement in the slave trade, the crusades.'[25] Gender oppression appears in his criticism of Christianity's patriarchy: 'its second-class view of women, its masculinization of God'. Taking these issues seriously in Black women's experience and theology has given rise to resistance and liberation categories of thought and action in womanist soteriology.

Womanist soteriology interprets the experience of Black women in the past and present in dialogue with the atoning work of God in Christ. There exist diverse perspectives; not all womanist traditions assert a 'masculinist liberation soteriology', where God intervenes directly in the world to automatically free all suffering and bondage. Other schools of thought promote a 'survival and quality-of-life' soteriology, where humanity must use the resources provided by God to effect human flourishing till liberation comes. Therefore, the womanist way of salvation is also on another level 'making a way out of no way' or salvation through spiritual awareness of salvific options here and now.[26] Articulating salvation as intersectional and therefore always inside of categories of 'race' and gender extends a desire for *salvation for all within the community and environment*. In sum, womanist soteriology proffers broader salvific praxis:

> As a form of liberation theology, womanist theologies aim for the freedom of oppressed peoples and creatures. More specifically, womanist theologies add the goals of survival, quality of life, and wholeness to Black theology's goals of liberation and justice.[27]

Illustration: Magnificat

Womanist soteriology, specifically the articulation of 'race' and gender liberation, is the centrepiece of the track 'Magnificat' on the *Jamaican Bible Remix* album.[28] The Magnificat, or Mary's song, occurs in the first chapter of Luke's Gospel. Upon discovering she is pregnant, Mary sings a song of praise to God. While there is some debate about whether Mary sang the song, Luke is confident that she did. A womanist soteriological option is evident in the lyricism of the track. The message track comprises two Black British women's articulation of 'race' and gender liberation. The foremost reflection comes from Birmingham hip-hop artist 'Justice' Williams. Justice's lyrical performance is a celebration of ordinary women in liberation struggles in history. The second articulation is a call for practical engagement with the political process or 'survival-in-life' thinking in samples at the start and finish of the track by the first Black female bishop in the Church of England, the Bishop of Dover, the Rev Rose Hudson-Wilkin. Finally, although the genre is not foregrounded here, it is important to note that this song's musical accompaniment or music track is the 'Lover's Rock' reggae genre. As Lisa Palmer suggests, this genre has an affinity with Black women's political consciousness in Britain.[29]

> **Rev. Rose Hudson-Wilkin** – I believe we need to hear more women's voices in public life, in particular for the next generation. If we are going to change the dynamics of what we have today, where it is still sort of a man's world. Then women today need to step forward, to enable their children and their grandchildren, in particular girls and actually boys, too. Boys need to see that

their counterparts can be equally respected in terms of the contribution that they bring to the table.

JNT – Luuk 1

... mi a Gad-bles uman,
kaaz di Muos Powaful Gad du da mirikl ya fi mi — im uoli!
Gad gud kyaahn don.

Chorus

Justice – Oh hear me ladies, oh hear me girls, 'cause God has chosen you to save the world. All Black women of the earth, skin like dirt, you need to know your worth.

JNT – Im tek im an du som powaful sitn;
im skyata skyata buosi piipl.
Gad aal dong ruula aafa dem ai chuon
an lif op piipl we nobadi neva tingk se mata.

Justice – I said its time for action, them slavery chains have a chain reaction, oh yes. I am a fighter resister, a daughter, a sister, I am a fraction of progress.
Some don't lift a finger, but I ride the storm like the queen Masinga.
Because all through the process, trust me its mommy that knows best.

Yo, we need justice and equal rights, want to rest in peace when we sleep at night.
Fight for the children, they use and abuse them, world of confusion enough so we lose them to the streets. Ain't no one to keep eyes out for them, no one to protect or vouch for them, let's reach out to them mothers of the earth, we do more than give birth, lets show what we worth.

JNT – Im gi onggri piipl uol iip a gud sitn,
bot rich piipl im sen we wid dem tuu lang an. Gad elp im ervant dem, Izrel.
Im memba fi bi gud an kain tu dem.

Chorus

Justice – Oh hear me ladies, oh hear me girls, 'cause God has chosen you to save the world. All Black women of the earth, skin like dirt, you need to know your worth.

Justice – Armed with a pen and a paper and strong mind.
I read for those who couldn't, and there was a long line.

I'm too tall, the sky ain't the limit, a jungle sometimes, I got a panther spirit. With or without a husband, I am freeing minds like Harriet Tubman.

The fact is, they deported and killed the activists, but they are a part of us, so we are attached to this.

Teacher, go teach the youth. Ananci, defend our people like the queens of Ashanti, bridge the gap for future generations, download our history and make our own stations. So many sayings left to be said, and so many books left to be read, we need to wake up the mentally dead, we need to lead so we won't be led, 'nough said.

Rev. Rose Hudson-Wilkin – For young women today who say that politics is rather boring and not for them,
I would like them to think of politics, as something that is going to impact on their lives,
whether they like it or not. So, in other words, they will need to ask themselves, 'Do I want to just sit and have something done to me, or do I want to be right there, at the cutting edge, making decisions, contributing to the decisions that are going to impact on society of which they are a part?'

Justice – I want to shout-out all my womanists: Valentina Alexander
Caroline Redfern
Dulcie McKenzie

Maxine Howell Lynette Mullings Let's go
Let's go
Let's go . . .

Womanist soteriology is not entirely new to this exploration. This concept is inherent in the social soteriology we explored in Chapter 2. However, in the case of womanist soteriology, the doctrine of salvation is embellished so that redemption is a holistic and intersectional practice of thought and action.

Option 2: Black biblical studies

The second option is Black biblical studies. Black biblical studies as an option emerges from an analysis of Jahaziel's critique of the Bible:

> its plagiarised Bible stories, characters and concepts, the many human errors of the Bible and its contradictions.

Questioning biblical validity is integral to contemporary biblical studies. Modern Western biblical studies foreground critical thought as a central feature of the late nineteenth-century historical-critical method. Unencumbered by ecclesiastical constraints, historical criticism sets out to identify the Bible's constructed-ness: how the compiling of books reflects ancient theological decision-making, rather than objective, other-worldly designs.[30] However, not all theologians succumb to the analytical vortex of Western biblical criticism. Black biblical scholars, for instance, while invested in criticizing sacred texts, still, from the vantage point of Black experience and history, also question the discipline's preoccupation with the ancient world, literary analyses and original meanings. Western trajectories unwittingly neglect the role of bias of interest in academic training, and consequently negate the power relations underlying all interpretation.[31]

Black biblical scholars proffer an alternative interpretive pathway to rectify the perceived deficiencies in the Western method by setting themselves the additional tasks of inter(con)textual interpretation.[32] In other words, these scholars seek to mediate between the issues and contradictions in the scriptures and the history and experience of the African diaspora. For instance, African American Hebrew Bible scholar Randall Bailey develops a critical reading of the conquest narratives in the Hebrew Bible.[33] For Bailey, the narrative's lack of historical verification raises critical questions about how the text is used today. He suggests that the text works metaphorically to justify religious conquest in the past and present. Bailey also turns his gaze to the contemporary context in the United States to consider how ideas about God as an oppressor continue to harass minorities in America.[34] Similarly, in *Womanist Sass and Talk Back: Social (In)justice, Intersectionality and Biblical Interpretation*, African American womanist biblical scholar Mitzi Smith engages in an intersectional analysis of scripture to re-evaluate the contemporary social, political and cultural concerns of Black women in society. In Britain, the emerging Black British biblical studies has resonance with womanist approaches. Gifford Rhamie, one of the first African Caribbean scholars to receive a PhD in biblical studies in England, contrasts Britain's convivial post-war culture with the ancient culture of the Book of Acts to reconsider the ethnicity and religion of the Ethiopian eunuch. [35]

Yet, despite this body of scholarly works, Jahaziel is oblivious to the Black theological academy, and innocently, his viewpoint aligns in some ways with the scepticism of Eurocentric biblical studies.

A Black biblical studies critique of Jahaziel's perspective produces the second option, Black biblical studies. In this option, we take seriously the need to challenge the contradictions in scripture; specifically, the ways interpretation has been misused to oppress peoples and groups in history. Hence, Chapter 9 makes a centrepiece of 'Di Jamiekan Nyuu Testiment' to achieve this second decolonial option.

Illustration: Incarnation: No Blacks, No Irish, No Dogs

Black biblical studies methods feature in the song 'Incarnation'. While the song was a focus for engaging with post-war migration in Chapter 4, the song is also an example of inter(con)textual reading – in this case a dialogue between Jan (John) 1.14 and post-Second World War racisms in Britain. Traditionally, in the mainstream church context, this text is read as the divine mission; namely, that Jesus came to save humanity. However, the incarnation has specific considerations for Black people. God becoming flesh underwrites the equality of all of God's children, including those of a darker hue. If all flesh is good, we cannot privilege one body over another. As German theologian Dietrich states:

> And in the Incarnation the whole human race recovers the dignity of the image of God. Henceforth, any attack even on the least of men is an attack on Christ, who took the form of man, and in his own Person restored the image of God in all that bears a human form.[36]

As womanist theologian Eboni Turman reminds us, there is an adverse history associated with the incarnation and racial hierarchies:

> Peculiar optics of morality have situated bodies difference to consistently aggravate the social and psychic formulations of human selves and society.[37]

The song focuses on the incarnation's constructive social meanings. The message track of the song has two parts. The first is questioning the meaning of the incarnation in conversation with Black post-war history by the song's narrator. The resolution is the necessity to view the incarnation as a call for inclusion. The second part is a fictional account of a colonial citizen's story performed by soul artist Darren Ellison. The music track is inspired by the 'Soul Britannia' soundscapes of soul artist and producer Junior Giscombe.

> **BBC News** – In 1954 about 10,000 West Indians came to Britain. In 1955, it is believed another 15,000 will make the long journey. Already their coming has caused a national controversy.

But one point must always be borne in mind. Whatever our feelings, we cannot deny them entry, for all are British citizens, and as such, are entitled to the identical rights of any member of the (British) Empire.

JNT – Jan 1
Nou, di wan we a di Wod ton man, im kom liv mongks wi, kom liv mongks wi. (x2)

Robert – John 1:14 tells the story of Jesus' incarnation. That the Word becomes flesh and lives amongst us.
It means that God who is fully God and fully man, takes on human form.
The incarnation means that unequivocally, all creation is good and that all flesh, no matter what colour, no matter what tone is good. My parents believed in this meaning of the incarnation, that their flesh was good.
They were immigrants from Jamaica who came to work in Britain after the Second World War.
But they soon came to realise that not everybody thought the same.
When they went to look for places to live, they were greeted with signs that said, 'No Blacks, no Irish and no dogs.'

Darren – Sailed 5,000 miles with the sun way off behind me. They said it's gonna be a while till I feel that warm again. Staring at the grey skies as the cold rain starts to soak me. Faces that I recognize but no one I'd call a friend. Just one class above how my fathers sailed before me. Still no wiser 'bout the days that lay ahead. Hands and feet are free but shackled by economy. Just a possibility of a better life instead. Maybe if you give me time just to let me tell my story. 'Bout how I came to be in the land of hope and glory. Moment that I touched the ground all I see is consternation. You never let me explain that I'm here by invitation.

Chorus

Came expecting arms to open wide. No Blacks, no Irish, and no dogs inside. The sign is plain, and you don't try to hide. No Blacks, no Irish, and no dogs inside.

BBC News – Much of the outcry against the immigrants arises from the Colour-Bar, which legally does not exist in Britain, does not exist in Britain.

JNT – im kom kom liv mongks wi, kom iiv mongks wi.

Darren – 5 years 3 days to go till I get back to my family. Got to find a place to stay with a people playing games. There's a lot of empty rooms and I know I've got the money. Funny how my currency doesn't seem to be the same. Working from 5-to-5 and the guys are always on me. Now the fight to stay alive, never figured in my plans. Tried to find the house of God, only made the people angry. Sadly, realised that I'm seen as less than just a man. Maybe if you give me time just to let me tell my story. 'Bout how I came to be in the land of hope and glory. Moment that I touched the ground all I see is consternation. You never let me explain that I'm here by invitation.

Robert – The strange thing is that in church history the brilliant minds of the church have spent a great deal of time trying to explain the doctrine of the incarnation, that Jesus had to be fully God and had to be fully man and use that as a way of countering heresy. But less time has been spent on the *meaning* of the incarnation, what it means to *practice* the equality of all humanity. If the church had spent more time on the meaning and the practice of the incarnation, we wouldn't have this terrible Post-War story: No Blacks, no Irish and no dogs.

Chorus
Came expecting arms to open wide. No Blacks, no Irish, and no dogs inside. The sign is plain, and you don't try to hide. No Blacks, no Irish, and no dogs inside.

Darren – God is not dead, He's still alive. (x2)
I can feel him in my hands,

I can feel him in my feet,
I can feel him all over,
Feel him all over me. (x3)

Option 3: Black history

The third decolonial option is relatively straightforward; it is Black history. Black history emerges as a concern in Jahaziel's first post-Christian single, 'Amen Ra' (2016). The song is a personal testimony, a confession of his new faith, ancient Kemitic religion:

> Hail up nature
> Hail up Amen
> Hail up the ancestors who taught us nature
> Using the netra
> You get me?[38]

He continues by noting Black history as a point of departure from the Christian tradition as a conflict:

> I was in the church baptising,
> When I went back to Black writers
> Said I'm backsliding.[39]

Intriguingly, the Black writers referred to in the song were books by authors of Black history.[40] While Jahaziel faced opposition in his church, centring Black history within Black religion is not new to Caribbean religions. In the twentieth century, the religious-cultural movements of Ethiopianism, Garveyism and Rastafari all insurrected aspects of Black history as a feature of Black redemption. Yet there is no equivalent in African Caribbean diaspora Christianity in Britain. In churches, Black history has generally remained on the sidelines, relegated to Black History Month or church-run supplementary schools. Integral to all of these movements is an existential wrestling with slavery, and this concern must also be addressed in contemporary gospel music.

The Black history option is a refinement of the third decolonial thought, 'loving blackness'. Loving blackness is, among other things, an appreciation of Black peoples, their histories and cultures. It is not, however, essentialist or supremacist. Loving blackness includes addressing complex or unpalatable issues in Black life, and this is examined in more detail in Chapter 10.

Illustration: Pay Back

An example of foregrounding Black history on *Jamaican Bible Remix* is the pro-slavery reparations gospel song 'Pay Back'. It explores the controversial and problematic question of recompense for Black suffering in the trans-Atlantic slave trade. The track's narrative revolves around the scripture track, a sample from the JNT from Paul's Letter to Failiiman (Philemon), where the Apostle offers to repay Philemon for damage done. The Philemon passage has reparations credentials. As Dwight Allen Callahan demonstrates, this New Testament book's anti-slavery subplot has resonance with the Black compensation narrative of the 1960s Civil Rights struggle.[41] In the song, a case for reparations is played out in the message track in the form of a conversation between the esteemed BBC broadcaster Andrew Marr and theologian Robert Beckford. The broadcast was originally aired on the 'Start of the Week' show on BBC Radio 4 in 2005. The claim for reparations is made in two verses in the song, supported by interventions by the former reggae DJ and professor of sociology Lez Henry. The music track is inspired by the Bristol hip-hop sound of Roots Manuva.

Lez – Introducing Dr Lesley Henry lyrics, on the Jamaican Bible Remix. **JNT** – Paal leta tu Failiiman

Andrew Marr – Should Britain pay reparations and make a formal apology to the descendants of slaves? Much of our imperial and business strength has its origins in the Slave Trade of the 18th and early 19th Century and the academic Robert Beckford, argues in a new television programme that the Empire should pay back.

Chorus

JNT – Ef im did du notn rang tu yu ar im uo yu, . . . wi pie yu bak , pie yu bak. (x2)

Andrew Marr – Let's start with the scale of slavery, you compare it in the programme to the Nazi Holocaust.

Robert Beckford – For several decades of the Slave Trade it was cheaper to bring in Africans, work them to death and then replace them. So, we are looking at genocidal conditions on the Caribbean plantations.

Lez – The complexity of our condition is what you fail to comprehend, historically turned into chattels, beasts of burden less than men, thinking the only way to survive is to pretend to be you, mocking our very existence, animals in your human zoo.

Chorus

JNT – Ef im did du notn rang tu yu ar im uo yu, . . . wi pie yu bak pie yu bak. (x2)

Andrew Marr – There are two almost instant default defences made by a lot of British people when this is raised. The first is, that actually, the Slave Trade was something that was driven from Africa itself, that it was Muslim, Arab slave traders moving down south and that people in the centre ground of West Africa in particular were behind the Slave Trade.

Robert – What we focus on is what the British did. I am not that concerned with what one ethic group did to another ethnic group in Africa. I am interested in how the British participated in it, the huge profits that were made, and the incredible economic benefit to this country, and also the underdevelopment of Africa. And more so, the brutalization of African people in the Caribbean.

Lez – Wearing your names in our brains, African cultures disrespected, educated against ourselves is why we wind up disaffected. The saddest case, in the saddest place, even these words leave a bitter taste in my mouth cos as an African to you I'm human waste.

Chorus

JNT – Ef im did du notn rang tu yu ar im uo yu, . . . wi pie yu bak pie yu bak. (x2)

Andrew Marr – The second defence mechanism people say is well it was Britain which ended the Slave Trade, it was Wilberforce and then it was the Royal Navy and that Britain's got a lot be proud of in stopping the Slave Trade.

Robert – When I was taught history, I was always told to approach it from a multi-dimensional perspective to look at what happened in the subjugated histories, and not just read history like TV history from the good and the great. In the Caribbean, they talk about the slaves who ended slavery, the fact that there were rebellions across the Caribbean in the 1830s that made slavery economically impossible and just not viable. So, we know that Britain ended the trade in 1807, we know that slavery was ended in 1834/38 – took a little bit of a while for it to work through. But we cannot discount the influence and the work of Africans in the Caribbean who helped to undermine slavery. So, it's a much more complex picture.

Lez – You try to confuse telling the world you set us free. Good old England, don't you know, we were anti-slavery. The Clapham sect should get respect because they showed a lot of class, another historical distortion like your William '*Wilber farce*'.

Chorus

JNT – Ef im did du notn rang tu yu ar im uo yu, mi . . . wi pie yu bak. (x2)

Andrew Marr – and probably most controversially, you say that there should be payback, there should be reparation.

Robert – I believe that as a mature, sophisticated post-industrialized nation, that we are in a very strong and dynamic position, and to be able to apologise for the past is not a sign of weakness but a sign of strength. And I also believe that things like compensation and an apology are psychosocial in their impact; they help to heal the nation and enable people to move on.

Lez – We've seen through your deception, and speak our truth in redemption songs, reparations transcend money it's about repairing historical wrongs. Britain as a nation needs to face one brutal fact, we need more than just a band aid to put the African on the map.

Chorus

JNT – Ef im did du notn rang tu yu ar im uo yu, mi . . . wi pie yu bak pie yu bak. (x2)

Rev. Jesse Jackson – There must be repay for damage done, repair for damage done. It's not a foreign concept: Israel is a state of reparations for damage done, justifiably so. The African victims of the Slave Trade, we must demand repay for damage done. It may take many forms, but the concept is legitimate, and the need is great.

Chorus

JNT – Ef im did du notn rang tu yu ar im uo yu, mi . . . wi pie yu bak pie yu bak. (x2)

We've got to know if we never touch this.
We don't have a faith if we don't have social justice. (x4)

Conclusion

To recap, this chapter ponders ways of delinking from colonial Christianity. To contextualize this process in Black musicality, I appropriate decolonial thought from the musicality of the Rastafari-inspired reggae band Steel Pulse. Next, turning to the borders of Black Church music, three decolonial options emerge from an analysis of the former gospel music artist Jahaziel. These are womanist soteriology, Black biblical studies and Black history. The next chapter aims to translate the decolonial options into production tools.

7

Black voices at the Royal Wedding
Translating decoloniality into music production

How do we translate the decolonial options into production tools for a decolonial contemporary gospel genre? More precisely, how might we conceive womanist soteriology, Black biblical studies and Black history as songwriting practices? After all, in light of the necessity to communicate with musicians, decolonial musicking must be practical, recognizable and doable, even though this study of it is overtly technical. To make the decolonial options practicable, I propose we return to the cultural theories of the Black Church. As mentioned in the Introduction, the Black Church is a source of overlooked cultural practices. Moreover, these practices are not benign; they are 'politics of transfiguration' developed outside of the oppressive systems of coloniality[1] and capable of doing the work of social transformation.[2]

My intention here is to mobilize Black orality. That is, to graft each of the decolonial options onto everyday Black Church orality: forms of singing, speaking and preaching.[3] Black Church orality is good to work with. It is malleable, versatile and polyvalent. It can 'get direction through indirection'; it is '(h)ideology'.[4] This fluidity of meaning allows us to work with oral traditions as modalities for producing music. The most public display of Black Church orality was the Royal Wedding of Prince Harry and Meghan Markle in 2018. This event offers us a unique opportunity to render three production tools. This chapter identifies three practices on which we can graft the decolonial options.

The Royal Wedding

Diverse examples of Black orality are evident at the Royal Wedding of Prince Harry and Meghan Markle in 2018, and a Barthian way of looking (denotation/connotation) makes them legible.[5] The Royal Wedding of 2018 was the most important public multicultural event in recent years and only surpassed in significance for the royals by the funeral of Queen Elizabeth II in 2022. Visually, the wedding was a multicultural triumph. Both guests and performers were from diverse communities in Britain and abroad. Undoubtedly, the role of Meghan was instrumental. As one commentator noted:

> Meghan Markle is an important figure in terms of representation – as a biracial woman her presence in and amongst the all-White royal family takes us one step closer to having people of colour represented in positions of power in the UK – especially traditional, monarchical power.[6]

Black British and African American Christians participated in the wedding ceremony. The Kingdom Choir, Britain's leading Black choir, performed 'Stand by Me' by Ben E. King; the prayers of intersession were led by the Jamaican-born Rev Rose Hudson-Wilkin; and the sermon was preached by the African American Episcopal Bishop, the Rev Dr Michael Curry. Why does the Black presence and positioning matter? In post-war British history, until recently it was rare to have even one Black person attending a royal event. Thus, having so many Black folk in presence, as both guests and playing important roles, was a powerful statement of intent from the Royal Family and the nation. But this hoped-for Royal conviviality has been short-lived. The controversy surrounding Harry and Meghan's departure from the Royal Family, and their veiled accusation of racism in the Royal household, has dented, if not derailed, the promise of a new royal family cosmopolitanism.[7]

Tool 1: Crossover

The first oral tool is crossover. It is registered in the *choice* of song by the Kingdom Choir. Their rendition of 'Stand by Me' is an example of a 'type' of crossover contemporary gospel music. As mentioned in Chapter 4, crossover gospel was a staple of the 1990s British contemporary gospel music scene, *but a nuanced version appears here.* While the 1990s version is characterized as a commercially astute yet lyrically ambiguous genre, at the wedding, crossover is a Christian appropriation, or poaching, and spiritual interplay with a secular song. This second crossover is a musical borrowing where the original meaning is reworked and repositioned in the new version. It is a form of appropriation where, by virtue of context and performance, the secular song's lyrics are imbued with sacred meaning, and consequently the connotation of the sacred song is transformed – not through lyrical ambiguity but instead by a sacralization of the secular song's lyrics. Within the specificity of this case, 'Stand by Me' was transformed from an individual love song into a Christian commitment for lifelong support and fidelity. To develop crossover style as a production tool, I will 'repeat it with a difference',[8] so that the tool focuses on merging the sacred and profane by laying lyrics from sacred and secular music – musicality located in the music performance of the 'West Indian front room'.

Tool 2: The Black vernacular

The second oral tool is the Black vernacular. This second theme is revealed in the *Black speech* at the wedding. There were numerous Black vernacular traditions at play in the service. The mid-Atlantic singing voice of the Kingdom Choir, the Jamaican-British accent of Rev Rose Hudson-Wilkin and the African American diction of the preacher, the Rev Dr Michael Curry, were audible. These vernaculars are not benign or neutral; they are the product of discrete histories of linguistic politics inside the violent settler colonialism prevalent in the Caribbean and North America. In plantation society, African and European language systems collided with plantocracy racism to forge a distinctive linguistic racial hierarchy.[9] Black speech was relegated to the base and White speech allowed to reach the apex. In the West Indies, therefore, the Black vernacular is always inside questions of colonial/postcolonial struggle, such as how one speaks and locates one's self in the history, culture and politics of British imperialism. As Frantz Fanon notes, the language of the colonizer continues as a measure of Black civility:

> The colonized is elevated above his jungle status in proportion to his adoption of the mother country's cultural standards.

The Black vernacular is the focal point for achieving Black biblical studies, the second decolonial option. As mentioned previously, Black biblical studies is concerned with inter(con)textual interpretation. *To achieve this second option, I graft the JNT onto the Black vernacular.* That is to say, the JNT translation exemplifies inter(con)textuality. Specifically, it is the product of a cultural dialogue between the social, historical and cultural experience of Jamaicans and scripture. Thus, when sampled and positioned in contemporary gospel songs, it achieves the aims of the second decolonial option; it registers a Black interpretation. But there is more meaning at work here for the JNT. The JNT version has an additional decolonial register beyond inter(con)textuality, and this additional meaning offers an additional connotation for every song which appropriates the JNT audio. In Chapter 9, I will identify additional theological meaning in relation to atonement theory.

Tool 3: Dangerous memories

Finally, the third oral tool is dangerous memories. 'Dangerous memories' describes the retrieval of Black historical memory.[10] As Nathaniel Murrell shows in the Caribbean context, dangerous memories are inextricably linked to the history of slavery and colonialism. They are the memory of suffering and its overcoming. Dangerous memories also have a particular purpose in Western theology. They challenge present understanding and falsehood:

> memories in which earlier experiences break through to the centre point of our lives and reveal new and dangerous insights for the present. They illuminate for a few moments and with a harsh and steady light the questionable nature of things we have apparently come to terms with and show up the banality of our supposed 'realism'. They break through the canon of the prevailing structures of plausibility and have certain subversive features. Such memories are like dangerous and incalculable visitations from the past. They are memories that we have to take into account, memories, as it were, with a future content.[11]

Dangerous memories emerge in the articulation of an aspect of slavery in Rev Dr Curry's sermon. Bishop Curry referred to the music of slavery as a defining moment in African American understanding of the power of love:

> If you don't believe me, well, there were some old slaves in America's Antebellum South who explained the dynamic power of love and why it has the power to transform. They explained it this way. They sang a spiritual, even in the midst of their captivity. It's one that says 'There's a balm in Gilead . . .' a healing balm, something that can make things right. 'There is a balm in Gilead to make the wounded whole,' and one of the stanzas actually explains why. They said: 'If you cannot preach like Peter, and you cannot pray like Paul, You just tell the love of Jesus, How he died to save us all.' Oh, that's the balm in Gilead! This way of love, it is the way of life. They got it!'[12]

Introducing dangerous memories of the slave narrative was courageous. Why? Because this small island's historical politics, characterized by the 'double whammy' of historical amnesia and postcolonial melancholia, produces a very British White fragility which often stifles, disavows or attacks mention of slavery's memory as legitimate Black suffering.[13] Explicit mention of slavery evades Black Church music. As I have expressed earlier, at the heart of this neglect is colonial Christianity's negative Black ontology (Chapter 2).

Dangerous memories in the preaching of the Black Church tradition are spiritual and material. Spiritual dangerous memory describes the histories of personal salvation. They retell how God has worked in the lives of believers and their communities of faith and their radical implications for today. The Black Christian is adept at communicating this first form. As shown in Chapter 3, the Black Church tradition of testimony is a context for the expression of tremendous stories of personal faith in the life of the believer. In contrast, material dangerous memory denotes the social and concrete history of the people. It encompasses the preaching and reflection on stories of slavery, colonialism, migration, settlement and social experience. In the best preaching, dangerous memories are a blend of the spiritual and material. Yet, tragically, contemporary gospel music in Britain has only wrestled with the former, the spiritual modes, and the material forms are less prevalent.

Grafting the Black history option onto dangerous memories facilitates a critical reflection in history in contemporary gospel music. It allows us to consider both the heroic and grotesque aspects of Black history in contemporary gospel music. To illustrate the use of the third tool, Chapter 10 makes a case study of the history of West Indian enslavement – specifically, how we remember slavery in contemporary gospel music.

Conclusion

In conclusion, to operationalize the decolonial options, that is, put them to use for music production, I graft the decolonial options onto Black orality to produce three production tools. The tools are crossover, the Black vernacular and dangerous memories. They are everyday features of Black orality and therefore practices that we can appropriate for producing the decolonial options. The next stage of this project is to show how each of these tools works in practice.

Part IV

Production tools

8

West Indian front room crossover

A crossover style is the production tool for producing womanist soteriology in contemporary gospel music. Previously, I identified two types of crossover music. I have acknowledged the lyrically ambiguous 1990s commercial gospel music version and also the borrowing and spiritualizing of a secular song's lyrics, exemplified by the Kingdom Choir at the Royal Wedding in 2018. Here, I will continue to work with the second type of crossover but in a more explicit way. Whereas the Choir blur the sacred and secular by appropriating and transforming the meaning of the secular song, here I propose another form of crossover as the best way of ingraining womanist soteriology in music production. This third type is the laying of sacred and secular lyrics. However, to demonstrate this specific crossover in lyricism, I turn not to theory nor overseas contexts but instead to Black British experience – specifically, crossover techniques from the West Indian front room stereogram record playing performativity.

Crossover remains a controversial musical strategy, and from the start, I will address these concerns as a symptom of a much deeper malaise, a continued conflict between the sacred and profane in Black Church life. This conflict underpins a division between traditionalists and progressives in contemporary gospel music. Next, to make evident the workings of first tool, I will return to the Windrush generation, but this time focusing on the music culture of the West Indian front room. The West Indian front room describes the aesthetic politics associated with the beautification of the front rooms of West Indian homes in the Windrush period. Integral to the room is the stereogram music player and a distinctive turntable technology. Finally, the illustration of the crossover practice is the track 'Caesarea Philippi' from *Jamaican Bible Remix*.

Central to this chapter's method is a participant observation of music practices from the West Indian front room. Participant observation is 'the systematic description of events, behaviours and artifacts in the social setting chosen for study'.¹ Participant observation is good to work with because it allows us to collect data from everyday cultural practices, or 'people ethnography'.² Appropriating participant observation, I will consider the soteriology embedded in the discrete crossover practice.

Traditional and progressive

Not every artist is content with crossover music as a gospel genre. While the criticism of each type of crossover differs, I will consider the criticism of the appropriation of secular songs. Take, for instance, the opposition to the Kingdom Choir's song choice at the Royal Wedding. Disagreement (but not bad faith) towards the choir's rendition came from an international gospel star. The journalist Marcia Dixon noted that African American gospel superstar Donnie McClurkin took to social media to register his reservations regarding the song choice in the ceremony.³ McClurkin's view matters because it arises from a traditionalist camp in contemporary gospel music. Theologically, traditionalists disavow a secular song's incorporation into the gospel repertoire because in their view the primary mission of gospel artists and their music is to promote the Christian faith. The genre's evangelical task is weakened, obfuscated and demeaned by the performance of secular songs.⁴ However, in contrast, progressives, armed with an incarnational theology of culture, broaden the gospel repertoire to include music with Christian significance, such as the crossover performance at the Royal Wedding.⁵ This 'family quarrel' might be a trivial concern to outsiders. Yet it matters in gospel music circles because beneath the surface of the dispute resides an uneasy history with the sacred and profane. Let me explain.

The debate between gospel music traditionalists and progressives fails to address the real cause of the discord. The real distress is an either/or rather than a both/and approach to the 'sacred and profane'. While the former (either/or) promotes a sharp distinction between the music of the church and the world, the latter (both/and) is more fluid, seeking to blend, incorporate, appropriate and rework musical thought from all spaces and places to service the needs of the Kingdom. Within the specificity of this study, taking the latter, 'both/and', seriously allows us to fold lyrics from subjects of sacred into the profane and thereby interpret the meaning of God as having social justice implications.

West Indian front room aesthetics and spirituality

The West Indian front room contains a historic example of the crossover method. This technique emerges in the interface of migration, culture and new music technology,[6] and as a politics of transfiguration, developed outside of the control of policing whiteness. There are two parts to detailing this method. First, I will identify the social and cultural context of the West Indian front room. Second, to unearth the features of this crossover method, I will show how playing music on the stereogram in the front room signifies a both/and approach to the sacred and profane.

The West Indian front room refers to the space associated with the adornment of the first-generation immigrant's homes in the post-war years. But the aesthetic belies a more complex history:

> The front room is a metaphorical 'frontline', because through its aesthetics and domestic practices, it displays a subtle 'politicised edge' between Black and White cultures. This edge is a performance of private 'backyard' imagined and reconstructed narratives, mediated by desire, status, difference, race, class, gender, and generation.[7]

A chronic housing shortage in post-war Britain led a racialized media to equate immigration with a national housing crisis. Therefore, dwelling space became a focal point for both racialized discrimination and resistance. Given the strategic importance of 'making a home' in Black women's political culture[8] once colonial citizens purchased their residences, the interior choices were inscribed with diasporic significance. Beautification signified the meaning of having a home away from home.[9] While the decoration and ornamentation were most often curated by women, the use of the space differed. My mother's time was devoted almost exclusively to religious pursuits. Conversely, my father only occupied the space on Sunday mornings to play music. For both of them, in dramatic contrast to the world outside, the home or the 'yard', as it was colloquially known, was a 'heterotopia': a shelter in a time of storm.[10] However, the 'yard' was more than a catharsis; it was also a productive space for Black creative production and spiritual re-existence, and the front room was integral.

Michael McMillan identifies several features of the front room. Among these are an aesthetic and respectability, to which I will add Christian spirituality.

As an aesthetic, the West Indian front room was mimesis with a difference. Like the English parlour, its status was measured by what it contained. Under the curation of the colonial citizens, the room developed a complex aesthetic:

> The front room was a contradictory space, where the efficacy of the display was sometimes more important than the authenticity of the objects, such as artificial flowers, plastic pineapple ice buckets, floral patterned carpet and wallpaper that never matched, and pictures of the scantily clad 'Tina' next to 'The Last Supper'.[11]

West Indian respectability has a long and complex history in Caribbean culture.[12] Originally a means of maintaining colonial Christian hegemony over colonized Blacks, the meaning of respectability is transformed in post-war Britain. Respectability, in the hands of the descendants of enslaved peoples, is no longer a tool for domination, but instead it is changed into a framework to counter the racialized stereotypes of Black family life:

> As a cultural institution of self-making, valorising the front room as a space of Black interiority, resists the racist trope that we live on the street, and have no homes to go to, with families and values. This interiority has shaped and been shaped by the cultural politics of Post-War Caribbean migration and reveals the rich complexity of 'Black domestic life' that the 'generality of society' rarely understands.[13]

Respectability as diaspora personal attainment was 'literally' framed in marriage and family portraits and educational certificates decorating the walls of the front room:

> For example, pictures on walls or shelving of men and women in their new work clothing from various industries, such as nursing, transport, and manufacturing (that were often sent back home), as well as family portraits from local photographic studios, signalled the transition to a new life in Britain, and confirmed that these immigrants were 'here to stay'.[14]

A 'politics of absences' is also signified in picture frames collage. As Michael Macmillan continues:

> Frozen in time, these photos composed studio environments, neither home nor work, reveal how the immigrants imagined themselves. A reconstructing out of the subject as document was sent 'back home,' to kinfolk and to real and desired spouses, in the form of photos and letters that often *omitted telling them about signs in windows reading No Irish, no dog, no coloureds, seen while searching for accommodation*. There is a structure of 'presences' in photographs, but also 'absences'.[15]

Christian spirituality was also a feature of the West Indian front room. For the early Black Christian settlers, the room was also a makeshift sanctuary. Set apart from the rest of the house, it was an ideal retreat for individual and familial devotions. A 'physical sanctification' elevated the room's status (not everyone was allowed to enter) for informal religious gatherings that eventually evolved into the first Black Pentecostal churches and denominations. All the major African Caribbean Pentecostal denominations can identify a specific house and front room where their tradition originates. For example, my mother birthed two churches for her denomination, the Pilgrim Holiness Church, from our front room in Northampton and Coventry, respectively.

Home entertainment

Home entertainment, especially playing records, was a pastime in the front room. Integral to this leisure pursuit was the coveted stereogram, a music centre pre-dating the mass consumer hi-fi units of the 1970s and 1980s. In the 1960s, a prized possession was the 'Blue-Spot' (made by the German manufacturer Blaupunkt) stereogram. Later, Decca, Hacker, Dynatron, Bush, Pye and HMV were some of the popular makes. The styling was important. Encased in natural or imitation wood, and designed to portray fashionable drinks cabinets, stereograms were the fruit of waged labour and the focal point for relaxation. They were not cheap to buy. In the 1960s, a good unit cost around £200 when the average wage was between £15 and £25 per week. A family had to save to purchase one or apply for financing options such as hire-purchase.

The arrival of West Indians in Britain created a ready market for Black music records in immigrant and host communities.[16] Recording studios and entrepreneurs capitalized on the new demographic by establishing local Black music record shops in major cities.[17] Living outside of London and Birmingham was a problem for procuring music. My father had to rely on work colleagues travelling to larger cities with more Black areas to provide him with new music from 'back home'. By the time I was able to study his musical rituals, he had already amassed an extensive collection of Trojan label ska and reggae singles and Euro-American and African Caribbean gospel albums. The period of music selection relevant to this study is when my family lived in a terraced house in the market town of Wellingborough in Northamptonshire in the late 1960s and early 1970s. It was a small dwelling with two rooms downstairs – one of which was our front room, the other was where we ate our meals and watched television. In a social context hostile to West Indians and their British-born children, our home and the church were the only guaranteed safe spaces for our bodies.[18] Spaces where we were not under surveillance by the local police and free from the threat of casual racism by passers-by on the street. The sanctuary of the space only served to intensify the importance of our activities, including playing music.

Selector

Participant observation of my father's music consumption and a *thick* or interpretive description is the source of knowledge for this crossover method. There are both substantive and functionalist dimensions of his actions.[19] I observe rituals and the interplay of theological ideas, but ultimately the function – that is, the outcome of the actions – is significant. Rituals are not benign; they have power, and they can momentarily challenge the social order.[20] In this case, my father's turntable technique was boundary-breaking, signifying a dissolving of a sacred/profane binary opposition of Black music lyricism.

I observed my father's weekly ritual of playing music, but *only* after completing my pre-church Sunday morning rituals of 'purification'.[21] The event was spiritual. The first act was an ablution, the cleansing; that is, washing and dressing for church, and therefore being suitably attired to gain access to the space. Second, I had to be positioned in the proper location. The front room was 'big people place'. So, I had to ensure that I was rightly stationed in a non-essential location, such as sitting in a corner or standing statuesque inside the doorway. Only then was I acceptable to gain access to the musical part of the ritual as a participant in the music culture. I observed my father re-territorialize the front room by lounging by the stereogram, opening its cupboards and pondering which records to play. His facial expression and posture were reminiscent of his Jamaican 'Saturday soup' preparation, choosing ingredients and laying them out while waiting for the pot to boil. His 'cooking music', however, was also a three-part process. The first part of the ritual is 'selection'. He carefully picked his records to play like a surgeon appropriating a surgical instrument to operate. Music selection is a dynamic process encompassing the construction of narratives full of tensions and their resolutions. Importantly, my father commandeered various music genres and lyricism from Jamaican ska, blue beat and rocksteady, American soul, and

Caribbean and African American contemporary gospel music (some of which belonged to my mother). The second part is preparation. Preparation describes the way he meticulously removed the record from its sleeve, ensuring that no fingerprints were deposited on the surface of the record before it was placed on the turntable. Gently lifting the needle onto the record was the end of the preparation. The final part was transcendence. He sat back, relaxed and let the music soak his body. For every track he played, he swayed and moved in time with the syncopated bass line. Occasionally, he broke out in a two-step dance routine, which, as religious dance theorist H. Patten demonstrates, is historically rooted in the African practice of the body and mind centring in African Traditional Religion.[22] On reflection, the melding of body, materials and machine was also a foreshadowing of Afro-futurism's melting of Black bodies into technology or 'mantronics'.[23] The pleasure my father derived from the ritual was infectious; this moment was one occasion of father and son, togetherness and enjoyment for both of us.[24]

Broad

There are two types of music selection. The first was derived from my father's pre-fundamentalist Christian life before he became more committed and joined a conservative church. The second type of experience appears later, after his conversion to Christianity.

The first type comes from his pre-fundamentalist Christian phase. Generally speaking, my father was motivated by a diaspora religiosity – the type which affirms belief in supernatural beings yet is suspicious of organized religion. He would slip away into the front room and tell us he was going to 'relax'. These words signalled the beginning of a suturing of gospel songs by Euro-American crooner Jim Reeves and Jamaican gospel sensation Joseph Niles, African American soul music by Sam Cooke and Nat King Cole, reggae music from Jamaica's Jimmy Cliff and a roster of Trojan label artists. Whether the primary consideration for his choices was sonic or textual is uncertain, but what interested me was the crossover of ideas in the lyricism of songs. I recall, for instance, my father playing Desmond Dekker and the Aces' '(Poor Mi) Israelite' (1968) followed by a message of divine liberation from Joseph Niles' 'Shadrack.'[25] The first song tells of the suffering of the Black poor in postcolonial Jamaica. The second song describes divine protection over evil in the story of Shadrach, Meshach and Abednego (Daniel 3). The sacred/profane binary was dissolved. The layering of the two song's subject content, as a consequence of playing one song immediately after the other, inadvertently suspended the traditional boundaries between what was otherwise known to be sacred and secular lyrics and, in the particularity of this music selection, presented a seamless relationship between the social world and divine protection. Another crossover example was a layering of Bob and Marcia's reggae version of Nina Simone's 'Young Gifted and Black' with the popular chorus 'God Is Not Dead' performed by the Black British gospel pioneers The Harmonizers. The first song was an affirmation of blackness or loving blackness. The second song was a praise of Jesus' resurrection power. In this second example, the layering practice *bonded* together the subjects of loving blackness and divine power.

The first type has resonance with the hip-hop turntable technology. While my father was operating with only one turntable, the method has a 'flow' consistent with the DJ's music selection:

> DJs layer sound literally one on top of the other, create a dialogue between sound and words. What is the significance of the flow . . . interpreting these concepts theoretically, one can argue that they create and sustain rhythmic motion, continuity and embellish this continuity through layering.[26]

We can make sense of the first type of crossover by identifying what it is not. Was it a chance happening? No, it was a regular event. Was it an experiment with sonic dynamics? Not quite, because the aesthetic of the music was always inclusive of lyricism and therefore the interplay of words across each record cannot be ignored. Given the ritualization of this event and the seamlessness to the flow of musical genres, I suggest we turn to African residual themes in Caribbean culture for interpretation.

The first type has resonance with aspects of ancient African Traditional Religion. It is the unconscious memory of a lost spirituality. 'African Traditional Religion' is a term used to describe the standard features of the diverse religions of West Africa.[27] It is essentially a holistic system, with few, if any, binary divisions. Take, for instance, the view of the spiritual world where the living and dead interplay.

> They are considered to be still part of their families. They are believed to live close to their homes where they lived when they were human beings. They show interest in their surviving families, and in return their families remember them

by pouring out parts of their drinks and leaving bits of food for them from time to time. The living dead may also visit their surviving relatives in dreams or visions, or even openly, and make their wishes known.[28]

In African Traditional Religion, religion is ubiquitous and inseparable from all other aspects of life. The supreme deity and lesser divinities are active in daily human existence. Further blurring of boundaries exists in the role of the deities. Take, for instance, the Yoruba *orisa* (god or spirit) Èṣù. As scholarship demonstrates, he is the messenger of the supreme god Olodumar, taking sacrifices to him and conversely communicating from God to humans. But Èṣù has his own complex and contradictory role and personality. He is also represented as a di-unital character with the capacity to do both good and evil.[29] He compels people to do evil or good; he is both an avenger and benevolent. Hence, the sacred and profane are both integral to Esu's character and mission.[30] Foregrounding the African repercussion in my father's practice makes legible a lengthier history of fusing faith and experience, 'unencumbered by spatial and temporal circumscription'.[31]

The first crossover I term a *broad* vision of the sacred. It represents my father's pre-fundamentalist Christian mixing ritual – one where lyricism travels across a range of subjects unencumbered by previously existing boundaries. The broad view has a biblical precedent. It is not outside of Christian thought. It reflects the belief that all creation is God's and therefore capable of reflecting God's glory: 'We know that the whole creation has been groaning as in the pains of childbirth right up to the present time' (Romans 8.22 NIV). It is also present in the belief in Christ's dominion over all the earth: 'God has put all things under the authority of Christ and has made him head over all things for the benefit of the church' (Ephesians 1.22 NIV).

This *broad* vision of music selection is not isolated; it has identification with the Black Christian sound system scene in the 1990s. There is a 'sonic migration'[32] from the front room to the Christian sound system[33] by young people from the churches to provide a Black Christian version of the Jamaican sound system culture in Britain.

The epoch of the Christian sound system movement begins with the inception of Shekinah Sound Ministries in 1996. This dynamic group of musical ministers had a passion and desire to share the Christian message through the medium of a sound system. Just like their secular counterparts, Shekinah had a sound system set complete with speaker boxes, amplifiers, equalizers, mixers and effects units. The selectors played the music to get the crowd moving and the MCs brought the musical 'vibes' on the microphone. According to its founder, Rico, what made Shekinah different from every other secular sound was the fact that it was focussed on outreach; their purpose was to 'minister the good news of Jesus Christ'. They also provided a service for Christians who needed a DJ/ sound system for their wedding receptions and other social celebrations.[34]

The Christian sound system scene was a sacred/secular binary of church hall and dance hall music:

> The Christian sound system movement in Britain represents an exchange between 'church hall' and 'dancehall' which started in the late 1990s. This contentious engagement between 'secular' and 'sacred' spaces is related to the wider discipline of theology and popular culture.[35]

This dynamic equivalent of the West Indian front room broad vision was Spirit-led:

> Participants expressed a reliance on the Holy Spirit for the ability to discern how to navigate the dancehall space and employ wisdom in their decision-making in all aspects of the sound system performance. The Spirit is guiding the selector to choose the right songs, the Spirit is inspiring the MC to speak appropriate words on the microphone and The Spirit does the work of conviction in the hearts and minds of the audience.[36]

Narrow

By the mid-1970s, my father's practice changed. The metamorphosis resulted from his conversion to fundamentalist Christianity; he became a Christian and joined my mother's church. At that time, the church's discipline forbade 'worldly' pleasures, including cinema-going and listening to popular music. These doctrinal dictates were the product of a Euro-American Christian imagination with deep roots in the nineteenth-century evangelical revival.

Fundamentalist Christianity has a profound impact on my father's performance of the sacred. The turntable/selector ritual was retained, but the pattern of consumption significantly altered. Sunday morning music became the exclusive domain of sacred music from African Caribbean and American recordings. Standing in the front room, I was only exposed to songs from the early 1970s gospel albums of the first UK gospel group, The Harmonizers, and

Caribbean gospel legends Joseph Niles and the Consolers, as well as gospel from Euro-American country music star Jim Reeves. Occasionally, he would 'backslide' and play a little reggae, but to secure his salvation, the secular music was banned, consigned to the annals of 'devil music' and a source of corruption. To demonstrate his transformation, he gave away his immaculate first-edition collection of Trojan single records to our neighbour's son.

I name the second type the *narrow* vision of the sacred. Here, the performance is restricted to the playing of 'explicitly' Christian music. It has resonance with both biblical and Eurocentric sociological traditions of thought. In the Bible, the sanctification narratives affirm that some things are meant to be set apart or sanctified – and the world rejected. Moreover, those who follow Christ commit to cleansing themselves to do God's work:

> Those who cleanse themselves from the latter will be instruments for special purposes, made holy, useful to the Master and prepared to do any good work. (2 Tim. 2.21)

This process includes abandoning the things of the world:

> Put to death, therefore, whatever belongs to your earthly nature: sexual immorality, impurity, lust, evil desires, and greed, which is idolatry. (Col. 3.5)

Classic sociological thought also explains the *narrow* vision. Rudolf Otto and Émile Durkheim represent the sacred as separate from the profane. While the work of these giants of the discipline has different views of the sacred, they are unified on its separateness from the profane. In *The Idea of the Holy* (1917), for Otto (1869–1937), the experience of the sacred was to become radically aware of one's profaneness.[37] The experience of the numinous is overpowering, and its *mysterium tremendum* makes evident God as 'wholly other'.[38] Similarly, in the *Elementary Forms of Religious Life* (1912), Durkheim (1885–1917), while refusing to associate the sacred with a non-rational entity (numinous), nonetheless divides the world into two domains of the sacred and profane,[39] though the sacred and profane interact and are dependent on each other, and the dichotomy does not always presuppose that the sacred is good and the profane bad. Even so, in the particularity of my father's case, the general division has resonance with his end point – a fundamentalist-inspired musical apartheid.

The *narrow* vision of the sacred is normalized in contemporary gospel music awards in Britain. A cursory glance at the lyrical content of recent contemporary gospel music winners' albums at the Music of Black Origin awards (MOBOs) underlines their limitations – the narrow view. On the 2015 Mobo-winning album by Faith Child, *Airborne*, the subject of the sacred is folded into personal ethics, personal empowerment and individuality. The tracks 'Tunnel Vision', 'Chosen Ones' and 'The Zone', for instance, all explore personal ethics and devotion within contexts marked by personal moral dilemmas. Only with the track 'Keeping Up with the Joneses,' featuring former artist Jahaziel, do we hear the sacred ripple over the social world in a critique of consumerism. But that track's narrative trajectory, like much of Christian hip-hop, is pietistic in its prognosis and omits structural critique of the causes of consumer culture. A similar narrative arch appears in the work of the 2016 winner Guvna B. The album *Secret World* is set in the Black urban space of twenty-first-century London. The artist makes a solitary reference to urban decay and the government's benign neglect.[40] Only on the track 'Let My People Go' is there a semblance of a broader soteriology. The 2017 winners, Volney Morgan and New Ye, do not venture beyond neo-Pentecostal themes of spiritual overcoming ('Sick and Tired') and intimacy with God. (There was no ceremony in 2018 or 2019.) The 2020 MOBO contemporary gospel music award winner was CalledOut Music, a talented singer and songwriter based in the UK. Not one song on his sophomore album, *In Due Time*, moves beyond the 'colonial boundaries' of personal salvation.[41] The 2021 winner Guvna B's album *Everywhere+Nowhere* rehearses the pattern of the previous albums. The album, though, makes the occasional reference to the social context of urban London ('straps', blades and other references to youth violence, etc.) and mentioned racism on the track 'Fall on Me'. Yet on the same track, he professes that he 'does not have the answers' except to defer to the power of prayer. Finally, the 2022 winner Still Shadey rehearses the personal salvation tropes associated with earlier generations of Christian hip-hop.[42]

The *broad* vision of music selection is the tool for the decolonization of contemporary gospel music. Translated into music lyricism, West Indian front room crossover's broad approach to lyrical concerns facilitates a thematic transformation: collapsing the gospel message into the socio-historical world to refuse the separation of the sacred and profane.

Illustration: Caesarea Philippi

The *broad* type of the sacred is evident in the song 'Caesarea Philippi'. The song reflects on Peter's answer to Jesus' question in Maak (Mark) 8.27: 'who do men say I am?' ('Uu pi ipl se mi bi?') In this exploration the rapper Juice

Aleem considers how various Black Atlantic communities have answered the same question in diverse sociopolitical and religious-cultural contexts. The purpose of the lyricism is to reveal various sociopolitical and religious-cultural considerations of Jesus as Messiah – and thereby dissolve the sacred/profane boundaries of Christian thinking in music-making. The scripture track is Maak (Mark) 8.27, and the message track consists of Juice's reflections and samples from American theologians and also from the motion movie *Malcolm X*.[43] The music is inspired by hip-hop musicality.

> **Juice** – Yes indeed, this is Juice Aleem.
> South Birmingham.
> Just chilling with my big brother Jesus.
> Jamaican Bible Remix.
> Listen good, listen good . . .
>
> **JNT** – Maak 8
>
> Chorus
>
> 'Uu pi ipl se mi bi?' (x4)
> uu unu tingk mi bi?
>
> **Juice** – Was a baby, born in a manger predicted?
> Three Wise Guys knew the Sun had been evicted?
> Essenes said: He would be in war
> with the wicked.
> Others said he joined this very same group of mystics.
> Black or White?
> Nazareth or Nazarite?
> Jasper skin.
> Eyes glow in a di night.
> Feet like burnt brass,
> turn water walker.
> Gospels, Apostles,
> Really who's the author?
> So many books.
> Took a look in Revelation.
> Black as the night.
> Is the first in creation
> Really Son of God?
> With dem African features?

Lesson for the learned
A poor righteous teacher.

Albert Cleage – I believe that Jesus is the black messiah, is a revolutionary teacher
send by God, sent by God. (x3)

Chorus

'Uu piipl se mi bi?' (x4)
uu unu tingk mi bi?

Juice – Young in the temple.
Some simple essentials.
Eighteen years.
Left studying the mental.
Lost in Egypt?
Must look the same like.
Black Madonna.
Dear Mama
Birthed a Kushite.
Middle Eastern?
When there was no Middle East.
Picture that you seen
Portrait of a beast?!
Maybe got married had a couple babies.
(**Robert** – Is he speculating that Jesus got married?
Tony – Yes but it's OK, he is just being historical critical).

Juice – Searchin' the histories
Can mek a man crazy.
I guess you were
Lookin' for a Yeshua,
Ha-Mashiakh.
Yes, you were convinced of that.
Messiah stats.
Covered in oils and fats.
Moisturize.
A trait known amongst the Blacks.
Son of Man.
Known in his habitat. (x3)

Chung Hyun Kyung – My image of God now is like a middle-aged Korean woman looking like my mother, very warm, and affirming. Very available, and strong and down to earth.

Chorus

'Uu piipl se mi bi?' (x4)
uu unu tingk mi bi?

Juice – So many words
Said about but never said by
The Logos.
Standing with the stars on his right side.
Peace!
He spoke as a sword
So, remember.
Two edges
One for the law and the lenders.
For revolution
A true rebel leader.
Smashed up the markets.
To Rah
He's a geezer.
Hunted by Romans.
Flippin' over tables.
Real livin' life
As opposed to the fables.
Hair like lamb's wool
skin pure sable.
Research in the works
If you true and livin' able.
But only if you're able.

Malcolm X, The Movie – Just a moment, just a moment. God is White, isn't it obvious, isn't it obvious. (x3)

Chorus

'Uu piipl se mi bi?'
uu unu tingk mi bi? (x4)

Conclusion

West Indian front room crossover, therefore, is a resource for songwriters, musicians and worship leaders. It represents a vision of writing songs about God within a broader world view where the songs about Christian experience explore all aspects of human life, including God's concern for justice over all of the earth (Amos 5.24).

9

The Black vernacular

The second tool for producing decolonial gospel music is the Black vernacular. The Black vernacular is the focal point for decolonizing interpretation. As noted in Chapter 7, language choice in the diaspora (Royal Wedding) is intimately related to decoloniality and therefore a good vehicle for communicating the interests of Black biblical studies. Language use matters in Black music. It can signal the legitimacy of local dialects (hip-hop in Black America), resistance to dominant imperial linguistics (reggae music in Britain) or gesture towards Black urban spiritualities (grime in the UK).[1] The agency of language choice justifies the question 'What language best conveys the interpretive interests of Black biblical studies?' There are several options because the Black British context is diasporic and its language practices characterized by diasporic flows from the Caribbean, North America and Africa. There is much to choose from, and many of the permutations have decolonial potential.

I propose the Jamaican 'patwa' (patois) of the JNT as the register for the interests of Black biblical studies. My decision is based on three premises. First, that the JNT is the product of decolonial biblical studies; it signifies decoloniality but in the form of vernacular hermeneutics. Second, Jamaican patwa in the form of the JNT carries additional decolonial meaning, which embellishes its inclusion. It is atonement for the oppression of colonial linguistics. Finally, Jamaican patwa is relatively easy to produce in contemporary gospel music and in the specificity of this case, the JNT is sampled on all of the tracks of *Jamaican Bible Remix*. However, the JNT represents *a model* rather than a definitive universal choice. The task of other diaspora communities is to consider how their language conventions might also signify biblical interpretation. For instance, an area to consider in West African gospel music is the signifying potential of code-switching.[2]

This chapter explains the mechanisms of the JNT as the second decolonial tool. First, I begin by contextualizing the politics of Jamaican patwa as part of the reappraisal of the Black vernacular in the postcolonial period. I consider the implications of these debates for postcolonial biblical interpretation, such as the JNT. However, Jamaican patwa carries additional decolonial/theological register, and this consideration leads to a second explanation: the JNT as an atonement. To parse this second decolonial/theological meaning, I engage in a cultural-theological dialogue, a conversation between two divergent views of Jamaican patwa and theories of atonement. The chapter ends with an illustration, 'Beatitudes', from *Jamaican Bible Remix*.

Language after empire

Language use matters in the postcolonial world. It surfaces as a significant linguistic issue in the twentieth century. It features among national independence movements across the continent and diaspora. The continuity of colonial linguistic imperialism of former colonial powers leads to a questioning of the hegemonic colonial language's place in postcolonial nation-building. Theorists, to paraphrase Audre Lorde, question if 'the former colonial tongue can ever destroy the neo-colonial house'. In continental African literary circles, a mid-twentieth-century, post-independence debate set out what I term as two generic responses to the predicament. These are 'reluctant to disavow' and 'assertive nativism'. 'Reluctant to disavow' describes the decision by some writers to foreground former colonial languages in literary production. For instance, writers such as Chinua Achebe publish in colonial English but comfort themselves in the knowledge that they are gaining as broad an audience as possible for their radical and provocative ideas. In his words, Achebe cautions: 'let us not in rejecting the evil, throw out the good with it.'[3] 'Assertive nativism', in contrast, stresses that only the native tongue can capture the visceral realities of the colonial and postcolonial world and therefore it must be foregrounded in literary works. By doing so, writers such as Ngũgĩ wa Thiong'o prioritize their African language as a political act. He states that African literature can only be 'written in the language of the peasantry and working class . . . the agency of the coming revolutionary break with neo-colonialism'.[4]

Language use is a political issue in the Anglophone Caribbean and its diaspora. A similar debate rages but with a difference. The dividing line in the Caribbean is between colonial English and bilingualism. The latter affirms the Creole languages of the descendants of formerly enslaved peoples. The debate is yet to reach a final resolution.[5] But what of contemporary Britain? On the one hand, standard English is the norm for education and commerce; on the other, there is a creeping recognition of the complex contribution of Jamaican patwa and other former colonial linguistics to language development. Jamaican patwa is now understood as a component of a broader sociolect; that is, Black British English (BBE).[6] However, BBE resides outside of mainstream professional acceptance.[7] Its marginalization is political. As Robert Phillipson reminds us, in colonial history, the Queen's English was not only constructed as superior but set the linguistic rules to marginalize the Black vernacular, such as 'pidgin' and 'creole', to 'reinforce Eurocentric myths and stereotypes' about Black people.[8] Suppression of the Black vernacular made national headlines in 2022 when a private school in London banned Black phrases:

> Ark All Saints Academy, in Camberwell, is also attempting to crackdown on phrases such as 'that's long' and 'he cut his eyes at me' which is of Caribbean origin and means to glance sharply at someone before turning away and closing their eyes. The private-run school was blasted by a professor as proof that 'very little has changed' over the decades with the schooling of Black children. The grassroots organisation Black Learning Achievement and Mental Health UK CIC (BLAM UK) is now spearheading for the immediate reversal of the decision to ban the use of 'Black British English' (BBE) among students in classrooms. BLAM UK argues that the school policy degrades and harms Black students by reinforcing anti-Black linguistic racism, classism, and White supremacist ideology while encouraging the elitist forms of English as the 'norm' to be used among pupils.[9]

The Black Church in Britain is not outside of these language debates. Unwittingly, it positions itself in the debate with a both/and proposition. A double consciousness of language use is played out in code-switching practices. Take, for instance, Black preaching. Many of the first-generation Windrush-era preachers performed code-switching in the pulpit.[10] Their κήρυγμα (kerygma) incorporates the mixing of Caribbean creoles and English. The practice was not benign. As Black British theologian Carol Tomlin demonstrates, code-switching in the Black pulpit also gestures towards the subversion of language.[11] Black preaching of the first generation was a carnivalesque 'play', which refused to disavow the mother tongue of the Caribbean in the interpretation and communication of divine truth.

Vernacular hermeneutics

Language use also matters for the theological reflection of formerly colonized peoples. Theorizing on language use gives rise to language use as a bearer of specific interpretive interests. Postcolonial theology, for instance, addresses language use within the discipline of vernacular hermeneutics.[12] These are 'mother tongue' hermeneutics comprising a variety of techniques to assist with the interpreting of scripture. As Sugirtharajah notes:

> The vernacular hermeneutics which privileges indigenous culture as an authentic site of doing theology, and which focuses on native characteristics.[13]

While there is no singular vernacular method, the scheme's general thrust is to challenge the hegemony of colonial languages imported as part of the colonizing project of Western nations in Africa and Asia. It does so by 'making links across the cultural divides by employing the reader's cultural resources and social experiences to illuminate the biblical narrative'.[14] I quote at length Michele Connolly's excellent exploration of vernacular hermeneutics in the postcolonial literary context of Australia as a helpful summary of Sugirtharajah's approach:

> Sugirtharajah has developed a methodology that focuses on culture, beginning with the culture of the interpreter which is therefore valued from the outset of any interpretive process, before moving to read the biblical text for its cultural content. Sugirtharajah has identified three large categories under which first, an interpreter's culture may be analysed and then, a biblical text may also be understood. In this way, working by analogy, sympathetic cultural resonances between an interpreter and a sacred text may be identified. These three categories deal with ideas or concepts; with behaviours, especially deeply significant ritual actions of a culture or a text; and the various material manifestations of a culture in which Sugirtharajah includes language and symbolism. In his words, the cultural content of the interpreter may be grouped under three headings, namely 'ideational (world views, values and rules), performantial (rituals and roles) and material (language, symbols, food, clothing, etc.).' Once the interpreting culture has been located in this way, it is possible to approach the text to be interpreted by what Sugirtharajah calls 'at least three modes of vernacular reading – conceptual correspondence, narrative [sic] enrichments and performantial parallels.' *The term 'conceptual correspondences' refers to conceptual similarities found in both the culture of production of a text and the culture seeking to interpret it.* 'Narrative enrichments' identify the various story-telling strategies by which a culture makes sense of the world to itself. . . . Such story-telling practices in the interpreting culture can be set beside narratives in the biblical text to be interpreted, as a way to access what both cultures have in common. 'Performantial parallels' refers to 'ritual and behavioural practices which are commonly available in a culture' and which thus provide a cultural commonality between the interpreting culture and that of the text to be interpreted (italics mine).[15]

Jamaican patwa is an example of vernacular hermeneutics – specifically, *biblical interpretation* as conceptual correspondence. That is to say, the *JNT is a dialogue between 'Jamaicana' and scripture.* Conceptual correspondence is not alien to Black biblical studies. I view it as a component of its broader quest for inter(con)textual interpretation. Yet, language use as decoloniality has different meanings in diverse contexts, and within the Caribbean/Caribbean diaspora contexts language has a deep resonance with colonial histories of oppression and resistance.[16] This consideration leads to an additional decolonial/theological register for patwa use in contemporary gospel music, and to explain it, I turn to atonement theory.

Atonement

Atonement is an excellent subject to illustrate the decolonial/theological register of Jamaican patwa. This is because of the uncanny death and resurrection correspondence between the atonement and the history of the language. The journey of Jamaican patwa is a death and resurrection story. In this linguistic drama, the African language suppressed by empire is resurrected to liberate Black people from the hegemony of colonial linguistic imperialism. As the forward of the JNT translation highlights, this language emerges in slavery to become the first or heart language of the majority of the country, especially its working classes.

> Jamaican is an English-based Creole, born over three hundred (300)years ago out of a contact language situation where Africans from various nations and language groups were brought to Jamaica, then an English colony, to work on sugar plantations. This origin and the inevitable association with slavery have led to a mistaken characterisation of the Creole as bad or broken English. Although this mis-conception has tainted the language and its speakers for a long time, research has disclosed that Jamaicans have begun to regard Jamaican as a symbol of national pride and as a useful and effective communicative tool. An All-Island Survey commissioned by the Jamaican Language Unit in 2005 disclosed that at least seventy-nine and a half percent (79.5%) of the one thousand (1000) respondents regard Jamaican as a language in its own right capable of communicating any thought, Idea, concept, or mental construct like any of the world's major languages. Jamaican, more commonly referred to as Jamaican Creole or Patwa, is the language indigenous to Jamaica and the mother tongue of eighty-five percent (85%) of the approximately 2.7 million citizens.

In this predominantly bilingual nation, Jamaican exists alongside English, the official language. (italics mine).[17]

The atonement viewpoint of patwa is not as implausible as it may initially appear. After all, re-reading atonement in response to the prevailing culture is a feature of Western Christianity. For instance, in classical theology atonement theory is constantly subjected to social and cultural influence, including the legal terminology, of feudal societies and antiquated criminal justice concepts.[18] So we are well within the parameters of Christian reasoning to entangle atonement and sociolinguistics.

Two views of Jamaican patwa help us to think about the JNT as an atonement. The first emerges after the riots of 2011[19] and is articulated by the British historian David Starkey. Here, Jamaican patwa is rejected, and within the atonement interpretation of the riots, the death of the Jamaican language will atone for the *sin* of civil disobedience. The second perspective comes from the Jamaican Language Movement, specifically the translation of the New Testament into Jamaican patwa and the production of *Di Jamiekan Nyuu Testiment*. This second view has identification with liberation atonement, and in contrast, Jamaican patwa's 'resurrection' is atonement for colonialism's linguistic imperialism.

Penal substitution

The first atonement view of the Jamaican patwa interplays the classic view of atonement with Jamaican patwa in the context of the aftermath of the 2011 riots in Britain – specifically, the British historian David Starkey's utterances on the Jamaican language and civil disorder. Before I add a theological interpretation to Starkey, I review the basic assumptions of atonement theory.

Atonement in the Christian tradition is understood as God's definitive means of reconciling sinful humanity to Godself by judging and forgiving sin and overcoming the power of evil that stems from sin. Although the New Testament bears witness to the death of Jesus as a saving event, it does not detail how the cross brings about reconciliation. Therefore, atonement theories have emerged throughout church history to explain how and why the crucifixion of Jesus results in sinful humanity's redemption. I will discuss liberation interpretations of atonement theory later, but the first theory is the classic approach. Atonement theory, what Gustaf Aulén termed the 'classic view', stressed the theme of victory.[20] The victory motif, informed by the time's social and intellectual climate, used the image of a cosmic struggle between good and evil, God and Satan, in which Jesus, God's son, was crucified, and the victory was presumed to be Satan's. However, the resurrection of Jesus turns defeat into victory. In contrast to the Christus Victor motif, which led some to raise questions about its view of God's power and character,[21] is the satisfaction model. Originating with Anselm of Canterbury (1033–1109), the satisfaction model seeks to underscore God's redemption of humanity in a manner that accords with God's righteous character. According to Anselm, God cannot overlook sin because it is an affront to God's majesty or honour. Therefore, 'satisfaction' or compensation is owed to God. Yet sin against God is so burdensome that no human being can offer appropriate satisfaction. Human beings must offer 'a debt of honour', yet only God can pay it. Therefore, Jesus, as the God-Man, the one who is fully human and divine, pays our debt. Accordingly, this model also posits the necessity of the incarnation.[22] Later, during the Reformation, Anselm's view of sin as an injury to God's majesty was replaced by the concept of sin as a violation of God's law. Calvin, who was influenced by Anselm's idea of debt payment and Roman conception of criminal law, views punishment as the only satisfaction that could be offered to affronted justice.[23] This view of punishment enables Calvin to develop a theory of 'penal substitution', in which Christ, who offers himself as a substitute, pays the debt that justice demands by bearing the requisite punishment in place of humankind. Although the concept of penal substitution is found neither in St Paul nor in Anselm, Calvin nonetheless extends it by equating it with 'propitiation', a sacrificial idea, which in Calvin's words 'appease[s] the righteous wrath of the Father'.[24] Calvin's legal tone, rooted in a 'retributive view of penalty',[25] informs today's retribution model for criminal justice.[26]

David Starkey's view of language in the riots of 2011 is central to the first atonement viewpoint. The background is the tragic death of Mark Duggan. He was a Black male of mixed heritage who was shot dead by the Metropolitan Police on 4 August. His death sparked social disturbances that spread across the boroughs of London and to the cities of Birmingham and Manchester, as diverse groups of young people confronted police and looted consumer goods from city centres, high streets and shopping outlets. In the aftermath, politicians, academics and social commentators began the arduous task of interpreting these tragic events. The following remarks were made by the historian David Starkey during a debate on an edition of the BBC's *Newsnight* programme:

> There has been a profound cultural change; I've just been re-reading Enoch Powell, the Rivers of Blood speech. His prophesy was absolutely right in one sense, the Tiber didn't foam with blood, but flames lambent, wrapped round Tottenham and Clapham, but it wasn't inter-communal violence, this is where

he was completely wrong, what's happened is a substantial section of the chavs you wrote about have become Black. The Whites have become Black; a particular sort of violent destructive nihilistic gangster culture has become the fashion and Black and White, boy and girl operate in this language together. This language, which is wholly false, which is a Jamaican patwa that's intruded in England. This is why many of us have a sense of literally a foreign country.[27]

A sympathetic reading of Starkey is that his comments, while emotive, were not representative. They are out of step with some of his previous remarks made earlier that year on the importance of diversity. For instance, months before this interview, he appeared on Channel 4 News to discuss the meaning of the Royal Wedding of Prince William and Kate Middleton. When asked by the interviewer, John Snow, about the potential of the wedding for reinventing the monarchy, Professor Starkey was quick to point out that the lack of diversity among the invited guests revealed that, on one level, the event had failed to represent the whole nation and thereby signify inclusivity. However, a less sympathetic reading of Starkey is that the *Newsnight* comments reflect a general pejorative perspective about Black people. For some, this second view is related to his remarks in 2020 about Africans.[28]

Starkey's views resonate with a Christus Victor atonement. He places the Jamaican language on 'trial', intimating that patwa is guilty of fomenting the disorder, and therefore the language users must be punished for the nation to be compensated (satisfied) and justice restored. Demonizing Black culture is not new. But after the riots, the Jamaican language and, by extension, Black culture(s) affronted the nation's honour.

In this first atonement drama, Jamaican patwa plays the role of the 'penal substitute', which takes the place of countless social actors who are guilty of rupturing the social compact. Folding language into civility or criminality is not new in British history. Normally, it is class-based or regional accents that are the register for either civility or criminality. 'Brummies' and 'Scousers' know all too well how accents relate to class, power and opportunity.[29] However, redemption for Blacks comes with an additional requirement. To be released, they must accept a racialized linguistic hierarchy, and Starkey *nods* towards the nature of this additional requirement when, in the same *Newsnight* interview, he refers to the diction of Black British politician David Lammy:

> Listen to David Lammy, an archetypical successful Black man, if you turn the [television] screen off, so you were listening to him on radio; you'd think he was White.

Standard English use for Blacks is thus a sign of redemption for the failings of their culture and heritage.

Liberation

The second atonement viewpoint is a liberation reading of the Jamaican language. It is founded on the publication and meaning of the *Di Jameikan Nyuu Testament*. The JNT, published by the Bible Society of the West Indies, is a translation of the New Testament into Jamaican patwa. It is the largest body of translated literature into Jamaican patwa and is more technically rigorous than previous works.[30] Not unlike my critique of Starkey's linguistic stance in relation to the Jamaican language, I use atonement discourse to discuss the JNT as an example of the Jamaican tongue but this time with emancipatory prowess. But first, I must elaborate on a theological stance that I refer to as 'liberation atonement'.

Liberation atonement foregrounds a broader soteriological significance and historicized notion of sin. Unlike the satisfaction theory, in liberation atonement, God is *not* one whose wrath must be appeased lest it falls upon sinful persons: quite the contrary. Through his Son, God endures the wrath of the Romans who crucified Jesus, who went to the cross to vanquish evil and redeem evildoers, *including* the enemies of God that oppress the weak and vulnerable.[31] Because God is totally committed to the struggle against human suffering and oppression, atonement is not separate from present human distress – it is more than a spiritual act. Liberation atonement emphasizes atonement's political dimension and its transformation of individuals within their sociopolitical context. James Cone surmises that there can be no reconciliation without justice and no sanctification without liberation.[32] Finally, since the gospels narrate Jesus' death as a historic event grounded in a first-century Greco-Roman context, liberation atonement is also grounded in history. It is God's redemptive act of delivering God's creation from sin and oppression in human history. Therefore, sin and oppression are neither abstract nor alien to human life but are concrete and historical. Considering this, racism, poverty, sexism and homophobia are the consequences of sin. Salvation, therefore, is not only reconciliation with God but also reconciliation with others (Eph. 2.14-18) and the destruction of the oppressive structures and forces that alienate people from each other. The prophets proclaimed this all-embracing view of salvation (Isa. 11.1-9) and apostles (Rev. 7.9-17).

The JNT version is an example of liberation atonement. This perspective is made possible as a result of the growing respect for Jamaican patwa as a legitimate language, paralleling the role of the postcolonial assertive nativism. Noel Erskine captures the contextuality of the translation when he notes:

> The translation of the New Testament into patwa begins the long journey of taking our social location seriously, and it highlights a context in which people are valued because we can point to divine revelation in our culture. There are now tangible clues of the divine in our situation. Revelation is given to the experience of a people who, for a long time, thought they were no people, but they now experience liberation as the divine word addresses them in their existential situation. The good news is that we do not have to go outside our culture or language to experience truth: God's call to communion and fellowship is related to Jamaicans in their culture and in their language. In our struggle to change the world we discover that God does not speak to us from afar but from within our culture. The Jewishness of Jesus opens the door to a new understanding that, with patwa as the bearer of Scripture, God speaks to Jamaican people from the depths of their culture. God does not speak Patwa with an accent as most foreigners do; instead, with *Di Jamiekan Nyuu Testiment* as our guide, we know that God is not a foreigner to the people of Jamaica: God is our friend and saviour.[33]

The JNT esteems the Black vernacular as a bona fide language, rather than a derivative dialect, which can express unambiguously the complex lived reality of its speakers. It also symbolizes the power and possibility of religious language to function in liberative ways, and like English translations of the NT, the JNT is not only a sacred religious text of spiritual value but also a sociocultural document of political significance. It is also deeply decolonial as it entails the overturning of centuries of dominance for Standard English in Bible translation.[34] The hegemony of Standard English in Jamaica is concomitant with the 200-year history of Britain's administration of slave/chattel labour camps in Jamaica. Like other European colonial powers, Britain imposed her national language on enslaved Africans and simultaneously prohibited communication in native tongues as part of the plantation mechanisms of control. Yet neither brutal conditions nor severe sanctions obliterated African languages. As a matter of necessity, a basic need for communication between owners and their slave workers created space for the retention of African languages.[35] This is the most likely explanation for the emergence of, first, so-called pidgin and then a creole language, known in Jamaica as patwa.[36] While neither linguistic system (English/African languages) was singular, there was sufficient linguistic similarity in forms of English among the colonizers and the varied ethnicities that formed the slave population (specifically, the underlying commonality of the Niger-Congo languages of Mande and Kwa) to facilitate a new structure.[37] Furthermore, there is always 'spill over' when a new language is absorbed.[38] For this reason, Jamaican linguists choose to describe patwa as an English vocabulary framed by an African linguistic structure (syntax, phonology and semantics).[39] Thus, the linguistics of the enslaved was more than a practicality: it was a political act of resistance; a desire to keep alive the memory of Africa in spoken language. When liberation atonement discourse is used to examine the role and function of the Jamaican language in its inscribed, disseminated and interpreted form within the JNT, the language of atonement throws off the vestiges of punishment and takes on the imagery and vision of liberation.

In this second atonement scenario, the Jamaican language, which earlier had been indicted as the sacrificial victim that bore the nation's wrath, is now cast in the personified role of the Redeemer/Reconciler. While the previous atonement analysis had implicitly labelled Jamaican language speakers as sinners, here, readers and listeners of the JNT are viewed as those who have been sinned against because of the island's 400 years of slave labour and colonialism. In this frame, the Jamaican language is a healing balm; it redeems the sin of linguistic oppression by mending the broken relationship between the Jamaican people and their language. It does so by elevating the language of the poor and despised, so that the language formerly known pejoratively as 'patwa' is liberated from the colonial miry clay of negative perception and placed on to the rocks of linguistic legitimacy.

The additional decolonial/theological register is the JNT as liberation atonement. The liberation view is decolonial in so much as it overturns colonial linguistics and its attendant language use and promotes local tongues and, concomitantly, local knowledge in the interpretation of scripture.

The JNT is relatively easy to produce in music. This is because these interests are made legible in the sampling of the JNT version in every song. For instance, all the songs on the album have samples from the JNT, but one track, 'Beatitudes', is comprised wholly of the JNT.

Illustration: Beatitudes

The 'Beatitudes' track makes legible the second option of Black biblical studies. The track is a complete sample of the JNT and therefore signifies inter(con)-textuality. Regarding the construction of the track, the scripture/message track is a sample Beatitudes from Matyu (Matthew) Chapter 5. The music track is inspired by the Jazz Warriors. There is also a solo performance from the international jazz saxophonist Soweto Kinch.

JNT – Matyu 5, Gad bles unu . . .

Aal a unu we nuo se unu niid Gad iina evri wie, Gad bles unu,
kaa di gud sitn dem we Gad gi wen im ruul piipl laif iina evri wie, a unu a-go get dem.

Chorus
Gad bles unu. (X6)

JNT – Aal a uu a baal nou, Gad bles dem,
kaaz di taim a-go kom wen Gad a-go osh dem an mek dem api agen. Aal a uu ombl demself, Gad bles dem,
kaa yu si di ort, a dem piipl de a-go kom get it.

Chorus
Gad bles unu. (X6)

JNT – Uu waahn du wa rait iina Gad yai so bad, dat it komiin laik se a ded dem a ded fi onggri an dem chuot jrai laik se dem no jringk waata ou lang, Gad bles unu,
kaa unu a-go get unu beli ful
Unu we paadn piipl, Gad bles unu,

kaaz im a-go paadn unu tu.

Chorus
Gad bles unu. (X6)

Children's Choir – Eternal Father bless our land.

JNT – Aal a uu onggl waahn fi du di sitn dem we mek Gad api, Gad bles unu,
kaaz wan die, wan die, unu a-go get fi si Gad.
Gad bles aal a uu elp piipl fi liv iina piis,
kaaz a piipl laik dem de Gad a-go kaal fi im pikni dem. Chorus
Gad bles unu. (X6)

JNT – Di piipl dem we ada piipl mek sofa jos kaaz dem liv ou Gad waahn piipl fi liv, Gad bles unu, kaa di gud sitn dem we Gad gi wen im ron piipl laif ou im waahn ron it, a dem sitn de unu a-go get.

Chorus
Gad bles unu. (X18)

Conclusion

Operationalizing the second option is straightforward. I sample the JNT version to register the interests of Black biblical studies. The JNT is an example of the conceptual correspondence of vernacular hermeneutics. However, JNT carries additional theological/decolonial meaning. The text also signifies a more extended history of struggle to overcome the linguistic oppression of British slavery in the West Indies. *The method is not limited to Jamaican speakers or gospel artists.* The tool has implications for the emerging West African churches in Britain. They must also consider the importance of the Black (African) vernacular in the ongoing struggle to decolonize biblical interpretation and thus, language use as a register for decoloniality in our songs about God. In other words, African songwriters and musicians in Britain must also question if the colonial language alone can dismantle colonial ideas about God in song.

10

Dangerous memories

The final tool for consideration is dangerous memories. This third tool is the culmination of loving blackness as exploration of Black history. This production tool refers to the stories we tell in gospel music songs. Stories of personal struggle, salvation, temptation and their overcoming are *regular* contemporary gospel music tropes. However, less prevalent are stories of salvation in regard to social history, social crises and their overcoming; that is to say, telling folks in song how 'God got us all over' as a people rather than just individuals. This second story category facilitates the exploration of Black history in music, and in this chapter, I want to make centrepiece the dangerous memories associated with West Indian enslavement. I have chosen the history of slavery because of its significance in the African Caribbean story. We cannot explore Black history in the African diaspora without reckoning with the racial capitalism, which created the West Indies. Moreover, the history of slavery is not outside of the earlier interest in this book for loving blackness. Black self-care must also reckon with the legacies of slavery and how we represent this history in our music and culture.

Dangerous memories concern the representation of the history of West Indian enslavement in songwriting. I don't want to position slavery in song as solely lament, though lamenting is necessary. Instead, I want to position slavery as history that also motivates action in the present. To achieve this goal, I propose that we explore this dangerous memory as an ethical theodicy. *That is to say, we represent this dangerous memory as an unresolved struggle for recompense.* To arrive at this perspective requires three moves. First, to underline the importance of this tool, I contextualize the problem of the difficulty of remembering slavery in contemporary British Christian communities. Next, I review the history and the development of Christian theodicy, and make my point of departure Black Christian theodicy. After this, I refine the meaning of Black theodicy through *the diagnostic of Black Pentecostal extemporaneous prayer.* Prayer, in this instance, clarifies the theodical thought for music production. To illustrate a theodical approach to the history, illustration is made of the track 'Go and Sin No More'.

White saviourism and Black suppressionism

British Christians have great difficulty talking about the history and legacy of enslavement. White and Black worshipping communities are culpable – both have specific troubles with incorporating a meaningful reflection of Black suffering into Christian education, much less musicality. The modern origins of the problem for White churches lie in a *White saviourism* and, for Black churches, a *Black suppressionism*.

White saviourism is the obstacle for White Christian communities; it is the obfuscation of violent settler colonialism by foregrounding a White saviour figure. The concealment is evident in education, from state schools to universities. For example, at state school, my generation's introduction to Christianity and the British Empire prioritized the stories of the nineteenth-century anti-slavery campaigner William Wilberforce and the mid-twentieth-century anti-apartheid activist and Anglican missionary Trevor Huddleston. The hegemony of these White saviour narratives evades discussion of Christian complicity with racial terror and leaves untroubled the myth of a benign, benevolent and compassionate empire.[1] A recent example of White saviourism in the context of higher education is, I suggest, the 'Ethics of Empire' project at the University of Oxford. The project's web page reveals the contradiction at play. Though it speaks of a desire for a complex history of British imperialism, the same text disavows any existential wrestling with the collective memory of Black suffering. The narrative evades the 300 years of theology's complicity with British racial terror in the West Indies by gesturing towards an enduring White saviourism, including the partial reading of the history of the slave trade which casts Britain as emancipators:

> In most reaches of contemporary academic discourse – not least in Theology, Religious Studies, Political Theory, Cultural Studies, and Post-Colonial Studies – the topic of ethics and empire raises no questions to which widely accepted answers are not immediately to hand. By definition, 'empire' is imperialist; imperialism is wicked; and empire is therefore unethical. Nothing of interest remains to be explored.
>
> This project begs to differ. First, it observes that, as an historical phenomenon as distinct from an ideological construct, 'empire' has meant all manner of ethical thing. In the British case, on the one hand, it presided over the 'genocide' of Tasmanian aboriginals in the early 1800s, the Irish Famine in 1845-52, and the massacre of unarmed civilians at Amritsar in 1919. *On the other hand, it*

suppressed the Atlantic and African slave-trades after 1807, granted Black Africans the vote in Cape Colony seventeen years before the United States granted it to African Americans, and offered the only centre of armed resistance to European fascism between May 1940 and June 1941 (italics mine).[2]

White saviourism has two primary forms. These are false equivalency and intellectual neglect. False equivalency describes the work of scholars who seek to downplay the genocidal horror and brutality of the slave and colonial world by claiming equivocation with the 'progress' brought by the civilizing mission. Take, for instance, Graham Ward's study of decolonizing theology in South Africa. In concluding this essay, and reflecting on the legacy of Christian mission, he *appears* to equivocate the benefits of Christian mission with the avaricious and rapacious designs of empire:

> The first challenge arises from the history of the relationship between Christian mission and colonization. The impact of that relationship is a considerable mixed bag – education and literacy have to be weighed alongside indoctrination and racism, patronizing at best, oppressive at worse. There is no getting round that history – though there would be neither the Bikos nor Mandelas without it.[3]

Intellectual neglect is a failure to meaningfully reflect on slavery by church and academic leadership. Regarding the church, take, for instance, Anglican leadership. The former archbishop of Canterbury Rowan Williams' study of theology in the public square evades reflection on the church's role in the trade and considers slavery only in relation to Christian ideas of personhood.[4] In his book *Reimagining Britain*, Williams' successor Justin Welby neglects Britain's role as an oppressor nation and therefore re-reads the Exodus story as outside of British experience: He notes:

> In the UK, the Exodus story is reduced in impact for most of us because – at least at the official, national level – we have not known slavery, occupation or oppression for a very long time.[5]

The statement is true in the sense that Britain has not experienced enslavement for a long time – one would have to go back to the Vikings or the White slave trade in North Africa to find a history of White slavery. But the statement is also problematic because Britain, including the Church of England, has a long history of involvement and benefit from the trans-Atlantic slave trade. Slavery is a part of its theological (colonial Christianity) and financial DNA. Regarding the latter, consider, for instance, how in 2022 the church acknowledged its financial benefit from the Queen Anne's Bounty. This fund was established to support poor clergy in the eighteenth century and made its profits from investing in a company that trafficked enslaved Africans.[6] Furthermore, the church's missionary arm, the Society for the Propagation of the Gospel, owned and ran a plantation in Barbados.[7] Hence, on a national level, we *have* known slavery, because Britain captured, enslaved, tortured and abused millions of Africans as part of the expansion and colonization of the so-called New World. Intellectual neglect among leadership has consequences. It produces an apology culture, rather than a reparation culture. Intellectual neglect is played out in academic leadership. For example, in the last seventy years, only two scholarly texts (excluding the work of Black British theologians) intersecting theology, 'race' and empire have been published.[8] Similarly, not one university research centre exists to contemplate the relationship between Christianity, slavery and racism. The consequence is a fudge – few texts, little interest – and naturally, the status quo is retained. Some Brits evade scrutiny by focusing on the Americas. What I am identifying here is the work of a few White British scholars, particularly those working in North America, who have attempted to address slavery as an exclusively African American concern.[9] This displacement maintains the myth that White British theology does not have a 'colour problem' and absolves it from any obligation. But the UK guild is not completely unaware or unconcerned. A few green shoots of interest in this theological predicament appeared after the murder of the African American George Floyd. In April 2021 the first 'Dismantling Whiteness' conference was organized by Black British theologian Anthony Reddie at Regent's Park College in Oxford. The keynote speakers (Rachel Starr and Paul Weller) set the tone for a new discourse on theology by shifting the focus from White saviourism to a critical whiteness. Time will tell whether this conference is the start of a radical transformation or a false dawn.

Black *suppressionsism* is the obstacle for Black Christian communities. It describes the response to the history of slavery in Black British churches. It is the spiritualizing of slavery memory in order to dampen or downplay its contemporary legacy or significance. However, the motivation for this response is benign. For instance, I know a multitude of parents from the Caribbean who refused to share their knowledge or histories of slavery and colonialism with their British-born children because they did not desire their young people to be enraged by their ancestors' experience. If the history of slavery was raised, it was quickly spiritualized. The Black story promptly became part of a divine plan to spread the gospel among 'heathen people'. Within this diaspora theodicy, a good God is protected, Black bodies are a site of struggle and White bodies absolved. As admirable an act of parental love as this was, on a social level it is a tragic failure. With no discussion, exploration or contemplation of the meaning of the slave past, there was no settled ethic for a redemption. In many cases, the strategy had the opposite to the desired effect. Many who encountered a sense of 'dread' upon hearing the horrors of the slave past were left with no explicit systems for redemption. We did not know how to transform our righteous anger into 'dangerous memories'.

Theodicy

Theodicy is a resource for thinking about how we remember enslavement in song. After all, theodicy guides the Black theological enterprise:

> How do we *dare* speak of God in a suffering world . . . in which Blacks are humiliated because they are Black . . . this question . . . occupies the central place in our theological perspective.[10]

Theodicy is also a feature of the biblical story and also foregrounded in Black British existence. The question of why people suffer excessive and enduring pain is the subject of Job's complaint against God (9.32; 10.1-22). Second Isaiah introduces the possibility of redemptive suffering (53.5). In the New Testament, Christ's suffering on the cross is interrogated in the atonement discourse (I Cor. 6.20; Rom. 5.6-15; I Thess. 5.10; Hebrews 9–10). African diasporic experience is also fecund with theodical contemplation. According to Clare Williams, the founder of 'Get Real', a Black apologetics organization in Britain, one of the most common apologetics questions from young Black people is, 'Why does God permit African people's suffering in history?'[11]

The Western Christian tradition coined 'theodicy' in the early eighteenth century. Theodicy frames the discussion of God's goodness amid evil.[12] While a diversity of positions exists, the classic formula asks, 'Why does a loving God allow evil?' The question reflects 'a logical tension between belief in divine goodness and omnipotence on the one hand, and on the other, the ubiquity of suffering'.[13] Two traditions have dominated the resolution to the problem of evil: the Augustinian and Irenaean schools of thought.[14] Put simply, the former proposes a free-will theory, which answers the problem of evil by speculating that God permits moral evil for the sake of human freedom. This way, the tension between divine goodness and evil is resolved and defended.[15] While this view has a basis in scripture (Genesis 1–3), it does not adequately explain evil's primordial origins.[16] The latter, often referred to as 'soul-making theodicies', explain evil through divine didacticism.[17] Grafted onto Irenaean teaching, this school presupposes that (1) being made in God's image is not the same as 'likeness' and (2) that suffering and evil play a role in closing the 'epistemic distance' between God and humankind – image and likeness. Dispensing with the mythology of the Fall in Genesis, and adapting a modern evolutionary world view, suffering and evil are recast as didactic – affording opportunity for moral growth. Suffering, therefore, is providential rather than punitive.[18] The strength of the second type is its integration into modern scientific thinking. Its weakness, however, is its instrumentalist view, which can downplay the brutality of radical evil.[19] Recently, a new wave of theodicy or anti-theodicy has challenged its premise; namely, that it cannot be resolved. As Karen Kilby states:

> My proposal ... is that these questions, these concrete and theological versions of the so called 'problem of evil' ought to be acknowledged as completely legitimate and utterly unanswerable.[20]

In anti-theodicy the issue is not that the problem of evil does not exist but that it cannot be rationally solved. Yet failing to answer the problem does not resolve it; instead, it leaves an image of a passable but ineffective deity.[21] Undeterred by this limitation, for anti-theodicy proponents the time and effort spent on theodical analysis is a 'fool's errand'. There is no meaningful rational solution, and the intellectual efforts obscure the power of meaningful therapeutic and material practices for addressing the manifestation of moral evil.[22] Subsequently, many anti-theodical perspectives promote concrete ethical responses to the problem of evil. For theodicy to be grounded in the liberation of humanity and secured in Christ's resurrection, it must be allied to a transformative action consistent with the struggle for liberation. In other words, theodicy must be ethical or praxis-oriented.[23]

Black liberation theology nuances the direction of theodicy. Considering collective historical Black suffering, it asks: 'Is God a White racist?' This question acknowledges the continuities of slavery's social death.[24] Once we pose the question 'Is God a White racist?', what practical theological options do we have? African American religious scholar Anthony Pinn, who writes extensively about North Atlantic slavery and Black theodicy, outlines three basic resolutions:

(1) Unmerited suffering is intrinsically evil yet can have redemptive consequences.

(2) God and humans are co-workers in the struggle to remove moral evil; and
(3) Black suffering may result from God being a racist.[25]

The first position represents 'soul-making' theodicy. As a frame of meaning, redemptive suffering gives strength to and empowers individuals to see transformation in their suffering. For instance, womanist theologians point out that theodicy in the lives of enslaved women was characterized by an unfailing belief that God existed and God's presence sustained them in their trials.[26] In Caribbean culture, this first position is captured in the popular refrain 'what people mek fi for bad, God tun fi good'. Redemptive suffering, however, has its critics. This category can legitimate *all* suffering, especially the historical disenfranchisement of Black women.[27] And the potential legitimation of *all* suffering leads some womanists to claim suffering is not the will of God, but an 'outrage that there is suffering at all'.[28]

The second position represents anti-theodicy. It acknowledges human agency and the persistence of evil, but does not seek to answer the dilemma through speculation, theory or philosophical consideration. Instead, it views the mission of the church as resistance to suffering, to protest and challenge it. For this reason, suffering is always oriented towards ethics, praxis and justice. A long history of Black Christian resistance and radicalism in anti-colonial struggles is encompassed in this second view. It may or may not seek to resolve the problem of evil, but ultimately makes its centrepiece the necessity of social justice action in Black communities.[29]

The third position questions God's goodness, thereby leaving open the possibility of divine hostility and divine racism. This position is intimately connected to Black humanism,[30] and while this final position raises important critical questions, especially regarding God's impartiality, its location is also its limitation. Its association with Black humanism confines its influence on the borders of Christian contemplation. However, as mentioned in Chapter 5, the borders are also fecund with creative possibilities. *Hence, to capture the third position's creative potential, I will appropriate it into my prayer as a legitimate starting point for reflecting on theodicy in the Black British context.*

Prayer

I turn now to Black extemporaneous prayer as a diagnostic for Black theodicy. I pray to *mediate* the Black theodical discussion by identifying the underlying tension and its resolution. This is not normative or regular methodology in theological studies, yet, in contrast, prayer as diagnostic is ubiquitous for the Black Church in Britain (Mt 6.6; I Thes. 5.16-18). Hence, we may question why this auto/ethnography is neglected in academic research. Furthermore, extemporaneous prayer is dynamic.[31] In Black Pentecostal 'speak', prayer is part of the experience of 'tarrying' or waiting with expectation for new understanding, knowledge and action. So, as I write this chapter, I pause to pray.

Let us pray.

'Dear God, are you a White racist?'

Dear God, unlike my forbears in the Black Church tradition, who did not dare to equate divine *will* with racism, I want to talk to you about the undoubted relationship that exists. I don't believe your *being* is racist, but I do believe that the tradition created in your name, in relation to African Caribbean descendants, is. My complaint is the tradition of colonial Christianity in which Christians in various ways have legitimated Black subordination. God, on reflection, this discrimination against us begins with the interpretation of the Bible. Even before European Christians encountered Africans in the age of European expansion, they'd already succumbed to interpretive practices which demonized Black flesh. God, while there is no evidence of pseudo-scientific racial theory in the Hebrew Bible's ancient narratives,[32] the remnants of one dangerous interpretation continues to be felt. The narrative is known as the Curse of Ham (Genesis 9.20-27, NRSV). As Black Biblical studies demonstrate, Canaan, not Ham, is cursed to be a slave (Gen. 9.25). Despite the real meaning of the passage gesturing towards the ancient taboo of disrespect, ideological bias and misinterpretation by scholars led to a reading of the text as divine blessing for African servitude.[33] The original sin of the Christian faith in the Caribbean, which *we* traditionally associate with earlier Chapters in Genesis, was the 'double fall': sin and blackness.[34]

God, the Curse justifies the punishment of Black bodies. The Curse of Ham infected the Christian imagination and made it possible for some to view Africans as unworthy of equality and, at best, beasts of burden. Therefore, a punishment theology underscored the British Christian mission in the New World. Furthermore, Christians sanctified slavery. Anglican priest Morgan Godwyn (1640-1690), a witness to the horror of the slave trade, proposed 'Christian slavery.' He argued that baptism did not imply manumission and the brutality of enslavement a saving grace for uncivilized Africans.

But the racialization of the Christian tradition was not accepted by all of the children of Africa in the Caribbean. There is another side to the story of racial terror: resistance and overcoming. I give you thanks God of Justice that African people who resisted this terror and, in so doing, left us a *witness* – a Black revolutionary tradition in their religious cultures. They combated racial terror through a variety of practices. Even before the advent of Christian mission, you inspired the rebel leaders Tacky and Nanny to resist. They understood enslavement to be anti-God and the slave system occult practice.

We also know that with the advent of Christian mission, African Christians rejected the Pauline injunction, 'Slaves obey your masters.' Through a variety of hermeneutical strategies that allowed them to either read against the biblical text or challenge disputed passages, they interpreted Scripture in ways that could not be curtailed. We locate this oppositional reading strategy in Paul Bogle's use of the Psalms and, in the post slave-world, in Marcus and Amy Garvey's underlining of the necessity of a Black gaze on Scripture.[35]

Lord, I thank you for this cloud of witnesses that watch over us today.

Amen.

Theodicy for remembering slavery

My prayer clarifies two juxtaposing theodical systems – punishment and ethical theodicy. Punishment theodicy protects the belief in God's goodness and implicates the Black sufferer in their predicament. Although the overdrawn synchronization of sin and suffering in punishment theodicy is not defended in scripture (Job 42.7; Jn 9.1-3; Lk. 13.4), the enslaved are either cursed by God or damned for misusing 'free will'. The stated goal of punishment is rehabilitation, and punishment as rehabilitation in Black history is often a legitimation for Black subjugation.[36] Punishment theodicy has much in common with earlier incarnations of the humanist position; namely, it underscores the possibility that God is silent on the suffering of Black people and therefore is absent or does not exist.[37] Punishment theodicy also renders possible the blaming of Black folks for their problems. Suffering is divine punishment for past or present sins of a people. In contrast, an ethical theodicy defends divine omniscience by focusing on human culpability, which includes the potential for misrule and oppression. Ethical theodicy is underlined in this prayer. The concrete reality of evil is foregrounded, as is resistance to it – by any means necessary. This second view maintains faith in a benevolent God but does not seek to answer the question explicitly of why an omniscient God would permit unmerited suffering. Instead, it mobilizes resources to resist suffering, including racial terror.

So where does this discussion leave us? I operationalize the dangerous memory of slavery in contemporary gospel music as an ethical theodicy. That means we don't seek to explain why it happened but instead concern ourselves with how we deal with its aftermath, the racialized injustice in the present. Thought of this way, slavery's dangerous memory projects forward into the present as an optic for fighting racism and resisting injustice.

Illustration: Go and Sin No More

The song 'God and Sin No More' from *Jamaican Bible Remix* is an example of the production of the third tool. The song explores the continued influence of the slave past on Black life in the present by questioning whether our notions of forgiveness are shaped by our history of enslavement. It places in tension traditional and radical views on forgiveness.[38] The scripture track is about forgiveness. It is based on Jan 8 (John 8), where Jesus tells the woman caught in adultery to 'go and sin no more'. The message track explores forgiveness but places Black forgiveness within a longer colonial history. It begins and ends with a sample from the African American psychologist Frances Cress Welsing. Between is a powerful sample, a narrative of Black forgiveness by the Walker family members in the aftermath of the murder of the Black teenager Anthony Walker. Anthony Walker was brutally attacked and killed in the city of Liverpool, England, in 2005. The unresolved tension between these two visions of forgiveness (Welsing/Walkers) is symbolized in the chorus: a mashup of Caribbean gospel singer Joseph Niles and the Consolers ('Neither do I condemn you') and Steel Pulse ('I'll never forgive'). Ultimately, the song asks the listener to consider which approach is best suited; that is, proffers the best ethical resources to address the legacy of slavery.

JNT – Jan 8

Frances Cress Welsing – I think that ah this automatic forgiveness ah when it comes to Black people being harmed or killed or injured by people who classify themselves as White. We don't hear people who are White if they have, ah feel they have sustained some injury or harm from a Black person, we don't hear them saying, 'I forgive, I forgive I forgive.'

Chorus

Neither do I condemn you. I'll never forgive. (X4)
Go and sin no more.

Gee Walker – When I expect the law to work for me, it's not up to me to take revenge.
Forgive those who sin against you, as we forgive, we expect to be forgiven, that's why I chose to forgive.

JNT – Eni wan a unu we neva sin yet, fling di fos stuon. (x2)

Chorus

Neither do I condemn you. I'll never forgive. (X4)
Go and sin no more.

Dominique Walker – I was approached by a reporter, and he asked me if I could find in my heart to forgive the killers of Anthony, knowing that I am a woman.... Obviously, a woman of God, woman of faith. And I said, I stopped for a second, and I was just like. I actually had to think. For me for me it probably seemed like I lifetime, I had to think, but it must have been less than a few seconds, and I said to him, I said, 'The Bible taught us and Jesus said seventy times seven we must forgive and that is what we must do.'

JNT – Eni wan a unu we neva sin yet, fling di fos stuon. (x4)

Chorus

Neither do I condemn you. I'll never forgive. (X4)
Go and sin no more.

Frances Cress Welsing – So I think that it is a part of Black peoples' tradition, tradition from the time of enslavement. Do you see when the slave master could beat the Black person and I can just envision the Black person being beaten and the slave master or the slave mistress would be saying, 'Say that you forgive me,' do you see and then giving them another lash. 'Say that you forgive me.' And so, the Black person doesn't have a choice but to say 'I forgive master, I forgive, I forgive, I forgive.'

Chorus

Neither do I condemn you. I'll never forgive.
Go and sin no more. (X8)

Conclusion

Dangerous memories are a way of producing Black history in contemporary gospel music. Through an ethical-theodical historiography, we focus on how the historical past motivates justice in the present. This third production tool has significant implications for lyricism, including the foregrounding of ethics in the exploration of Black history. Wrestling with Black history falls within the decolonial motif of loving blackness. The last three chapters demonstrate how we operationalize and produce the decolonial options in contemporary gospel music. Crossover technique facilitates the broader soteriology of womanist theology, the Black vernacular a focus for Black biblical studies and dangerous memories facilitate Black history. The final question to consider is the effect of *Jamaican Bible Remix* on gospel artists. Namely, can the album trigger a move from soulful gospel music to music that reflects the soul of the Gospel?

Part V

Impact

11

Mercy, Mercy Me

What is the impact of Jamaican Bible Remix? If impact occurs, how do we measure it? Conversely, if there is no impact, what can we learn from this musicological enterprise? To test the book's intention to be a practical guide for decolonizing contemporary gospel music (p.2), I present two case studies.

Case studies are a useful way of assessing the impact. Case studies explain the links between theory and practice as well as identify gaps and failings.[1] Hence, they are a valuable method of critically exploring value and influence in real-life settings,[2] though some discussion exists on their reliability and replicability.[3] The first case study is the response of an elite group of church musicians who participated in a public symposium called 'The West Indian Front Room' (2018). The second is a joint music venture with Karen Gibson and the Kingdom Choir to re-version Marvin Gaye's classic environmental song 'Mercy, Mercy Me (the Ecology)' for the United Nations Cop26 Global Conference on Climate Action in Glasgow, Scotland, in November 2021. *Concerning impact, the first case study exemplifies transformation in thinking, and the second, transformative action.*

The Front Room event

The first case study is 'The West Indian Front Room' event. This conference was a dialogue organized between prominent contemporary gospel musicians, academics and Black Church members. As noted previously, the West Indian front room was the space for an encounter between sacred and secular music, and in some cases a broadening of the meaning of the sacred (Chapter 8). Furthermore, for many Black Church musicians of African Caribbean heritage, the front room was where they encountered the sonic textures of Black music and listened to their first contemporary gospel music albums. There were several presenters on the day and the event comprised two parts: lectures and musical performances.

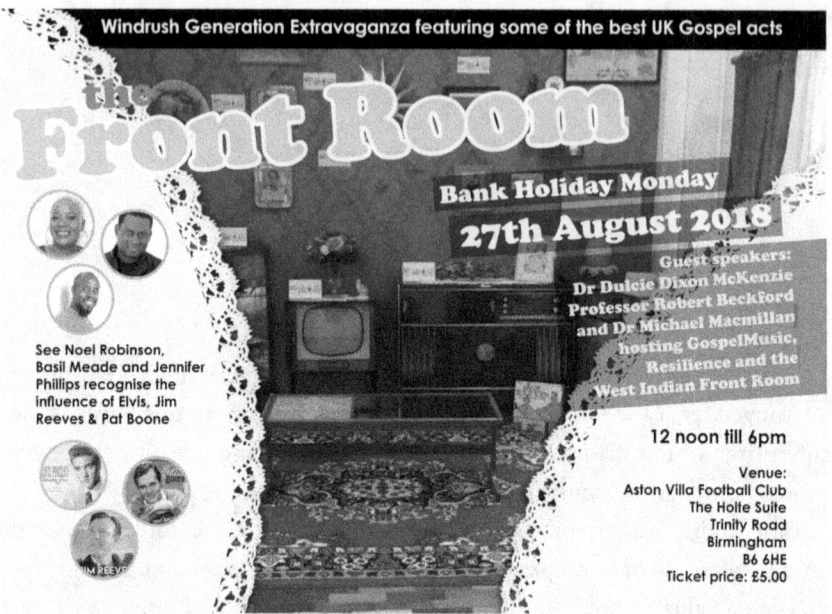

The day began with a talk by Dr Michael McMillian. He launched the proceedings with an analysis of the history and meaning of the West Indian front room. As mentioned previously, for McMillian, beneath the surface of the disparate collection of artefacts lurks a discrete diaspora cultural politics. Next, Dr Dulcie McKenzie revealed the heritage of Black Christian music. Drawing on her doctoral research, she contoured the diverse musical traditions that flowed into the West Indian front room from the Caribbean, North America and Europe. The penultimate presentation was from the musicologist Dr Pauline Muir. Muir spoke about the sonic dynamics of Black Church music, specifically those of West African diaspora churches in London. She contended that an overemphasis on upbeat musical styles and sounds limits the range of emotional expression and restricts the songwriting to songs of joy, celebration and jubilation. I contributed the final presentation, and naturally, my topic was the decolonizing of contemporary gospel music. I began by reviewing the theological concepts of decoloniality and moved on to contour the decolonial theological orientation (Chapter 3). By way of illustration, I played two songs from the album: first, 'Incarnation: No Blacks, No Irish, No Dogs', and second, the song 'Magnificat'.

The album impacted the thinking of the gospel artists. I noted several responses to my presentation from the musicians. Bazil Meade from the London Community Gospel Choir told me that everything I presented was new to him and caught him off-guard. Similarly, Noel Robinson, one of Britain's leading gospel artists, was equally engaged with the ideas and, like Bazil, suggested that we continue the discussion after the conference. The ensuing discussions with these two giants of Black Church music led to two conclusions. First, the artists accepted decoloniality as a legitimate consideration for contemporary gospel music. Second, this positive response is conditioned by the reality of the contemporary gospel music market. Songs of praise and worship dominate the market of consumers who are mostly racialised as White and Christian, and these economic realities militate against the promotion of a decolonial genre.[4] I decided to take their responses seriously and consider experimenting with a more commercial approach; that is to say, balancing decolonization with a mainstream commercial viability. This ambition was realized in collaboration with the Kingdom Choir, the development charity Christian Aid and the Marvin Gaye Estate.

The Kingdom Choir

The second case study concerns the Kingdom Choir. I contacted the Choir's leader, Karen Gibson, in the summer of 2021 to explore if the Choir would work with me on a musical production for the United Nations Summit on Climate Change in November of the same year. Initially, I pitched a musical project to the charity, Christian Aid. I suggested that we ask the Choir to write and perform a new song to engage with the racial justice/climate justice agenda of Christian Aid. As Childish Gambino illustrates in the music video for his 2019 release 'Feels Like Summer', working-class, working poor Black communities are literally on the front line of those feeling the heat of global warming. As climate change campaigner Jeremy Williams puts it in more forthrightly in a global context, 'Climate Change is Racist.'[5]

> What we're talking about here is structural racism: patterns of disadvantage that emerge from the overall functioning of the global system, often accumulated over centuries. This is inequality at its broadest and least visible because it functions without perpetrators or intent, unfolding through the structures of the global economy. Many White people are unaware of structural racism. It lies outside the most common definition of racism as personal prejudice, and they have never experienced it for themselves.[6]

However, when I discussed the project with a friend and colleague, Roy Akerman of Zinc Media, he originated the idea of re-versioning Marvin Gaye's early 1970s hit song, 'Mercy, Mercy Me (the Ecology)'. Gaye's song was ahead of its time, a soulful reflection on the impending ecological crisis caused by the human destruction of natural habitats and pollution. Aside from the technical issues of securing rights and sourcing funding, it was crucial to get the Choir on board.

Engaging the Choir required a careful negotiation. Karen responded to my request with a question. She asked me if I was the same 'Robert Beckford' who wrote a critical piece on the Kingdom Choir in a recent book. I was caught unprepared and could not immediately locate the source of my analysis. I racked my brain to remember, and initially I thought it must be someone else and said so to Karen. After a few minutes, I remembered that I had indeed mentioned the Choir in an essay in a book about reggae music, edited by Lez Henry at Thames Valley University.[7] Within a developmental piece exploring decoloniality in reggae music, I compared the music production of the Kingdom Choir with the rap artist Stormzy after the Grenfell Tower disaster.[8] (A revised version of the comparison appears earlier (Chapter 1).) I explained to Karen how, within the context of the essay, the criticism is not of the Choir but of Black theology's failure to engage with contemporary gospel musicians and performers. I continued by stating that it was my hope that, by working together on a climate change song, we might begin a process of redemption. Karen questioned who was being redeemed by the process, but nonetheless was happy to go ahead and continue to work on this crossover gospel project. It is important to recognize that the *Jamaican Bible Remix* album was again the catalyst for our discussion, but her first encounter was with the written form of a song.

I collaborated with the Kingdom Choir for their performance of Marvin Gaye's 'Mercy, Mercy Me (the Ecology)' at a special service held at Glasgow Cathedral on 8 November 2021. In my introduction to the Choir, I interpreted Gaye's song through the lenses of climate and racial justice. I proposed that if we juxtapose the song with other social issues on the album *What's Going On?* (militarism, poverty, state violence against Black people),[9] then climate issues are folded into racial justice. Furthermore, I also ventured that there is an underlying religious influence on the album: Marvin's Black Pentecostal roots. I quote the improvised introduction at length.

> 50 years ago, Marvin Gaye writes and produces his classic album *What's Going On?* This album is significant for a variety of reasons. One is because of its technological advances. First time a multi-track studio is used to produce a solo album. It's also significant because it represents the birth of the Black protest tradition in soul music and is followed later by other artists such as Sly and the Family Stone. I think the album is most significant because of

what he has to say about the ecology. Marvin Gaye folds racial justice into climate justice and suggests to us that the two are wed together and cannot be separated.

How does Marvin Gaye do that? Why does Marvin Gaye do that? Well, the way in which he does it is that he juxtaposes climate justice with three evils of his day, militarism, poverty, and racism. His brother comes back from Vietnam and tells him about the carpet bombing of innocent women and children. His brother tells him about the disproportionality of African American men who were sent to Vietnam. African Americans represented around 12% of the population but represent 24% of the population who are drafted. Marvin Gaye responds to that by writing the song 'What's Happening Brother?' The other evil of his day is poverty. Marvin takes two years out of recording. Goes back into the ghetto. We called them hoods now, to understand what's going on. He realizes that the community continues to be disenfranchised. 40% of all African Americans live below the poverty line. How does Marvin respond? With the song, 'What's Going On?' Militarism, poverty, also racism. Marvin knows that racism hasn't ended in America and wants the deal with it, and to reflect on its nuances; he produces the song, 'Inner City Blues.'

He folds these three evils into the ecological destruction that he sees around him in Black communities and produces the song, 'Mercy, Mercy Me (The Ecology).'

The question I ask myself as a Black Pentecostal is how does Marvin reach that point? Because there are politicians today, there are theologians today who haven't realized the interconnectedness of racial justice and climate justice. How does Marvin reach that point? I think there are three things which enable him to make these connections and they all come out of the Black Pentecostal tradition; we must remember that Marvin Gaye's father was a Pentecostal preacher.

Three things that come out that [Pentecostal] tradition makes this song possible.

The first one is the retention of an African cosmology. In African Traditional Religion there is belief in the connectedness of all things, and the interrelatedness of all things, and therefore it is a requirement of the human species to teach us to treat all life equitably and equally. That sense of connectedness extends into the other world. That's why in African Traditional Religion there is a reverence for the ancestors because they are also seen as being interconnected with this world. The tragedy is that slavery and colonialism remove that sense of connectedness from Black religion. And what Marvin is trying to remind us . . . of is the interconnectedness of all things. Racial justice, climate, justice.

The second thing is . . . Black women's ways of knowing. Two things that influence Marvin Gaye's capacity . . . the first is experience: experience is the criterion of meaning in Black feminist thought.... Brothers and sisters, come to my church on a Sunday morning, and the women will always tell you 'who feels it knows it.' Marvin puts himself in a position for two years. Takes hiatus from Motown in order to experience urban life and make these connections. The Second theme is ... not only that experience matters but also that there is a place for emotion. Marvin just doesn't want to sing about this. He wants to feel it and he wants you to feel it. That's why in the song 'Inner City Blues,' he says; 'It makes me wanna holler, throw up my hands.' He wants us to feel our way through this situation, and that's how he's able to make this connection.

[Third] The Reason Marvin gets to this place when politicians haven't got to yet, and where many theologians have not got to yet is because he stands within the tradition of the Black Church's commitment to social justice. It's only two years prior that King is assassinated. It's only six months prior that the FBI have 'done in' the Black Panthers, and Marvin realizes that he has the opportunity to embody the Civil Rights Movement. In fact, Mark Anthony Neal, the African American sociologist, argues that this album is the embodiment of the Civil Rights Movement of King's [I have a Dream] speech in 1963. This is significant. Because we often forget. In order to get to 'the dream,' the last 34 words of the speech, you have to work through the nightmare – the first 1500 words of the speech where, King talks about poverty injustice and the need for reparations.

'Mercy, Mercy Me' is not just a song. It is a call for revolutionary action.[10]

The second case study illustrates another impact of *Jamaican Bible Remix*. Moving beyond the raising of awareness in the first case study, in this case the Choir do the work of producing a broader soteriology in song. Though the method was the appropriation of a secular song, this second case evidenced the desired impact – socially engaged lyricism.

Conclusion

So, what can we learn from these case studies? There are three considerations. First, we learn that *Jamaican Bible Remix* fulfils its mission as a communicative bridge between theologians and gospel artists, musicians and songwriters. In both case studies, the album and its reckoning are the focus of conversation and dialogue. Second, that crossover was the easiest way to produce decolonial thinking, though the type of crossover was an appropriation of a secular song rather than the specific front room approach as in Chapter 8. Finally, the work of writing lyrics requires more practical consideration. A way must be found to engage the songwriters and artists of church with a context for writing lyrics consistent with the soul of the Gospel of Jesus.

Conclusion
Resurrection revolution

This book has demonstrated a praxis for decolonizing contemporary gospel music in Britain. Colonial Christian thinking about soteriology, interpretation and Black ontology is set aside and replaced by decolonial thinking; that is, a womanist soteriology, Black biblical studies and Black history. I have argued that coloniality remains a feature of contemporary Black British gospel music. From the arrival of the *Empire Windrush* to the outbreak of Covid-19, our lyricism has failed to break free from colonial missionary theology. I have also produced decolonial theological thinking, first from narrative theology, then, with support from Rastafari-inspired reggae and a former gospel rapper, developed three decolonial options (Chapter 6). To make these options productionable, I appropriate banal, everyday Black orality as production tools for processing the options. The tools are crossover, the Black vernacular and dangerous memories (Chapter 7). Decolonized contemporary gospel music exemplifies the 'soul of the Gospel of Jesus' (Introduction). Jesus' radical, holistic message of salvation is inscribed in songs on the decolonial contemporary gospel album *Jamaican Bible Remix*.

Dialogue with Black British gospel artists reveals the limitations of the contemporary gospel music industry. It has yet to cultivate audiences and congregations to engage with social justice songs. However, crossover techniques, including poaching socially explicit contemporary songs, provide a commercial opportunity for gospel artists; for instance, the Kingdom Choir's revisioning of Marvin Gaye's 'Mercy, Mercy Me' (Chapter 11). But musical poaching does not confront the necessity for a wholesale questioning, rewriting and transforming of the ideas about God that continue to shape our musicians and songwriters. Until this gap is bridged, and there is more consistent sharing of ideas and the cultivation of new audiences, decolonized contemporary gospel music is likely to be a voice in the wilderness, 'speaking truth to power' from the margins of the church.

To normalize decolonial gospel music, we need consistent, engaged and reciprocal dialogue and sharing of ideas between theologians, musicians, songwriters and artists of contemporary gospel music in Britain. Only through more dialogue and conversation, especially in the context of music production, can we find creative commercially viable ways of confronting colonial Christianity in Christian music. In 2023, I will be addressing the Gospel Music Association of Great Britain, and my hope is that my lecture will be the start of a new conversation.

We cannot afford for there *not* to be any change in our Christian musicality. Good Christian music, like good theology, must engage with the existential questions posed by the communities we inhabit. Failure to do so has catastrophic consequences for the mission of the church. The musical responses to the Grenfell Tower fire (Chapter 1) and Covid-19 (Chapter 2) show the inadequacies of our lyricism and, by extension, the continued influence of colonial Christian thinking.

In closing, I turn to the final track on the *Jamaican Bible Remix* album, 'Resurrection'. The track embodies the soul of the Gospel of Jesus. The resurrection of Jesus demands meaningful reflection on social justice in contemporary gospel music in Britain. The resurrection exemplifies God's power to overcome evil and death and therefore emancipate all things. The resurrection has meaning beyond the traditional Black Church personal salvation perspective, where we sing about Christ's death and resurrection as exclusively freedom from sin and shame. The resurrection's liberating power also extends into the social sin and social world in which we live. Decolonized contemporary gospel music is resurrection music.

Illustration: Resurrection

The scripture track is an edited version of the Luuk (Luke) account of Jesus' resurrection (Chapter 24) and the message track performed by Birmingham-based gospel artist Jerome Bucknor. Each verse juxtaposes the resurrection with a range of global social issues such as environmental degradation and the Middle East peace process crisis. The tension invites the listener to question the meaning of the resurrection in wider, holistic, sociopolitical terms for our often fractured and disunited world. As Mark Davis notes:

> The hermeneutics of resurrection is not a fatalistic capitulation to the inevitable death of all things. It increases the value of life – life of the earth, life of the community, even life of the enemy – because where there is life, there is God.[1]

Finally, the music track is an intermingling of African burra drumming from Jamaica fused with classical strains from European stringed instruments.

JNT – Luuk 24
'Wa mek unu a luk fi di wan we a liv mongks di wan dem we ded? Im no de ya, im kom bak alaiv!, im kom bak alaiv!'

Jerome – Resurrection revolution.
Christ is risen, sin and shame done.
Satan can't win.
Christ is risen. (x2)

JNT – Afta dem kom bak fram di tuum, di uman dem tel Jiizas ilevn apasl an aal di res a falara dem wa did apm. Nou a did Mieri Magdaliin, Juowana, Mieri we a Jiemz mada, an di ada uman dem, uu did tel di apasl dem wa dem si. Bot di apasl dem neva biliiv di uman dem, kaaz we dem did a se soun laik fuulinish.

Jerome – Resurrection revolution.
Christ is risen, gun and gang done.
No vexation immigration.
Christ is risen. (x2)

JNT – Piita get op an ron go a di tuum. Im ben dong, bot di onggl ting im si a di piis a linin klaat wan, so im go we, a wanda wa apm.

Jerome – Resurrection revolution.
Christ is risen, end pollution.
Palestinian peace solution.
Christ is risen. (x2)

Jerome – Up from the grave He arose.
With a mighty triumph for His foes.
He arose the victor from the dark domain.
And He lives forever with the saints to reign.
Christ is risen. (x4)

Notes

Introduction

1 Contemporary gospel music refers to the interplay of Black Atlantic Christian thought with contemporary music genres. It is the religious music of African Americans appropriated by African diaspora communities in Europe and the Caribbean.
2 Long, W. C. and Dyer, Bryan R. (2016) *The Bible and Social Justice: Old Testament and New Testament Foundations for the Church's Urgent Call*. Eugene: Pickwick Publications; Portier-Young, A., Sterling, G. E. et al., eds. (2018) *Scripture and Social Justice: Catholic and Ecumenical Essays*. Lanham: Lexington Books/Fortress Academic.
3 For discussion on the intersection of 'race', colonialism and climate change, see Williams, J. (2021) *Climate Change Is Racist: Race Privilege and the Struggle for Climate Justice*. London: Icon Books.
4 See, for example, Gushee, D. and Stassen, G. (2018) *Kingdom Ethics: Following Jesus in Contemporary Contexts*; 2nd ed. Grand Rapids: Wm. B. Eerdmans Publishing Company.
5 Gordon, L. R. (2018) 'Black Aesthetics, Black Value'. *Public Culture*, 30 (1), 19–34.
6 For discussion on the double meaning of the African American Spirituals, see Cone, H. J. (1972) *The Spirituals and the Blues: An Interpretation*. New York: Orbis Books; Kirk-Duggan, C. A. (1997) *Exorcising Evil: A Womanist Perspective on the Spirituals*. New York: Orbis.
7 Informal conversation with Jo-Ann Richards online, 15 September 2020.
8 Gilroy, P. (1993) *Black Atlantic: Modernity and Double Consciousness*. London: Verso, p. 187 ff.
9 See, for instance, the positioning of Blacks over centuries of White British hegemony over Black bodies in Fryer, P. (2021) *Black People in the British Empire*. London: Pluto Press.
10 *Jamaican Bible Remixed* (2018) [Radio programme] BBC World Service 8 July.
11 For discussion on the waves of Christian migration in the Caribbean, see Wilkinson, J. L. (1993) *Church in Black and White: The Black Christian Tradition in 'Mainstream' Churches in England: A White Response and Testimony*. Edinburgh, Scotland: Saint Andrew Press.
12 For an example of the European hegemony, see Dayfoot, A. C. (1999) *The Shaping of the West Indian Church, 1492-1692*. Barbados: University of the West Indies

Press. For an example of the Euro-American hegemony and complicity, see Austin-Broos, D. J. (1997) *Jamaica Genesis: Religion and the Moral Orders*. Chicago: University of Chicago Press.

13 Mukherjee, S. R. (2018) 'Make America Great Again as White Political Theology'. *Revue LISA/LISA e-journal*, 16 (2). Available online (accessed 8 December 2022).

14 Fanon, F. (1986) *Black Skin, White Mask*. London: Pluto Press, p. 116.

15 Cooper, C. (1995) *Noises in the Blood: Orality, Gender, and the 'vulgar' Body of Jamaican Popular Culture*. Durham: Duke University Press, pp. 117–36.

16 Henry, W. and Worley, M. (2020) *Narratives from Beyond the UK Reggae Bassline: The System Is Sound*. Basingstoke: Palgrave Macmillan, pp. 7–29.

17 See discussion in Back, L. (2017) *New Ethnicities and Urban Culture Social Identity and Racism in the Lives of Young People*. London: Routledge.

18 Clarke, Johnny (1976) *Rockers Time Now*. [LP] London: Virgin Records.

19 See Hoffman, A. (2008) 'Interview with Walter Mignolo/Part 2: Key Concepts'. *E-International Relations*, Available online: https://www.e-ir.info/2017/01/21/interview-walter-mignolopart-2-key-concepts/.

20 For a good discussion on alternative epistemes from the Global South, see Santos, B. D. S. (2018) *The End of the Cognitive Empire: The Coming of Age of Epistemologies of the South*. Durham: Duke University Press; Medina, J. (2013). *The Epistemology of Resistance: Gender and Racial Oppression, Epistemic Injustice and Resistant Imaginations*. New York: Oxford University Press.

21 Beckford, R. (2021) *My Theology: Duppy Conqueror*. London: Darton Longman & Todd; Beckford, R. (1998) *Jesus Is Dread: Black Theology and Black Culture in Britain*. London: Darton Longman & Todd.

22 Bourne, R. and Adkins, I. (2021) *A New Introduction to Theology: Embodiment, Experience and Encounter*. London: T&T Clark, p. 1.

23 The whole album is located on Soundcloud. See *Jamaican Bible Remix* (2017) [Soundcloud] 5AM Records. See https://soundcloud.com/user-765185353/sets/the-jamaican-bible-remix-project. Playlist with lyric sheet available at: https://www.canterbury.ac.uk/arts-and-humanities/school-of-humanities/religion-philosophy-and-ethics/research/jamaican-bible-remix.aspx.

24 I am referring to the MA and PhD programmes at the Queen's Foundation in Birmingham, UK.

Chapter 1

1 See, for example, Damiola Babarinde's analysis of the hybridization of gospel and church songs, concerts and worship. Babarinde, D. M. (2019) 'Emergent Issues

in the Hybridisation of Christian Gospel Music in South-West Nigeria'. *Cajolis-Calabar Journal of Liberal Studies*, 21 (1), 81–8. Also, Deborah Smith's reflection on contemporary gospel music. Pollard, D. S. (2008) *When the Church Becomes Your Party*. Detroit: Wayne State University Press, pp. 17–53.
2   Pollard, D. S. (2008) *When the Church Becomes Your Party*.
3   See Hebdige, D. (1987) *Cut 'n' Mix: Culture, Identity and Caribbean Music*. London: Comedia.
4   Ibid.
5   *The Battle for Christianity* (2016). [TV Programme] BBC1, 8 April 2016.
6   Woodhead, L. (2016) 'The Rise of "No Religion" in Britain: The Emergence of a New Cultural Majority'. *Journal of the British Academy*, 4 (8), 245–61.
7   See Ostwalt, C. (2012) *Secular Steeples: Popular Culture and the Religious Imagination*. London: Bloomsbury, p. 77.
8   See, for further discussion, Marti, G. (2012) *Worship Across the Racial Divide: Religious Music and the Multiracial Congregation*. New York: Oxford University Press.
9   See, for example, https://hillsong.com/uk/Black-lives-matter/.
10 Compare in the wake of George Floyd's murder the commitment to anti-racism at https://hillsong.com/uk/Black-lives-matter/ with the visual politics at play in the leadership team https://hillsong.com/uk/centrallondon/meet-the-team/.
11 Riches, T. (2010) 'The Evolving Theological Emphasis of Hillsong Worship (1996–2007)'. *Australasian Pentecostal Studies*, 13, 87–118, p. 91.
12 Evans, M. (2015) 'Hillsong Abroad: Tracing the Songlines of Contemporary Pentecostal Music'. In M. M. Ingalls and A. Yong, *The Spirit of Praise: Music and Worship in Global Pentecostal-Charismatic Christianity*. Pennsylvania: The Pennsylvania State University Press.
13 Nketia, J. H. K. (1979) 'African Roots of Music in the Americas: An African View'. *Jamaica Journal*, 43, 12–17.
14 See Smith, R. D. et al. (2014) *Churches, Blackness, and Contested Multiculturalism: Europe, Africa, and North America*. New York: Palgrave Macmillan. See the introduction.
15 Rodreguez, K. D. (2008) *Black Dance in London, 1730-1850: Innovation, Tradition and Resistance*. Jefferson: McFarland & Co; Gilroy, P. (1987) *There Ain't No Black in the Union Jack*. London: Routledge. For the United States, see Neal, M. A. (1999) *What the Music Said: Black Popular Music and Black Public Culture*. London and New York: Routledge Press.
16 Rogers, A. (2016) 'How Are Black Majority Churches Growing in the UK? A London Borough Case Study'. *LSE Blogs*. https://blogs.lse.ac.uk/religionglobalsociety/2016/12/how-are-Black-majority-churches-growing-in-the-uk-a-london-borough-case-study/.
17 See Glendhill, R. (2016) 'The Remarkable Impact of London's Flourishing Megachurches'. *Christianity Today* 2. https://www.christiantoday.com/article/the-remarkable-impact-of-londons-flourishing-megachurches/99624.htm.

18 Kwiyani, H. C. (2020) *Multicultural Kingdom: Ethnic Diversity, Mission and the Church*. London: SCM Press; Ofinjana, I. (2010) *Reverse in Ministry and Missions: Africans in the Dark Continent of Europe: An Historical Study of African Churches in Europe*. Milton Keynes: AuthorHouse; Kwyani, H. (2017) *Blessed Reflex: African Christians in Europe*. University of Groningen Press. Internet resource. https://www.researchgate.net/publication/349420187_A_Blessed_Reflex_Migration_African_Christianity_and_Missio_Dei_in_Freddy_Macha%27s_The_Drunk_and_the_Preacher.

19 Rhoden, H. R. (2003) 'The Essence of Pentecostal Worship'. *Enrichment Journal*, March, http://enrichmentjournal.ag.org/200303/200303_018_essence.cfm.

20 Ibid.

21 Woods, R. and Walrath, B. (2007) *The Message in the Music: Studying Contemporary Praise and Worship*. Nashville: Abingdon Press, pp. 96–7.

22 Allen-McLaurin, L. (2021) *A Womanist Theology of Worship: Liturgy, Justice, and Communal Righteousness*. New York: Orbis Books.

23 Pauline Muir discusses this phenomenon. It is the main point of her study of Black (African) Church worship in London. See Muir, P. E. (2018) 'Sounds Mega: Musical Discourse in Black Majority Churches in London'. PhD Dissertation, Birkbeck College, University of London.

24 Drane, John W. (2000) *The Mcdonaldization of the Church: Spirituality, Creativity, and the Future of the Church*. London: Darton Longman & Todd, p. 100.

25 McKenzie, D. A. D. (2014) 'The Future of the Past: Forging a Historical Context for Black Gospel Music as a Tradition Amongst African Caribbean Pentecostals in Post-War Britain'. Dissertation University of Birmingham; Muir, P. (2018) 'Sounds Mega'.

26 Pollard, D. S. (2008) *When the Church Becomes Your Party*, p. 17.

27 Butler, M. (2019) *Island Gospel: Pentecostal Music and Identity in Jamaica and the United States*. Champaign: University of Illinois Press, p. 1.

28 See Abbington, J. (2014) *Readings in African American Church Music and Worship*. Chicago: GIA Publications, Inc.

29 Kroeker, C. Y. (2002) 'Music Pedagogy and the Christian Faith: A Twenty-Year Journey of Discovery'. In Arlin C. Migliazzo (ed.), *Teaching as an Act of Faith: Theory and Practice in Church-Related Higher Education*. New York: Fordham University Press.

30 Darden, B. (2015) *People Get Ready! A New History of Black Contemporary Gospel Music*. New York and London: Bloomsbury Academic, pp. 70–94.

31 Hendricks, O. (2011) *The Universe Bends Toward Justice: Radical Reflections on the Bible, the Church, and the Body Politic*. Maryknoll: Orbis Books, pp. 1–38.

32 Chitando, A., Chikowero, J. and Madongonda, A. M., eds (2015) *The Art of Survival: Depictions of Zimbabwe and the Zimbabwean in Crisis*. Newcastle: Cambridge Scholars Press, p. 125ff.

33 Lindenbaum, J. (2013) 'The Neoliberalization of Contemporary Christian Music's New Social Gospel'. *Geoforum*, 44, 112–19.
34 See, for example, the flow of ideas across continents in Mahler, A. G. (2018) *From the Tricontinental to the Global South: Race, Radicalism, and Transnational Solidarity*. Durham: Duke University Press.
35 Preston, J. (2019) *Grenfell Tower: Preparedness, Race and Disaster Capitalism*. London: Palgrave; Shildrick, T. (2018) 'Lessons from Grenfell: Poverty Propaganda, Stigma and Class Power'. *The Sociological Review*, 66 (4), 783–98.
36 See Beaumont-Thomas, B. (2018) 'Stormzy asks "Theresa May, Where's the Money for Grenfell?" at Brit awards.' *The Guardian*, 21 February.
37 Ibid.
38 The Kingdom Choir (2018) [CD] *Stand by Me*. UK: Sony Music.
39 Hendricks, O. M. (2011) *The Universe Bends Toward Justice*. Maryknoll: Orbis Books, pp. 1–38.
40 Wilmore G. S., (2007) 'Black Theology at the Turn of the Century'. In D. N. Hopkins, *Black Faith and Public Talk: Critical Essays on James H. Cone's Black Theology and Black Power*. Waco, TX: Baylor University Press, p. 232ff.
41 The potential and limitations of Black theology as a mass movement are explored in Howard, C. (2016) *Black Theology as Mass Movement*. London: Palgrave Macmillan.
42 David Muir (Roehampton), Anthony Reddie (Oxford) and Andrew Boakye (Manchester). At the time of writing, I was teaching in Sustainability and working as a professor of climate and social justice.
43 Lincoln, C. and Mamiya, L. H. (1990) *The Black Church in the African American Experience*. Durham: Duke University Press. p. 346.
44 Santos, B. (2017) *Epistemologies of the South: Justice against Epistemicide*. London: Routledge.
45 Beckford, R. (2014) *Documentary as Exorcism: Resisting the Bewitchment of Colonial Christianity*. London: Bloomsbury.
46 Reddie, A. G. (2006) *Dramatizing Theologies: A Participative Approach to Black God-Talk*. London: Routledge.
47 McClure, J. S. (2011) *Mashup Religion: Pop Music and Theological Invention*. Waco: Baylor University Press, pp. 43–50.
48 Fishbane, M. (2008) *Sacred Attunement: A Jewish Theology*. Chicago: University of Chicago Press, p. 4.
49 Fulani, I., ed. (2012) *Archipelagos of Sound: Transnational Caribbeanities, Women and Music*. Kingston: University of the West Indies Press, pp. 1–2.
50 Hebdige, D. (1987) *Cut 'n' Mix*, pp. 56–8.
51 This point is made by MacRobert, I. (1989) 'Black Pentecostalism: Its Origins, Functions and Theology: With Special Reference to a Midland Borough'. PhD Dissertation, University of Birmingham. MacRobert describes 'artistry' as a function of the church.

52 Informal conversation with Tony Bean, 12 January 2018.
53 Roots Manuva (1999) *Brand New Second Hand* [CD] Big Dada Records, London.

Chapter 2

1 A description of the method appears in Green, L. (2001) *Let's Do Theology: A Pastoral Cycle Resource Book*. London: Continuum. Chapter 2.
2 Graham, E., Walton, H. and Ward, F. (2018) *Theological Reflection Methods*. London: SCM Press. p. 216. Kindle Edition.
3 See, for example, Elliott-Cooper, A. (2018) *Black Resistance to British Policing*. Manchester: Manchester University Press.
4 Lartey, E. Y. (1997) *In Living Colour: An Intercultural Approach to Pastoral Care and Counselling*. London: Cassell, pp. 94–102.
5 Crouch, A. 'Soon and Very Soon' (1976). [LP] Crouch Music Corp. Bud John Songs, Inc.
6 Alexander, M. J. (2005) *Pedagogies of Crossing: Meditations on Feminism, Sexual Politics, Memory, and the Sacred*. Durham: Duke University Press, pp. 7–8.
7 Turner, V. (1996) *The Ritual Process: Structure and Anti-Structure*. London: Routledge, pp. 94–165.
8 Alexander, M. J. (2006) *Pedagogies of Crossing*, p. 6.
9 Alexander, V. (1998) '"Breaking Every Fetter"? To What Extent Has the Black Led Church in Britain Developed a Theology of Liberation?' PhD Dissertation, University of Warwick, p. 227.
10 Ibid.
11 Ibid., 125.
12 See Spencer, J. M. (1990) *Protest & Praise: Sacred Music of Black Religion*. Minneapolis: Fortress Press. 1990.
13 Ibid.
14 For a review of the politics of reggae music in Britain, see Henry, W. and Worley, M. (2021) *Narratives from beyond the UK Reggae Bassline: The System Is Sound*. Cham, Switzerland: Palgrave Macmillan.
15 Steel Pulse, 'Klu Klux Klan' (1978) *Handsworth Revolution*, [LP]. UK: Island Records.
16 Rice, C. M. 'Great Is Thy Faithfulness' lyrics © Clumsy Fly Music, Hope Publishing Company, So Essential Tunes, Hill and Range Songs, Inc.
17 See 'Disparities in the Risk and Outcomes of Covid-19' (2020) Public Health England, PHE Publications, pp. 39–50.
18 An argument for the racialization of the British media is made in Law, I. (2002) *Race in the News*. Basingstoke: Palgrave.

19 See also for Christian press response to 'The Blessing Song' and the prime minister's response. Available at https://premierchristian.news/en/news/article/prime-minister-gives-tim-hughes-award-and-labels-uk-blessing-video-a-sensational-singing-masterpiece.
20 For a further discussion of 'The Blessing Song', see https://www.premierchristianity.com/Blog/Explained-The-meaning-of-The-Blessing-lyrics
21 See https://www.youtube.com/watch?v=PUtll3mNj5U.
22 Ibid.
23 Hill, C. (2020) *Beyond the Pandemic: Is There Any Word from the Lord?* UK: Wilberforce Publications.
24 See, for example, Jordan, W. D. (1968) *White over Black: American Attitudes Toward the Negro, 1550–1812*. Chapel Hill: University of North Carolina Press, pp. 81–98.
25 See the reflection on mission and slavery in Simpson, G. E. (1978) *Black Religions in the New World*. New York: Columbia University Press.
26 This point is the thesis of Perkinson, J. W. (2004) *White Theology: Outing Supremacy in Modernity*. New York: Palgrave Macmillan. P. 51–87.
27 Ibid.
28 Quoted in Lampe, A. (2001) *Christianity in the Caribbean: Essays on Church History*. West Indies: University of the West Indies Press, p. 91.
29 Woolverton, J. F. (1984) *Colonial Anglicanism in North America*. Detroit: Wayne State University Press, pp. 72–3. Gerbner, K. (2018) *Christian Slavery: Conversion and Race in the Protestant Atlantic World*. Pennsylvania: University of Pennsylvania Press, p. 3.
30 Vaughan, A. T. (1995) *Roots of American Racism: Essays on the Colonial Experience*. New York: Oxford University Press, p. 57.
31 The remark was made during the debate between Biggar, me and Esther Stanford but edited out in the final broadcast programme. The full version has the remarks.
32 Kidd, C. (2006) *The Forging of Races: Race and Scripture in the Protestant Atlantic World, 1600-2000*. Cambridge: Cambridge University Press, p. 168.
33 Whitford, D. M. (2014) *The Curse of Ham in the Early Modern Era: The Bible and the Justifications for Slavery*. Farnham: Ashgate; Carson, Marion L. S. (2014) 'Difficult Texts: Colossians 3.22 – Slaves, Obey Your Earthly Masters in Everything'. *Theology*, 117 (3), 203–5.
34 Murrell, S. (2000) 'Dangerous Memories: Underdevelopment, and the Bible'. In G. Gossai and N. S. Murrell, *Religion, Culture and Tradition in the Caribbean*. Basingstoke: Macmillan, p. 12.
35 See Quijano, A. and Ennis, M. (2000) 'Coloniality of Power, Eurocentrism, and Latin America'. *Nepentla: Views From the South*, 1 (3), 533–80.
36 Hutton, J. E. (1992) *A History of Moravian Missions*. London: Moravian Publications Office, p. 44.
37 Godwyn, M. (1680) *The Negros and Indians Advocate, Suing for their Admission to the Church, or, A Persuasive to the Instructing and Baptizing of the Negro's and Indians in Our Plantations Shewing that as the Compliance therewith can Prejudice no Man's just Interest,*

so the Wilful Neglecting and Opposing of it, is No Less than a Manifest Apostacy from the Christian Faith: To Which is Added, a Brief Account of Religion in Virginia. London.
38 Gerbner, K. (2018) *Christian Slavery*, p. 3.
39 Goldenberg, D. M. (2003) *The Curse of Ham: Race and Slavery in Early Judaism, Christianity and Islam*. Princeton; Oxford: Princeton University Press; Whitford, D. M. (2012) *The Curse of Ham in the Early Modern Era: The Bible and the Justifications for Slavery*. Farnham: Ashgate.
40 Park, W. (2021) 'The Blessing of Whiteness in the Curse of Ham: Reading Gen 9:18–29 in the Antebellum South', *Religions* 12 (11), 928.
41 Shields, M. W. (2022) 'The Terror of White Hermeneutics: Black and Enslaved Bodies Interpreted in the Context of Whiteness'. In Smith, J. M., Parker, A. N. and Dunbar Hill, E. S., *Bitter The Chastening Rod: Africana Biblical Interpretation After Stony the Road We Trod in the Age of BLM, SAYHERNAME and METOO*. Lanham: Lexington Books/Fortress Academic, p. 110.
42 See Clark, J. (2012) *Indigenous Black Theology: Toward an African-Centered Theology of the African American Religious Experience*. USA: Palgrave Macmillan, pp. 55–74.
43 Dadzie, S. (2021) *A Kick in the Belly: Women Slavery and Resistance*. Brooklyn: Verso.
44 Ming, D. G. (2020) 'What Is "Decoloniality"? A Postcolonial Critique'. *Postcolonial Studies*, 23 (4), 596–600.
45 Mignolo, W. D. (2000) *Local Histories/Global Designs: Coloniality, Subaltern Knowledges, and Border Thinking*. Princeton: Princeton University Press, pp. ix–x.
46 Ibid.
47 See Manuva, *Brand New Second Hand*.

Chapter 3

1 Grosfoguel, R. (2007) 'The Epistemic Decolonial Turn'. *Cultural Studies*, 21 (2–3), 211–23.
2 Ibid., 212.
3 See Karla, A. A. (2014) 'Anancy Stories Beyond the Moralistic Approach of the Western Philosophy of Being'. *Boletín De Literatura Oral*, (4), 43–52.
4 Ibid., 43–4.
5 Day, K. (2021) *Notes from a Native Daughter: Testifying in Theological Education*. Eugene: Eerdmans Publishing, p. 3.
6 Meunier, J. B. (2012) 'Trans-Atlantic Circulation of Black Tropes: Èsù and the West African Griot as Poetic References for Liberation in Cultures of the African Diaspora'. LSU Doctoral Dissertations.
7 Allen-McLaurin, L. (2021) *A Womanist Theology of Worship*, pp. 119–23.
8 Jones, L. G. (1993) 'Art. Narrative Theology'. In Alister E. McGrath (ed.), *The Blackwell Encyclopaedia of Modern Christian Thought*. Oxford: Blackwell, pp. 395–8.

9 Hauerwas, S. and Jones, L. G., eds (1987) *Why Narrative? Readings on Narrative Theology*. Eugene: Wipf and Stock Publishers, p. 2.
10 Hall, D. (2021) *Black British Pastoral Theology*. UK: SCM Press, p. 64.
11 Grant, J. (1994) '"Come to My Help Lord for I'm in Trouble": Womanist Jesus and the Mutual Struggle for Liberation'. *Journal of Black Theology in South Africa*, 8 (1), 21–34.
12 Niebuhr H. R. (2006) *The Meaning of Revelation*. Louisville: Westminster John Knox Press, p. 23.
13 See the general themes in Beckford, R. (2000) *Dread and Pentecostal: A Political Theology for the Black Church in Britain*. London: SPCK, pp. 187–208.
14 Anderson, V. (2018) *Beyond Ontological Blackness*. London: Bloomsbury, p. 120ff.
15 Oakes, E. (1992) 'Apologetics and the Pathos of Narrative Theology'. *The Journal of Religion*, 72 (1), 37–8.
16 See Coard, B. (1971) *How the West Indian Child Is Made Educationally Sub-Normal in the British School System*. London: New Beacon Books; Richardson, B. and Coard, B. (2007) *Tell It Like It Is: How Our Schools Fail Black Children*. London: Bookmarks Publications; John, G. (2004) *The Crisis Facing Black Children in the British Schooling System: A Call to Independent Action by Black Students and Black Parents*. Rawtenstall: The Gus John Partnership Ltd.
17 Sanders, J. (2016) *Theology in the Flesh: How Embodiment and Culture Shape the Way We Think About Truth, Morality, and God*. Minneapolis: Fortress Press, pp. 175–90.
18 Pearce, L. G. (2019) 'Black Students in England 1950-2000: Representation, Identity and Barriers to Success'. *New Vistas*, 45 (2), 4.
19 See Rollock, N. et al. (2015) *The Colour of Class: The Educational Strategies of the Black Middle Classes*. London: Routledge.
20 Sölle, D. (2007) *Creative Disobedience*. Eugene: Wipf & Stock Publishers.
21 See Dinerstein, J. (2017) *The Origins of Cool in Postwar America*. Chicago: University of Chicago Press.
22 Beckford R. (2022) 'After the Flood: Christianity, Slavery and Reconciliation'. [Film] UK: Movement for Justice and Reconciliation.
23 Reardon, T. W. (2021) *Politics of Salvation: Lukan Soteriology, Atonement, and the Victory of Christ*. London: T&T Clark, Bloomsbury Publishing Plc, pp. 33–63.
24 See a summary of New Testament debates in Zahl, S. (2021) 'Beyond the Critique of Soteriological Individualism: Relationality and Social Cognition'. *Modern Theology*, 37 (2), 336–61.
25 See, for example, Hall, S. and Jefferson, T. (1983) *Resistance Through Rituals: Youth Subculture in Post-War Britain*, 2nd edn. London: Routledge.
26 *Subnormal* (2020) BBC Documentary. [TV] Lammas Park Productions.
27 Duncanson-Hales, Christopher J. (2017) 'Dread Hermeneutics: Bob Marley, Paul Ricœur and the Productive Imagination'. *Black Theology*, 15 (2), 156–75.

28 See Murrell, N. S., McFarlane, A. and Spencer, W. (1998) *Chanting Down Babylon: The Rastafari Reader*. Philadelphia: Temple University Press, p. 326ff.
29 Murrell, N. L. and Williams, L. (1998) 'The Black Biblical Hermeneutics of Rastafari'. In Murrell, McFarlane and Spencer, *Chanting Down Babylon*, p. 328.
30 Smith, M. J. (2018) *Womanist Sass and Talk Back: Social (in)Justice, Intersectionality, and Biblical Interpretation*. USA: Wipf and Stock Publishers, p. 8.
31 Bevans, S. B. (2002) Models of *Contextual Theology*. New York: Orbis, p. XVI.
32 Earl, R. E. (2012) 'Black Theology and Human Purpose'. In D. Hopkins and E. Antonio (eds), *The Cambridge Companion to Black Theology*. Cambridge: Cambridge University Press, pp. 132–3.
33 Carter, J. K. (2014) 'Humanity in African American Theology'. In K. G. Cannon and A. B. Pinn, *The Oxford Handbook of African American Theology*. Oxford: Oxford University Press, p. 176.
34 Turner, C. (2020) *Overcoming Self-negation: The Church and Jankanoo in Contemporary Bahamian Society*. UK: Pickwick.
35 hooks, b. (2015) *Black Looks: Race and Representation*. New York: Routledge, p. 20.
36 See Akala (2019) *Natives: Race and Class in the Ruins of Empire*. London: Two Roads.
37 See, for example, McDonald, C. (2021) *God Is Not a White Man and Other Revelations*. London: Hodder & Stoughton.
38 Goffman, E. (1975) *Frame Analysis: An Essay on the Organization of Experience*. Harmondsworth: Penguin; Lakoff, G. (2014), *The All New Don't Think of an Elephant! Know Your Values and Frame the Debate*. White River Junction: Chelsea Green Publishing, pp. xi–xii.
39 Gadamer, H. and Smith, P. C. (1980) *Dialogue and Dialectic*. London: Yale University Press, p. 119.
40 Epstein, H. (2005) *Melting the Venusberg: A Feminist Theology of Music*. New York: Continuum, pp. 11–32.
41 Whitla, B. (2021) *Liberation, (De)Coloniality, and Liturgical Practices: Flipping the Song Bird*. Cham: Palgrave Macmillan Springer Nature Switzerland.
42 See Hendricks, O. M. (2006) *The Politics of Jesus: Rediscovering the True Revolutionary Nature of the Teachings of Jesus and How They Have Been Corrupted*. New York: Doubleday.
43 Roni Size (1997) *New Forms*. [CD] London: Talking Loud.

Chapter 4

1 See Feld, S. (1984) 'Sound Structure as Social Structure'. *Journal of Ethnomusicology*, 28 (3), 383–409.

2 See, for example, Broughton, V. (1996) *Too Close to Heaven: The Illustrated History of Gospel Music*. London, England: Midnight Books.
3 Muir, P. E. (2018) *Sounds Mega*; Charles, Monique (2016) 'Hallowed Be Thy Grime? A Musicological and Sociological Genealogy of Grime Music and Its Relation to Black Atlantic Religious Discourse'. University of Warwick Dissertation.
4 This study is an evolution of my previous exploration of Black music as an interpretive tool for theological studies. See Beckford, R. (2006) *Jesus Dub: Theology, Music, and Social Change*. London: Routledge.
5 Bidnall, A. (2017) *The West Indian Generation: Remaking British Culture in London, 1945-1965*. Cambridge: Cambridge University Press, pp. 22-3.
6 Rush, A. (2007) 'Reshaping British History: The Historiography of West Indians in Britain in the Twentieth Century'. *History Compass*, 5 (2), 463-84, p. 477.
7 Ibid.
8 See, for instance, McLean-Farrell, J. A. (2016) *West Indian Pentecostals: Living Their Faith in New York and London*. London: Bloomsbury Academic, pp. 67-70.
9 Paul, K. (1997) *Whitewashing Britain: Race and Citizenship in the Postwar Era*. New York: Cornell University Press, p. 111.
10 Ibid.
11 Ibid.
12 See, for example, Bourne, S. (2012) *The Motherland Calls: Britain's Black Servicemen and Women, 1939-45*. Stroud: History Press.
13 See Akala (2019) *Natives*.
14 See Paul, K. (2007) *Whitewashing Britain Race and Citizenship in the Postwar Era*. New York: Cornell University Press, p. 114.
15 The British Nationality Act of 1948 defined British nationality to include citizens of the colonies. See, https://www.legislation.gov.uk/ukpga/Geo6/11-12/56/enacted
16 Hall, S. (1984) 'Reconstruction Work: Stuart Hall on Images of Post War Black Settlement'. *Ten-8*, 16 (4), 2-9.
17 See Dayfoot, A. C. (1999) *The Shaping of the West Indian Church, 1492-1692*; Wilkinson, L. (1993) *Church in Black and White*.
18 Muir, D. (2018) 'From Tilbury to the Pew and Pulpit: How the Church Met the Empire Windrush'. *Church Times* 22 (June).
19 Ibid.
20 Paul, K. (1997) *Whitewashing Britain*, p. 13.
21 For a comprehensive history, see Back, L. and Solomos, J. (2007) *Theories of Race and Racism: A Reader*. London: Routledge.
22 See Small, S. (2014) *Racialised Barriers: The Black Experience in the United States and England in the 1980s*. London: Routledge.
23 Perry, K. H. (2018) *London Is the Place for Me: Black Britons, Citizenship and the Politics of Race*. Oxford: Oxford University Press, pp. 63-71.

24 Ibid.
25 Ibid.
26 Ibid.
27 *Black Messiah* (2001) [TV Documentary] BBC 4.
28 Lambeth Council (1998) *Forty Winters On*. London: South London Press, p. 39.
29 Pathé News Report (1955) [TV] 'Our Jamaican Problem'.
30 See, for example, the study of employment in post-Windrush Britain in James, W. and Harris, C. (1993), *Inside Babylon: The Caribbean Diaspora in Britain*. London: Verso, pp. 73–97.
31 James, C. (1993) 'Post-War Migration and the Industrial Reserve Army', in James and Harris, *Inside Babylon*, pp. 1–9.
32 Ramdin, R. (2017) *The Making of the Black Working Class in Britain*. London: Verso, pp. 241–6.
33 Glass, R. and Pollins, H. (1961) *London's Newcomers: The West Indian Migrants*. Cambridge, MA: Harvard University Press; Lass, R. and Westergaard, J. (1965) *London's Housing Needs: Statement of Evidence to the Committee on Housing in Greater London*. London: Centre for Urban Studies, University College.
34 *Daily Herald*, 4 November 1955.
35 *News Chronicle*, 1 March 1954.
36 Sherwood, Harriet (2020) 'Church of England Urged to Apologise for Windrush Racism'. *The Guardian*, 24 January. https://www.theguardian.com/world/2020/jan/24/church-of-england-urged-to-apologise-for-windrush-racism.
37 Pentecostal Credit Union (2020), 'Anglican Church Offers Moving Apology', 10 December. See https://www.pcuuk.com/Church-apologises-for-racist-rejection-and-humiliation-meted-out-to-Windrush-generation-teenager.
38 Ferris, Lesley (2010) 'Incremental Art: Negotiating the Route of London's Notting Hill Carnival'. *Social Identities*, 16 (4), 519–36.
39 Ramdin, R. (2017) *The Making of the Black Working Class in Britain*, pp. 410–25.
40 Panayi, P. (2014) *An Immigration History of Britain: Multicultural Racism since 1800*. London: Routledge, p. 43.
41 Hiro, D. (1996) *Black British White British*. Michigan: UMI Books, p. 44ff.
42 Fryer, P. (2018) *Staying Power, the History of Black People in Britain*. London: Pluto Press, p. 376ff.
43 See discussion of informal micro finance in Black communities at http://learningunlimited.co/files/FinLiCoDocs/Ex59_Microfinance_activity.pdf.
44 Perry, K. H. (2018) *London Is the Place for Me*, pp. 129, 136.
45 Foster, E. (1992) 'The Inverted Pyramid'. In G. Saghal and N. Yuval-Davis, *Refusing Holy Orders: Women and Fundamentalism in Britain*. London: Women Living Under Muslim Laws, p. 42ff.
46 Beckford, R. (1998) *Jesus Is Dread: Black Theology and Black Culture in Britain*. London: Darton, Longman and Todd, p. 45ff.

47 Becket, A. (2020) 'Synod Apologises to Windrush Generation for C of E Racism'. *Church Times*. See, https://www.churchtimes.co.uk/articles/2020/14-february/news/uk/synod-apologises-to-windrush-generation-for-c-of-e-racism
48 Lindsay, B. (2019) *We Need to Talk about Race: Understanding the Black Experience in White Majority Churches*. London: SPCK.
49 Thomas, T. (2021) *Kincraft: The Making of Black Evangelical Sociality*, Durham, London: Duke University Press.
50 See Gerloff, R. I. H. (1992) *A Plea for British Black Theologies: The Black Church Movement in Britain in Its Transatlantic Cultural and Theological Interaction with Special Reference to the Pentecostal Oneness (Apostolic) and Sabbatarian Movements 2. 2*. Frankfurt am Main: Peter Lang, p. 65.
51 See Althusser, L. (2014) *On the Reproduction of Capitalism: Ideology and Ideological State Apparatuses*. London: Verso, p. 191.
52 McKenzie, D. A. D. (2014) 'The Future of the Past.'
53 Ibid.
54 Ibid.
55 McClurkin, D. (2000) 'Caribbean Melody'. Warner Chappell Music, Inc.
56 Burgess, Stanley M. (2006) *Encyclopaedia of Pentecostal and Charismatic Christianity*. New York: Routledge. p. 291.
57 See for a social reading of Acts, Jennings W. J. (2017) *Acts*, First edn. Louisville: Westminster John Knox Press.
58 Derricks, C. (1934) 'Will Soon Be Done with Troubles and Trials'. Stamps-Baxter Music.
59 Sankey, Ira D. (1957) *Sacred Songs and Solos: 1200 Pieces*. London: Marshall, Morgan & Scott, Ltd; Joint Redemption Hymnal Committee (1951) *Redemption Hymnal*. London: Joint Redemption Hymnal Committee.
60 Gundry, S. N. (1999) *Love Them In: The Life and Theology of D.L. Moody*. USA: Moody Publishers, p. 117.
61 Ibid.
62 Ade, I. E. (1958), *What Constitutes Worldliness? The Lust of the Flesh, the Lust of the Eyes, the Lust of Life*. Bedford: The Full Gospel Press, p. 31ff.
63 Donnellan, P. (1965) *The Colony* [TV Documentary]. BBC.
64 Ibid.

Chapter 5

1 Francis, R. N. (2019) *How to Make Contemporary Gospel Music Work for You: A Guide for Contemporary Gospel Music Makers and Marketers*. Croydon: Filament Publishing, p. 78ff.

2   See Smith, A. M. (1994) 'Thatcherism, the New Racism and the British New Right: Hegemonic Imaginary or Accidental Mirage?' In *New Right Discourse on Race and Sexuality: Britain, 1968–1990*. Cambridge: Cambridge University Press, pp. 28–69.

3   Hiro, D. (1992) *Black British, White British: A History of Race Relations in Britain*. London: Paladin, pp. 289–90.

4   Tomlinson, S. (2018) 'Enoch Powell, Empires, Immigrants and Education'. *Race Ethnicity and Education*, 21 (1), 1–14.

5   Ibid.

6   Stratton, J. (2019) *When Music Migrates: Crossing British and European Racial Faultlines, 1945-2010*. London: Routledge, pp. 81–3.

7   Ibid.

8   Stratton, J. (2014) *Black Popular Music in Britain since 1945*. Farnham: Ashgate, p. 27ff.

9   Ibid.

10 Quoted in *Byline Times* (2020), 'White Riot: Why We Need a New Rock Against Racism', 30 April. https://bylinetimes.com/2020/04/30/review-White-riot-why-we-need-a-new-rock-against-racism/.

11 For a detailed study, see Rachel, D. (2017) *Walls Come Tumbling Down: The Music and Politics of Rock Against Racism, 2 Tone and Red Wedge, 1976-1992*. London: Picador.

12 Potter, T. (2016) 'When David Bowie and Eric Clapton flirted with the Far-Right and Inspired an Anti-fascist Movement'. *Public Reading Rooms Online*, August https://prruk.org/when-david-bowie-and-eric-clapton-flirted-with-the-far-right-and-inspired-an-anti-fascist-movement/.

13 Out of Darkness (1972) 'Wordpool'. *The Celebration Club*. [LP] London: Plankton.

14 Smith A. M. (1994) *New Right Discourse on Race and Sexuality in Britain 1968-1990*. Cambridge: Cambridge University Press, pp. 1–28.

15 Bourne, J. (2013) '"May We Bring Harmony"? Thatcher's Legacy on "Race"'. *Race & Class*, 55 (1), 87–91, p. 81.

16 Hiro, D. (1992) *Black British, White British*, pp. 67–8.

17 Scott-Samuel, A., Bambra, C., Collins, C., Hunter, D., McCartney, G. and Smith, K. (2014) 'The Impact of Thatcherism on Health and Well-Being in Britain'. *International Journal of Health Services*, 44 (1), 53–71.

18 Scarman, L. G. (1981) *The Scarman Report: The Brixton Disorders 10-12 April 198*. London: Penguin; Hall, S. et al. (2013) *Policing the Crisis: Mugging the State and Law and Order*, Second edn. Houndmills, Basingstoke; Hampshire: Palgrave Macmillan-Harmondsworth: Penguin.

19 Ibid.

20 See Law, I. (2015) 'Scarman Report'. In X. Smith et al., *The Wiley Blackwell Encyclopaedia of Race, Ethnicity, and Nationalism*. Oxford: Wiley, Blackwell.

21 Civil, D. and Himsworth, J. J. (2020) 'Introduction: Meritocracy in Perspective. The Rise of the Meritocracy 60 Years on'. *The Political Quarterly*, 91 (2), 373–8.
22 See Stan, F., Stetson, B., Joseph, G. and Conti, J. G. (1997) *Black and Right: The Bold New Voice of Black Conservatives in America*. Westport: Praeger, 1997.
23 Kerwick, J. (2011) '"Black Conservatism": The Philosophy of Thomas Sowell'. *E-LOGOS*, 18, 1–24.
24 See the study on Black Christian education and aspiration by Channer, Y. (1995) *I Am a Promise: Achievement of British African-Caribbeans*. Trentham: Stoke-on-Trent.
25 See the *Guardian* comment piece on Asians and the Conservative Party. https://www.theguardian.com/commentisfree/2020/feb/27/how-did-britih-indians-become-so-prominent-in-the-conservative-party.
26 Weber M. (2014) *The Protestant Ethic and the Spirit of Capitalism*, New edn. Kettering: Angelico Press.
27 Gerloff, R. I. H. (1992) *A Plea for British Black Theologies*, pp. 61–6.
28 This argument is made by C. L. R. James in his study of cricket and values in the colonial West Indies. See James, C. L. R. (2019) *Beyond a Boundary*. London: Vintage Books.
29 Paradise (1982) 'Success'. *World's Midnight*. [LP] London: Ebony Records.
30 London Community Gospel Choir (1984) 'Fill My Cup'. [CD] London: Island Records.
31 See Cathcart, B. (2000) *The Case of Stephen Lawrence*. London: Penguin.
32 Ibid.
33 Burnett, J. (2012) 'After Lawrence: Racial Violence and Policing in the UK'. *Race & Class*, 54 (1), 91–8.
34 Ibid.
35 Brackett, D. (1994) 'The Politics and Practice of "Crossover" in American Popular Music, 1963 to 1965'. *The Musical Quarterly*, 78 (4), 774–97.
36 Francis, R. N. (2019) *How to Make Gospel Music Work for You*, p. 94.
37 Harold, C. N. (2020) *When Sunday Comes: Gospel Music in the Soul and Hip-Hop Eras*. Urbana: University of Illinois Press, p. 165.
38 Nu Colours (1993) 'Unlimited'. [CD] PolyGram Records. Nu Colours (1996) 'Nu Colours'. [CD] Wildcard.
39 Nu Colours (1992) 'Power'. [CD] London: Wildcard.
40 Nu Colours interview (1996) *Cross Rhythms Magazine*. https://www.crossrhythms.co.uk/articles/music/Nu_Colours_Living_on_their_knees/40595/p1/.
41 Doward, J. (2008) 'Key Report Says Labour Has Failed on Youth Crime'. *The Guardian*, 31 May.
42 See Cooper, V. and Whyte, D. (2017) *The Violence of Austerity*. London: Pluto Press.
43 See Beckford. R (2004) *God and the Gangs: An Urban Toolkit for Those Who Won't be Bought Out, Sold Out or Scared Out*. London: DLT.
44 Witness (1990) 'Ghetto Cry'. UK: Witness Dis Music.

45 Ibid.
46 Ibid.
47 Jahaziel (2007) 'In My Neighbourhood'. *Ready to Live*. UK: Preacha Boy Music.
48 Ibid.
49 See Olofinjana, I. O. (2020) *World Christianity in Western Europe: Diasporic Identity, Narratives and Missiology*. Oxford: Regnum Books.
50 This is discussed in Olofinjana, I. O. (2010) *Reverse in Ministry and Missions: Africans in the Dark Continent of Europe*. Milton Keynes: AuthorHouse, p. 41.
51 See Soji-George, J. (2004) *The Contemporary Issues in the Nigerian Church: Healing, Signs & Wonders, Deliverance, Anointing Oil, Miracles, Prosperity*. Lagos, Fislol Nig.
52 See Quebedeaux, R. (1976) *The New Charismatics: The Origins, Development, and Significance of Neo-Pentecostalism*. Garden City: Doubleday.
53 Babatunde, A. (2012) *Coat of Many Colours: The Origin, Growth, Distinctiveness and Contributions of Black Majority Churches to British Christianity*. Blackpool: Wisdom Summit, 2012, pp. 149–55.
54 For a full discussion see Roberts, D. (2011) *Reading the Riots: Investigating England's Summer of Disorder*. London: Guardian Books.
55 Briggs, D. (2012) *The English Riots of 2011: A Summer of Discontent*. London: Waterside Press, p. 10.
56 Triple O. (2017) 'I'm Not About That'. *Zero Not Equal to One*. [CD] UK: Triple O Music.
57 Ben Okafor, 'About Ben' on official website. See http://www.benokafor.com/about.html
58 Ibid.
59 S.O. (2019) 'White Jesus' Augustine's Legacy [CD] USA: Lamp Mode Recordings.
60 Ibid.
61 Villafañe E. (1993) *The Liberating Spirit: Toward an Hispanic American Pentecostal Social Ethic*. Grand Rapids: W.B. Eerdmans.
62 Ron Kenoly (1992) 'Anointing Fall on Me'. *Lift Him Up*. Colorado: Integrity Music.

Chapter 6

1 Walsh, C. E. (2018) 'Decolonial in/as Praxis'. In W. D. Mignolo and C. E. Walsh, *On Decoloniality: Concepts, Analytics, Praxis*. Durham: Duke University Press, pp. 15–102.
2 See, for example, the consideration of new thought in Caribbean theology. N. L. Erskine (1998) *Decolonizing Theology: A Caribbean Perspective*. Trenton: Africa World Press.
3 See Keating, A., ed. (2005) *Entre Mundos/Among Worlds: New Perspectives on Gloria Anzaldúa*. New York: Palgrave Macmillan.
4 Mignolo, W. D. (2007) 'Delinking'. *Cultural Studies*, 21 (2), pp. 449–514.

5 Achinte, A. A. (2013) 'PEDAGOGÍAS DE LA RE-EXISTENCIA. Artistas indígenas y afrocolombianos'. In C. Walsh (ed.), *Pedagogias Decoloniales Tomo I. Practicas Insurgentes De Resistir (Re)Existir Y (Re)Vivir*, vol. 1. Quito: Ediciones Abya-Yala, pp. 443–68.
6 As a contextual Black British music, Rastafari-inspired reggae is rooted in the Caribbean diaspora spirituality, language and culture, and marks it as qualitatively different from African American hip-hop's American centrism and hegemony of discourse of Black life. Consequently, the centring of Black British reggae facilitates a more democratic and global imagining of religious meanings in music of the African diaspora. See Goldson, R. R. (2005) 'Liberating the Mind: Rastafari and the Theorization of Maroonage as Epistemological (Dis) engagement'. *Journal of Black Studies*, 51 (4), 368–85.
7 Mignolo, W. D. (2007) 'Delinking', p. 459.
8 Mignolo, W. D. and Tlostanova, M. (2006) 'Theorizing from the Borders Shifting to Geo and Body-Politics of Knowledge'. *European Journal of Social Theory*, 9, 205–21, p. 208.
9 Ibid., 205–21.
10 Mignolo, W. D. (2011) 'Geopolitics of Sensing and Knowing: On (De)coloniality, Border Thinking and Epistemic Disobedience'. *Postcolonial Studies*, 14 (3), 273–83, p. 274.
11 Mignolo, W. D. and Tlostanova, M. (2006) 'Theorizing from the Borders', p. 210.
12 Mignolo, W. D. (2002) 'The Geopolitics of Knowledge', *South Atlantic Quarterly*, 12 (1), 57–96, p. 67.
13 Ibid.
14 Mignolo W. D. (2007) 'Delinking' , pp. 459–60.
15 See Clarke, P. B. (1997) *Black Paradise: The Rastafarian Movement*. San Bernardino: R. Reginald.
16 Mignolo, W. D. (2007) 'Delinking', p. 453.
17 Waters. A. M. (2017) *Race Class and Political Symbols: Rastafari and Reggae in Jamaican Politics*. London: Routledge, p. 134.
18 Steel Pulse (1978) *Handsworth Revolution*.
19 Ibid.
20 Daniel, J. L., Smitherman-Donaldson, G. and Jeremiah M. A. (1987) 'Makin' a Way Out of No Way: The Proverb Tradition in the Black Experience'. *Journal of Black Studies*, 17 (4), 482–508, p. 490.
21 Ngara, C. (2007) 'African Ways of Knowing and Pedagogy Revisited'. *JCIE*, 2 (2), 7–21.
22 Hodges, H. (2008) *Soon Come: Jamaican Spirituality, Jamaican Poetics*. Charlottesville: University of Virginia Press, p. 65.
23 Mignolo, W. D. and Tlostanova, M. (2006) 'Theorizing from the Borders', pp. 220–1.
24 David Daniels (2015) 'Legendary UK Rapper Jahaziel Renounces Christian Faith'. *Rapzilla*, 23 (December). http://www.rapzilla.com/rz/news/38-backstage/12223-legendary-uk-rapper-jahaziel-renounces-christian-faith.

25 See Jones, W. R. (1998) *Is God a White Racist? A Preamble to Black Theology*. Boston: Beacon Press; Pinn, A. B. (1999) *Why, Lord? Suffering and Evil in Black Theology*. New York: Continuum.
26 Coleman, M. A. (2008) *Making a Way Out of No Way: A Womanist Theology*. Minneapolis: Fortress Press, p. 32.
27 Ibid., p. 11.
28 See https://www.canterbury.ac.uk/arts-and-humanities/school-of-humanities/religion-philosophy-and-ethics/research/jamaican-bible-remix.aspx.
29 See Palmer, L. (2012) '"Ladies A Your Time Now!": Erotic Politics, Lovers' Rock and Resistance in the UK'. In I. Fulani (ed.), *Archipelagos of Sound Transnational Caribbeanities, Women and Music*, Kingston Jamaica: University of the West Indies Press, pp. 258–78.
30 See Brown, M. J. (2004) *Blackening of the Bible: The Aims of African American Biblical Scholarship*. Harrisburg: Trinity Press International.
31 Ibid.
32 Thomas, O. A. (2014) *Biblical Resistance Hermeneutics within a Caribbean Context*. London: Routledge. p. 8.
33 Bailey, R. (1995) 'They're Nothing but Incestuous Bastards: The Polemical Use of Sex and Sexuality in Hebrew Canon Narratives'. In F. F. Segovia and M. A. Tolbert (eds), *Reading from this Place Volume 1: Social Location and Biblical Interpretation in the United States*. Minneapolis: Fortress Press, pp. 121–38.
34 Ibid., pp. 121–38.
35 See Rhamie, G. (2019) *Whiteness, Conviviality and Agency: The Ethiopian Eunuch and Conceptuality in the Imperial Imagination of Biblical Studies*. Unpublished PhD Dissertation. UK: Canterbury Christ Church University.
36 Bonhoeffer, D. (2015) *The Cost of Discipleship*. London: SCM Press, p. 231.
37 For a full discussion see Turman E. M. (2013) *Toward a Womanist Ethic of Incarnation: Black Bodies, the Black Church, and the Council of Chalcedon*. New York: Palgrave Macmillan.
38 Jahaziel (2016) 'Armen Ra'. https://www.youtube.com/watch?v=R5KW1ZFopyo.
39 Ibid.
40 Informal conversation with Jahaziel, June 2019.
41 See Callahan, D. A. (1997) *Embassy of Onesimus: The Letter of Paul to Philemon*. Valley Forge: Trinity Press International, pp. 56–62.

Chapter 7

1 Gilroy, P. (1993) *Black Atlantic*, p. 37.
2 This point is made in Shapiro and Barnard's re-reading of modernism and religion, and the centring of Pentecostal origins as a modernist sociocultural movement. See

Barnard, P. and Shapiro, S. (2017) *Pentecostal Modernism: Lovecraft Los Angeles and World-Systems Culture*. London: Bloomsbury Publishing.

3 West, C. (1988) *Prophetic Fragments: Illuminations of the Crisis in American Religion and Culture*. Trenton: Africa World Press, p. 5.

4 Cooper, C. (1995) *Noises in the Blood*, pp. 137–71.

5 Sturken, M. and Cartwright, L. (2009) *Practices of Looking: An Introduction to Visual Culture*, 2nd edn. New York: Oxford University Press, pp. 25–30.

6 See https://warwick.ac.uk/newsandevents/knowledgecentre/society/sociology/royalwedding.

7 Neal, A. (2019) 'Mexit'. *Guardian (Sydney)*, p. 9.

8 Repetition and development are features of Black culture in the West. See Nealon, J. T. (1998) 'Refraining, Becoming-Black: Repetition and Difference in Amiri Baraka's Blues People'. *Symplokē*, 6 (1–2), 83–95, pp. 84–6.

9 Paton, D. (2006) 'Gender, Language, Violence and Slavery: Insult in Jamaica, 1800–1838'. *Gender & History*, 18 (2), 246–65.

10 See a Caribbean reflection on 'dangerous memories' in Hemchand and Murrell, *Religion, Culture and Tradition in the Caribbean*, pp. 1–32.

11 Metz, J. B. (1986) *The Emergent Church*. New York: Crossroad, p. 105.

12 Curry, Bishop Michael, 'The Power of Love', The Archbishop of Canterbury Website, https://www.archbishopofcanterbury.org/speaking-and-writing/sermons/power-love-bishop-michael-currys-sermon-wedding-prince-harry-and.

13 Gilroy, P. (2004) *After Empire: Melancholia or Convivial Culture?* London: Routledge, pp. 108–16.

Chapter 8

1 Marshall, C. and Rossman, G. B. (1989) *Designing Qualitative Research*. Newbury Park: Sage, p. 79.

2 Fine, G. A. (2003) 'Towards a Peopled Ethnography Developing Theory from Group Life'. *Ethnography*, 4 (1), 41–60.

3 Informal discussion with Marcia Dixon 2018.

4 Claudrena, H. (2012) 'Almighty Fire: The Rise of Urban Contemporary Gospel Music and the Search for Cultural Authority in the 1980s'. *Fire!!!*, 1 (1), 25–48.

5 Ibid.

6 McMillan, M. (2009) 'The West Indian Front Room: Reflections on a Diasporic Phenomenon'. *Small Axe: A Caribbean Journal of Criticism*. 13 (1), 135–56.

7 See McMillan, C. M. (2009) *The Front Room: Migrant Aesthetics in the Home*. London: Black Dog Publishing.

8 Beckles-Raymond, G. (2020) 'African-Caribbean Women, (post)Diaspora, and the Meaning of Home'. *African and Black Diaspora: An International Journal*, 13 (2), 202–14.

9   Beckford, R. (2014) *Documentary as Exorcism*, pp. 117–30.
10 See Foucault, M. and Faubion, J. D. (2019) *Aesthetics, Method, and Epistemology*. London: Penguin, p. 178.
11 McMillan, M. (2009) 'The West Indian Front Room', p. 138.
12 Austin-Broos, D. (1997) *Jamaica Genesis*, pp. 177–26.
13 McMillan, M. (2019) 'Dub in the Front Room: Migrant Aesthetics of the Sacred and the Secular'. *Open Cultural Studies*, 3, 184–94, p. 185.
14 Hall, S. (1984) 'Reconstruction Work'.
15 Macmillan, M. (2009) 'The West Indian Front Room', p. 141.
16 Stratton, J. (2014) *Black Popular Music in Britain since 1945*.
17 Ibid.
18 This subject is the theme of this book. See Beckford, R. (2006) *Jesus Dub: Faith, Culture and Social Change*. London: Routledge.
19 See Berger, P. L. (1974) 'Some Second Thoughts on Substantive versus Functional Definitions of Religion'. *Journal for the Scientific Study of Religion*, 13 (2), 125.
20 Gluckman, M. (2014) *Order and Rebellion in Tribal Africa*. London; New York: Routledge.
21 Hellholm, D. (2010) *Ablution, Initiation, and Baptism: Late Antiquity, Early Judaism, and Early Christianity*. Berlin: De Gruyter, pp. 3–40.
22 Patten, H. (2019) 'The Spirituality of Reggae Dancehall Dance Vocabulary: A Spiritual, Corporeal Practice in Jamaican Dance'. PhD Thesis, Canterbury Christ Church University.
23 See Eshun, K. (2018) *More Brilliant Than the Sun*. London: Verso.
24 Dent, G. (1992) 'Black Pleasure, Black Joy: An Introduction'. In G. Dent (ed.), *Black Popular Culture*. USA: Bay Press, pp. 1–19.
25 Joseph Niles and the Consolers, 'Gospel Ship' [LP] Redemption, 1973.
26 Rose, T. (1994) *Black Noise: Rap Music and Black Culture in Contemporary America*. Hanover and London: Wesleyan University Press, p. 39.
27 Mbiti, J. S. (1975) *Introduction to African Religion*. Praeger: New York, pp. 55–6.
28 Ibid., pp. 55–6.
29 Esu (Eshu-Elegba) mediates the relationship between humanity and the deities. He is the messenger of the supreme god Olodumare. The role of messenger is important and includes tricking humans. While missionaries came to associate Esu with Satan, the Yoruba view this deity, like all others, as capable of good and harm.
30 Kirk-Duggan, C. A. (2014) 'Sacred and Secular in African American Music', in F. B. Brown (ed.), *The Oxford Handbook of Religion and the Arts*, Oxford Handbooks: online edn, Oxford Academic.
31 Reed, T. L. (2003) *The Holy Profane: Religion in Black Popular Music*. Kentucky: University Press of Kentucky, pp. 2–3.

32 Henriques, J. (2008) 'Sonic Diaspora, Vibrations and Rhythms: Thinking through the Sounding of the Jamaican Dancehall Session'. *African and Black Diaspora*, 1 (2), 215–36.
33 Ibid.
34 Tracy, C. (2019) 'Christian Sound Systems in Britain: Its Origins, Functions and Theology'. MA Thesis, Canterbury Christ Church University, p. 3.
35 Their style was a more sophisticated technological version of what my father performed in the front room. As Tracy notes, 'as one operator told me, "In the early days we played a mi of gospel and conscious songs by reggae artists such as Sanchez, and George Nooks etc."' Tracy, C. (2019) 'Christian Sound Systems in Britain', p. 3.
36 Ibid., p. 71.
37 Otto, R. (1959) *The Idea of the Holy: An Inquiry into the Non-Rational Factor in the Idea of the Divine and Its Relation to the Rational: Translated [from the German] by John W. Harvey*. Harmondsworth: Penguin Books.
38 Ibid.
39 Durkheim, É. and Swain, J. W. (2015) *The Elementary Forms of the Religious Life*. Oxford: Benediction Classics, p. 84.
40 For instance, 'Easy Road' speaks of the plans of the devil 'proving deliverance', the 'blood of the lamb' and the joy of touring the world. 'Nothing but the Blood' speaks of Satan's voice, blessings, mistakes and salvation/grace. Also, 'Never Too Late' focuses on deliverance in terms of salvation, and speaks of the threat demons and the blessings bestowed by God on the artist. 'Show Me the Way' begins with a prayer for deliverance in terms of God being the 'peace in the storm' and speaks of the devil winnings. 'Remember Me' speaks of the devil's attacks.
41 CalledOut Music (2018) 'Heaven'. [CD] London: HFP music.
42 See, for example, the single 'Shadey's Sermon', 2019. https://www.youtube.com/watch?v=bFTgiWIVOq4.
43 *Malcolm X* (1992). [Movie] 40 Acres and a Mule.

Chapter 9

1 Cutler, C. (2007) 'Hip-Hop Language in Sociolinguistics and Beyond'. *Language and Linguistics Compass*, 1, 519–38.
2 See Chimene-Wale, N. C. (2019) 'Code Switching and Mixing in Nigerian Gospel Music'. *Scholarly Journal of Science Research and Essay*, 9 (1), 11–17.
3 Achebe, C. (1975) 'English and the African Writer'. In A. Mazuri, *The Political Sociology of the English Language*. The Hague/Paris: Mouton (Appendix B), pp. 216–23.

4 wa Thiong'o. N. (1985) 'The Language of African Literature'. *New Left Review* 150 (March/April), 109–27, p. 125.
5 Morren, R. C. and Morren, D. M. (2007) *Are the Goals and Objectives of Jamaica's Bilingual Education Project Being Met?* http://www.sil.org/resources/archives/7822.
6 Sutcliffe, D. (1983) *British Black English*. Oxford: Basil Blackwell, p. 210. Review by D. Craig in *Language in Society,* 12 (4), 542–8.
7 See Russel, J. and Cohn, R. (2015) *Multicultural London English*. Lavergne: CPSIA.
8 Phillipson, R. (1992) *Linguistic Imperialism*. Oxford: Oxford University Press, p. 38.
9 Javid, S. (2021) 'Secondary Schools Ban Students from Using Slang Terms Such as "Like" and "Bare"'. *The Independent*, 1 October.
10 Tomlin, C. (2019) *Preach It: Understanding African-Caribbean Preaching*. London: SCM Press, p. 46.
11 Ibid.
12 Sugirtharajah, R. S. (1999) *Vernacular Hermeneutics*. Sheffield: Sheffield Academic Press, p. 15.
13 Ibid., p. 12.
14 Ibid., p. 97.
15 Connolly, M. A. (2019) 'Antipodean and Biblical Encounter: Postcolonial Vernacular Hermeneutics in Novel Form'. *Religions*, 10 (6), 21.
16 Beckford, R. (2014) *Documentary as Exorcism,* Chapter 5.
17 *Di Jamiekan Nyuu Testament* (2012) Kingston, Jamaica: Bible Society of the West Indies, pp. viii–ix.
18 Fiddis, P. S. (1989) *Past Event and Present Salvation: The Christian Idea of Atonement*. London: DLT, pp. 7–13.
19 BBC News Website (2011) 'England Riots: "The Whites Have Become Black" says David Starkey', 13 August. http://www.bbc.co.uk/news/uk-14513517.
20 Aulén, G. (1970) *Christus Victor: An Historical Study of the Three Main Types of the Idea of the Atonement*. London: SPCK.
21 McGrath, A. E. (1997) *Christian Theology: An Introduction*, Second edn. Oxford: Blackwell Publishers, pp. 300–401; Weaver, J. D. (2001) *The Nonviolent Atonement*. Grand Rapids: Wm. B. Eerdmans Publishing Co, pp. 16–18.
22 Fiddes, P. S. (1989) *Past Event and Present Salvation: The Christian Idea of Atonement,* p. 97.
23 Ibid., p. 70.
24 Ibid., p. 98.
25 Ibid., p. 102.
26 See Gorringe, T. (1996) *God's Just Vengeance*. Cambridge: Cambridge University Press.
27 BBC *Newsnight*, 2011.
28 See BBC News (2020), 'David Starkey: Historian Apologises for "Clumsy" Slavery Comments', 6 July. https://www.bbc.co.uk/news/entertainment-arts-53308061.

29 Kerswill, P. (2014) 'The Objectification of "Jafaican": The Discoursal Embedding of Multicultural London English in the British Media'. In J. Androutsopoulos (ed.), *Mediatization and Sociolinguistic Change*. Berlin: De Gruyter, pp. 428–55.
30 The translators note in the introduction of the JNT that 'The translation of the Bible into Jamaican goes further than previous works in extending the functions and use of the language. This effort requires a more structured representation of the language in writing and a system that reflects the individuality of this language. To that end, the spelling used in Di Jamiekan Nyuu Testament is the Cassidy-JLU orthography. This writing system was developed by Frederic Cassidy, a Jamaican linguist in the 1960's and later modified by the Jamaican Language Unit at the University of the West Indies.'
31 Weaver, J. D. (2001) *The Nonviolent Atonement*, p. 78.
32 Cone, J. H. (1975) *God of the Oppressed*. USA: HarperSanFrancisco, p. 108ff.
33 Erskine, N. L. (2013). 'Di Jamiekan Nyuu Testament', *International Journal of Public Theology*, 7 (4), 389–97, p. 397.
34 See Devonish, H. (1986) *Language and Liberation: Creole Language Politics in the Caribbean*. Great Britain: Karia Press; Deuber, D. (2014) *English in the Caribbean: Variation, Style and Standards in Jamaica and Trinidad*. Cambridge: Cambridge University Press.
35 Slaves working in close proximity to the colonizers picked up words and concepts that were carried to slaves who, through the differentiation of labour, were more distant from English speakers.
36 Sakoda, K. and Siegel, J. (2003) *Pidgin Gramar: An Introduction to the Creole Language of Hawaii*. USA: Bess Press Incorporated.
37 For broader discussion see Alleyne, M. (1980) *Comparative Afro-American*. Ann Arbor: Karoma Publishers.
38 Devonish, H. (1986) *Language and Liberation*, p. 41.
39 Alleyne, M. (1980) *Comparative Afro-American*, p. 109.

Chapter 10

1 Gilroy, P. (2004) *After Empire*, p. 77.
2 See https://www.mcdonaldcentre.org.uk/ethics-and-empire.
3 Ward, G. (2017) 'Decolonizing Theology'. *Stellenbosch Theological Journal*, 3 (2), 561–84, p. 578.
4 Williams, R. (2012) *Faith in the Public Square*. London: Bloomsbury, pp. 151–4.
5 Welby, J. (2021) *Reimagining Britain: Foundations for Hope*. London: Bloomsbury, p. 5.
6 See Church Commissioner's Research into Historic Links to the TransAtlantic Chattel Slavery. https://www.churchofengland.org/sites/default/files/2022-06/Church%20Commissioners%20research%20report%20final.pdf.

7   Beckles, H. (1987) *Black Rebellion in Barbados: The Struggle against Slavery 1627-1838*. Bridgetown: Carib Research & Publications; Sherwood, H. (2021) 'Church of England Investigates Possible Slave Trade Origins of 9.2bn Fund'. *The Guardian*, 16 June.
8   These are Wilkinson, J. L. (1993) *Church in Black and White*; Leech, K. (1987) *Churches Fighting Racism in the '80s*. Cambridge: Great St. Mary's, the University Church.
9   See, for example, Bretherton, L. (2022) *Christ and the Common Life: Political Theology and the Case for Democracy*. Grand Rapids: William B. Eerdmans Publishing Company, pp. 82–119.
10 Cone, J. H. (1970) *A Black Theology of Liberation*. New York: Orbis Books, p. 115.
11 See Beckford, R. (2022) 'After the Flood: Christianity, Slavery and Reconciliation'.
12 See Leibniz, G. W. (2017) *Theodicy: Essays on the Goodness of God, the Freedom of Man, and the Origin of Evil*. Whithorn: Anodos Books.
13 Scott, M. S. M. (2015) *Pathways in Theodicy: An Introduction to the Problem of Evil*. Minneapolis: Fortress Press, p. xi.
14 For a comprehensive discussion see Hick, J. (2010) *Evil and the God of Love*. Basingstoke: Palgrave Macmillan.
15 Platinga, A. (1974) *God, Freedom and Evil*. New York: Harper & Row.
16 Hick, J. (2010) *Evil and the God of Love*, pp. 62–3.
17 Ibid.
18 Ibid., p. 256.
19 Davis, S. T. (2001) *Encountering Evil: Live Options in Theodicy*. Edinburgh: T&T Clark, p. 62.
20 Kilby, K. (2022) *God, Evil and the Limits of Theology*. London: Bloomsbury, T&T Clark, p. 24.
21 Ibid.
22 Swinton, J. (2018) *Raging with Compassion: Pastoral Responses to the Problem of Evil*. London: SCM Press, pp. 3–4.
23 Ibid.
24 Pinn, A. B. (1995) *Why Lord?: Suffering and Evil in Black Theology*. New York: Continuum, p. 13.
25 Ibid., p. 15.
26 Martin, C. J. (1993) 'Biblical Theodicy and Black Women's Spiritual Autobiography: "The Miry Bog, the Desolate Pit, a New Song in My Mouth"'. In E. M. Townes (ed.), *A Troubling in My Soul: Womanist Perspectives on Evil and Suffering*. Maryknoll: Orbis Books, pp. 13–36.
27 Williams, D. S. (2013) *Sisters in the Wilderness: The Challenge of Womanist God-Talk*. Maryknoll, New York: Orbis Books, p. 161ff.
28 Towns, E. M., ed. (2019) *A Troubling in My Soul: Womanist Perspectives on Evil and Suffering*. Maryknoll: Orbis Books, p. 84.

29 See Grant, J. (1989) *White Women's Christ and Black Women's Jesus: Feminist Christology and Womanist Response*. Atlanta: Scholars Press.
30 See Pinn, A. B. (2014) *Writing God's Obituary: How a Good Methodist Became a Better Atheist*. Amherst: Prometheus Books.
31 See Crawley, A. T. (2017) *Blackpentecostal Breath: The Aesthetics of Possibility*. New York: Fordham University Press, pp. 93–4.
32 See Bernal, M. (1992) *Black Athena*. Ithaca: Cornell Alumni Federation.
33 Goldenberg, D. M. (2003) *The Curse of Ham,* p. 170. While the ancient ethnographic aetiology may originally have referred to Ham and his error, later versions of the story were embellished to support the sociopolitical manoeuvrings in ancient Palestine: to legitimate the subjugation of the Canaanites by Shem's descendants (Israel) and those of Japheth (Philistines), Stony the Road.
34 Douglas, K. B. (2015) *Stand Your Ground: Black Bodies and the Justice of God*. New York: Orbis Books.
35 See Thomas, O. A. W. (2014) *Biblical Resistance Hermeneutics within a Caribbean Context*.
36 See Meister, C. and Dew, J. K., Jr (2017) *God and the Problem of Evil Five Views*. Westmont: InterVarsity Press, pp. 28–9.
37 See Jones, W. R. (1998) *Is God a White Racist?*.
38 Carter, J. K. (2018) Conference Paper, Society of the Study of Theology, Nottingham, April.

Chapter 11

1 Northcott, M. S. (1990) 'The Case Study Method in Theological Education'. *Contact*, 103 (1), 26–32. These case studies use two data collection methods: the first is informal conversations and the other field notes.
2 Yin, R. K. (2009) *Case Study Research, Design and Method*. London: Sage Publications Ltd, p. 4.
3 Ibid.
4 See Francis, R. N. (2019) *How to Make Contemporary Gospel Music Work for You*.
5 Williams, J. (2021) *Is Climate Change Racist?* p. 166 Kindle Edition.
6 Ibid.
7 Henry, W. and Worley, M. (2021), *Narratives from Beyond the UK Reggae Bassline: The System Is Sound*. p. 289ff.
8 Ibid.
9 See Dyson, M. E. (2005) *Mercy, Mercy Me: The Art Loves and Demons of Marvin Gaye*. New York: Basic Civitas Books; Neal, M. A. (1999) *What the Music Said: Black Popular Music and Black Public Culture*. London: Routledge, p. 55ff.

10 Beckford, R. (2021) 'Introduction to the Kingdom Choir.' Glasgow Cathedral's Christian Aid Event for Cop26, November.

Conclusion

1 Davis, M. (2015) 'The Politics of Resurrection Hermeneutics – Luke 24:36-48'. *Political Theology Network Online.* https://politicaltheology.com/the-politics-of-resurrection-hermeneutics-luke-2436-48/.

Bibliography

Abbington, James (2014) *Readings in African American Church Music and Worship.* Chicago: GIA Publications, Inc.

Ade, I. E. (1958) *What Constitutes Worldliness? The Lust of the Flesh, the Lust of the Eyes, the Lust of Life.* Bedford: The Full Gospel Press.

Adi, Hakim (2018) *Pan-Africanism: A History.* London: Bloomsbury.

Akala (2019) *Natives: Race and Class in the Ruins of Empire.* London: Two Roads.

Alexander, M. Jacqui (2005) *Pedagogies of Crossing: Meditations on Feminism, Sexual Politics, Memory, and the Sacred.* Durham: Duke University Press.

Allen-McLaurin, Lisa (2021) *A Womanist Theology of Worship: Liturgy, Justice, and Communal Righteousness.* New York: Orbis Books.

Alleyne, Mervyn (1980) *Comparative Afro-American.* Ann Arbor: Karoma Publishers.

Althusser, Louis (2014) *On the Reproduction of Capitalism: Ideology and Ideological State Apparatuses.* London: Verso.

Anderson, Victor (2018) *Beyond Ontological Blackness: An Essay in African American Religious and Cultural Criticism.* London: Bloomsbury Publishing.

Androutsopoulos, Jannis, ed. (2014) *Mediatization and Sociolinguistic Change.* Berlin: De Gruyter, pp. 428–55.

Aulén, Gustaf (1970) *Christus Victor: An Historical Study of the Three Main Types of the Idea of the Atonement.* London: SPCK.

Austin-Broos, Diane J. (1997) *Jamaica Genesis: Religion and the Moral Orders.* Chicago: University of Chicago Press.

Babatunde, Adedibu (2012) *Coat of Many Colours: The Origin, Growth, Distinctiveness and Contributions of Black Majority Churches to British Christianity.* Blackpool: Wisdom Summit.

Back, Les (2017) *New Ethnicities and Urban Culture Social Identity and Racism in the Lives of Young People.* London: Routledge.

Back, Les and John Solomos (2007) *Theories of Race and Racism: A Reader.* London: Routledge.

Barnard, Philip and Shapiro Stephen (2017) *Pentecostal Modernism: Lovecraft Los Angeles and World-Systems Culture.* Bloomsbury Publishing.

Beckford, Robert (1998) *Jesus is Dread: Black Theology and Black Culture in Britain.* London: Darton, Longman and Todd.

Beckford, Robert (2000) *Dread and Pentecostal: A Political Theology for the Black Church in Britain.* London: SPCK.

Beckford, Robert (2004) *God and the Gangs: An Urban Toolkit for Those Who Won't Be Bought Out, Sold Out or Scared Out.* London: DLT.

Beckford, Robert (2006) *Jesus Dub: Faith, Culture and Social Change*. London: Routledge.
Beckford, Robert (2014) *Documentary As Exorcism: Resisting the Bewitchment of Colonial Christianity*. London: Bloomsbury.
Beckford, Robert (2021) *My Theology: Duppy Conqueror*. London: DLT.
Beckles, Hillary (1987) *Black Rebellion in Barbados*. Barbados Carib Research & Pub.
Bernal, Martin (1992) *Black Athena*. Ithaca: Cornell Alumni Federation.
Bevans, S. (2002) Models of *Contextual Theology: Faith and Cultures* (Revised and Expanded Edition). New York: Orbis Books.
Bidnall, Amanda (2017) *The West Indian Generation: Remaking British Culture in London, 1945–1965*. Liverpool: Liverpool University Press.
Bonhoeffer, Dietrich (2015). *The Cost of Discipleship*. London: SCM Press.
Bourne, S. (2012) *The Motherland Calls: Britain's Black Servicemen and Women, 1939–45*. Stroud: History Press.
Bourne, Richard and Imogen Adkins (2021) *A New Introduction to Theology: Embodiment, Expeirence and Encounter*. London: t&tclark.
Bretherton, Luke (2022) *Christ and the Common Life: Political Theology and the Case for Democracy*. Grand Rapids: William B. Eerdmans.
Briggs, Daniel (2012) *The English Riots of 2011: A Summer of Discontent*. London: Waterside Press.
Broughton, Gospel (1996) *Too Close to Heaven: The Illustrated History of Goospel Music*. London: Midnight Books.
Brown, Michael J. (2004) *Blackening of the Bible: The Aims of African American Biblical Scholarship*. Harrisburg: Trinity Press International.
Burnett, Jon (2012) 'After Lawrence: Racial Violence and Policing in the UK'. *Race & Class* 54(1): 91–8.
Butler, Melvin L. (2019) *Island Gospel: Pentecostal Music and Identity in Jamaica and the United States*. Urbana: University of Illinois Press.
Callahan, Dwight A. (1997) *Embassy of Onesimus: The letter of Paul to Philemon*. MarshaValley Forge: Trinity Press International.
Carter, J. K. (2014) "Humanity in African American Theology." In Katie G. Cannon and Anthony B. Pinn, *The Oxford Handbook of African American Theology*. Oxford: Oxford University Press.
Cathcart, Brian (2000) *The Case of Stephen Lawrence*. London: Penguin.
Channer, Yvonne (1995) *I am a Promise: Achievement of British African-Caribbeans*. Stoke-on-Trent, Staffordshire: Trentham Books.
Charles, Monique (2016) *Hallowed Be Thy Grime? A Musicological and Sociological Genealogy of Grime Music and Its Relation to Black Atlantic Religious Discourse*. Dissertation, Coventry: University of Warwick.
Chitando, A., J. Chikowero and A. M. Madongonda, eds (2015) *The Art of Survival: Depictions of Zimbabwe and the Zimbabwean in Crisis*. Newcastle: Cambridge Scholars Press.

Clark, Jawanza E. (2012) *Indigenous Black Theology: Toward an African-Centered Theology of the African American Religious Experience*. London: Palgrave Macmillan.
Clarke, Harold D., et al. (2016) *Austerity and Political Choice in Britain*. London: Palgrave Macmillan UK.
Clarke, Peterwat B. (1997) *Black Paradise: The Rastafarian Movement*. San Bernardino: R. Reginald.
Coard, Bernard (1971) *How the West Indian Child Is Made Educationally Sub-Normal in the British School System*. London: New Beacon Books.
Coleman, Monica A. (2008) *Making a Way Out of No Way: A Womanist Theology*. Minneapolis: Fortress Press.
Cone, James H. (1970) *A Black Theology of Liberation*. New York: Orbis Books.
Cone, James H. (1972) *The Spirituals and the Blues: An Interpretation*. New York: Orbis Books.
Cone, James H. (1975) *God of the Oppressed*. USA: HarperSanFrancisco.
Cooper, C. (1995) *Noises in the Blood: Orality, Gender, and the 'vulgar' Body of Jamaican Popular Culture*. Durham: Duke University Press.
Cooper, Vickie and David Whyte (2017) *The Violence of Austerity*. London: Pluto Press.
Crawley, Ashton T. (2017) *Blackpentecostal Breath: The Aesthetics of Possibility*. New York: Fordham University Press.
Dadzie, Stella (2021) *A Kick in the Belly: Women Slavery and Resistance*. Brooklyn: Verso.
Daly, Mary (1985) *Beyond God the Father: Toward a Philosophy of Women's Liberation* Boston: Beacon Press.
Darden, Robert D. (2015) *People Get Ready! A New History of Black Contemporary Gospel Music*. New York and London: Continuum.
Day, Keri (2021) *Notes from a Native Daughter: Testifying in Theological Education*. Grand Rapids: William B. Eerdmans Publishing Company.
Dayfoot, Arthur C. (1999) *The Shaping of the West Indian Church, 1492–1692*. Barbados: University of the West Indies Press.
De Sousa Santos, Boaventura (2014) *Epistemologies of the South: Justice against Epistemicide*. London: Routledge.
De Sousa Santos, Boaventura (2018) *The End of the Cognitive Empire: The Coming of Age of Epistemologies of the South*. Durham: Duke University Press.
Dent, Gina, ed. (1992) *Black Popular Culture*. USA: Bay Press.
Deuber, Dagmar (2014) *English in the Caribbean: Variation, Style and Standards in Jamaica and Trinidad*. Cambridge: Cambridge University Press.
Devonish, Hubert (1986) *Language and Liberation: Creole Language Politics in the Caribbean*. Great Britain: Karia Press.
Di Jamiekan Nyuu Testiment (2012) Kingston, Jamaica: Bible Society of the West Indies.
Dinerstein, J. (2017) *The Origins of Cool in Postwar America*. Chicago: University of Chicago Press.

Douglas, Kelly B. (2015) *Stand Your Ground: Black Bodies and the Justice of God.* Maryknoll, New York: Orbis Books.

Drane, John W. (2000) *The Mcdonaldization of the Church: Spirituality, Creativity, and the Future of the Church.* London: Darton Longman & Todd.

Drew Smith, R., W. Ackah and A. Reddie, eds (2014) *Churches, Blackness, and Contested Multiculturalism: Europe, Africa and North America.* New York: Palgrave Macmillan.

Durkheim, Émile and Joseph W. Swain (2015) *The Elementary Forms of the Religious Life.* Oxford: Benediction Classics.

Dyson, Michael E. (2004) *Mercy Mercy Me: The Art and Love of Marvin Gaye.* New York: Basic Civitas Books.

Edmonds, E. B. and M. A. Gonzalez (2010) *Caribbean Religious History: An Introduction.* New York: New York University Press.

Elliott-Cooper, Adam (2018) *Black Resistance to British Policing.* Manchester: Manchester University Press.

Epstein, Heidi (2005) *Melting the Venusberg: A Feminist Theology of Music.* New York: Continuum.

Erskine, Noe L. (1998) *Decolonizing Theology: A Caribbean Perspective.* Trenton: Africa World Press.

Evans, Mark (2015) 'Hillsong Abroad: Tracing the Songlines of Contemporary Pentecostal Music', in Monique M. Ingalls and Amos Yong, *The Spirit of Praise: Music and Worship in Global Pentecostal-Charismatic Christianity.* Penn State: The Penn State University Press.

Fanon, Frantz (1986) *Black Skin, White Mask.* London: Pluto Press.

Faryna, Stan, Brad Stetson and Joseph G. Conti (1997) *Black and Right: The Bold New Voice of Black Conservatives in America.* Westport: Praeger, 1997.

Fiddis, Paul S. (1989), *Past Event and Present Salvation: The Christian Idea of Atonement.* London: DLT.

Fishbane, Michael (2008) *Sacred Attunement: A Jewish Theology.* Chicago: University of Chicago Press.

Foster, Elaine (1992) 'The Inverted Pyramid', in Gita Saghal and Nira Yuval-Davis, *Refusing Holy Orders: Women and Fundamentalism in Britain.* London: Virago.

Foucault, Michel (2019) *Aesthetics, Method, and Epistemology.* London: Penguin.

Francis, Roy N. (2019) *How to Make Contemporary Gospel Music Work for You: A Guide for Contemporary Gospel Music Makers and Marketers.* Croydon: Filament Publishing.

Fryer, Peter (2018). *Staying Power, the History of Black People in Britain.* London: Pluto Press.

Fryer, Peter (2021) *Black People in the British Empire.* London: Pluto Press.

Fulani, Ifeona, ed. (2012) *Archipelagos of Sound: Transnational Caribbeanities, Women and Music.* Kingston: University of the West Indies Press.

Gadamer, Hans-Georg and P. Christopher Smith (1980) *Dialogue and Dialectic: Eight Hermeneutical Studies on Plato.* New Haven: Yale University Press.

Gerbner, Katherine (2018) *Christian Slavery: Conversion and Race in the Protestant Atlantic World*. Pennsylvania: University of Pennsylvania Press.

Gerloff, Roswith (2008) *The African Diaspora in the Caribbean and Europe from Pre-emancipation to the Present Day*. Cambridge: Cambridge University Press.

Gerloff, Roswith H. (1992) *A Plea for British Black Theologies: The Black Church Movement in Britain in Its Transatlantic Cultural and Theological Interaction with Special Reference to the Pentecostal Oneness (Apostolic) and Sabbatarian Movements 1. 1*. Frankfurt: Peter Lang.

Gilroy, Paul (1987) *There Ain't No Black in the Union Jack*. London: Routledge.

Gilroy, Paul (1993) *Black Atlantic: Modernity and Double Consciousness*. London: Verso.

Gilroy, Paul (2004) *After Empire: Melancholia or Convivial Culture?* London: Routledge.

Glass, Ruth (1961) *London's Newcomers: The West Indian Migrants*. Cambridge, MA: Harvard University Press.

Gluckman, Max (2014) *Order and Rebellion in Tribal Africa*. London: Routledge.

Goffman, Erving (1986) *Frame Analysis: An Essay on the Organization of Experience*. Boston: Northeastern University Press.

Goldenberg, David M. (2003) *The Curse of Ham*. Princeton, Oxford: Princeton University Press.

Goldson, Randy R. (2005) 'Liberating the Mind: Rastafari and the Theorization of Maroonage as Epistemological (Dis) Engagement'. *Journal of Black Studies* 51(4): 368–85.

Gordon, Lewis R. (1995) *Bad Faith and AntiBlack Racism*. Atlantic Highlands: Humanities Press.

Gorringe, Timothy (1996) *God's Just Vengeance*. Cambridge: Cambridge University Press.

Graham, Elaine, Heather Walton and Frances Ward (2018) *Theological Reflection Methods*. London: SCM Press.

Grant, Jacquelyn (1989) *White women's Christ and Black Women's Jesus: Feminist Christology and Womanist Response*. Atlanta: Scholars Press.

Green, Laurie (2001) *Let's Do Theology: A Pastoral Cycle Resource Book*. London: Continuum.

Gundry, Stanley N. (1999) *Love Them In: The Life and Theology of D.L. Moody*. USA: Moody Publishers.

Gushee, David and Glen S. Stassen (2018) *Kingdom Ethics: Following Jesus in Contemporary Contexts*, 2nd edn. Grand Rapids: Wm. B. Eerdmans Publishing Company.

Hall, Delroy. (2021) *Redemption Song: Black British Pastoral Theology and Culture*. London: SCM Press.

Hall, Stuart and Tony Jefferson (1983) *Resistance Through Rituals: Youth Subculture in Post-War Britain*, 2nd edn. London: Routledge.

Hall, Stuart, Chas Critcher, Tony Jefferson, John Clarke and Brian Roberts (2013) *Policing the Crisis: Mugging the State and Law and Order*, Second edn. Houndmills, Basingstoke and Hampshire: Palgrave Macmillan Harmondsworth: Penguin.

Harold, Claudrena N. (2020) *When Sunday Comes: Gospel Music in the Soul and Hip-Hop Eras*, 165. Urbana: University of Illinois Press.

Harris, Clive and Winston James (1993) *Inside Babylon: The Caribbean Diaspora in Britain*. London: Verso Books.

Hauerwas, Stanley and L. Gregory Jones, eds (1997) *Why Narrative? Readings on Narrative Theology*. Eugene: Wipf and Stock Publishers.

Hebdige, Dick (1987) *Cut 'n' Mix: Culture, Identity and Caribbean Music*. London: Comedia.

Hellholm, David (2010) *Ablution, Initiation, and Baptism: Late Antiquity, Early Judaism, and Early Christianity*. Berlin: De Gruyter.

Hendricks, Obery M. (2006) *The Politics of Jesus: Rediscovering the True Revolutionary Nature of the Teachings of Jesus and How They Have Been Corrupted*. New York: Doubleday.

Hendricks, Obery M. (2011) *The Universe Bends Toward Justice: Radical Reflections on the Bible, The Church, and the Body Politic*. Maryknoll: Orbis Books.

Henry, William and Matthew Worley (2020) *Narratives from beyond the UK Reggae Bassline: The System is Sound*. Basingstoke: Palgrave Macmillan.

Hick, John (2010) *Evil and the God of Love*. Basingstoke: Palgrave Macmillan.

Hill, Clifford (2020) *Beyond the Pandemic: Is there Any Word from the Lord?* UK: Wilberforce Publications.

Hill Collins, Patricia (1990) *Black Feminist Thought: Knowledge, Consciousness and the Politics of Empowerment*. New York: Routledge.

Hiro, Dilip (1971) *Black British, White British*. London: Paladin.

Hodges, Hugh (2008) *Soon Come: Jamaican Spirituality, Jamaican Poetics*, 65. Charlottesville: University of Virginia Press.

hooks, b. (2015) *Black Looks: Race and Representation*, Second edn. New York: Routledge.

Howard, Charles (2014) *Black Theology as Mass Movement*. London: Palgrave Macmillan.

Hutton, J. E. (1922) *A History of Moravian Missions*. London: Moravian Publications Office.

James, C. L. R. (2019) *Beyond a Boundary* London: Vintage Books.

Jennings, Willie (2017) *Acts: A Theological Commentary on the Bible*. Knoxville: Westminster John Knox Press.

John, Gus (2004) *The Crisis Facing Black Children in the British Schooling System: A Call to Independent Action by Black Students and Black Parents*. Rawtenstall: The Gus John Partnership Ltd.

Jones, J. I. (1993) 'Art. Narrative Theology', in Alister E. McGrath (ed.), *The Blackwell Encyclopaedia of Modern Christian Thought*. Oxford: Blackwell, pp. 395–8.

Jones, William R. (1999) *Is God a White Racist? A Preamble to Black Theology*. Boston: Beacon Press.

Jordan, W. D. (1968) *White Over Black: American Attitudes Toward the Negro, 1550–1812*. Chapel Hill: University of North Carolina Press.

Keating, AnaLouise, ed. (2005) *Entre Mundos/Among Worlds: New Perspectives on Gloria Anzaldúa*. New York: Palgrave Macmillan.

Kidd, Colin (2006) *The Forging of Races: Race and Scripture in the Protestant Atlantic World, 1600–2000*. Cambridge: Cambridge University Press.

Kilby, Karen (2022) *God, Evil and the Limits of Theology*. London: Bloomsbury, T&T Clark.

Kirk-Duggan, Cheryl A. (1997) *Exorcising Evil: A Womanist Perspective on the Spirituals*. New York: Orbis Books.

Kroeker, C. Y. (2002) 'Music Pedagogy and the Christian Faith: A Twenty-Year Journey of Discovery', in Arlin C. Migliazzo (ed.), *Teaching as an Act of Faith: Theory and Practice in Church-Related Higher Education*. New York: Fordham University Press.

Kwiyani, Harvey C. (2017) *Blessed Reflex: African Christians in Europe*. University of Groningen Press.

Kwiyani, Harvey C. (2020) *Multicultural Kingdom: Ethnic Diversity, Mission and the Church*. London: SCM Press.

Lakoff, George (2014) *The All New Don't Think of An Elephant! Know Your Values and Frame the Debate*. White River Junction: Chelsea Green Publishing.

Lambeth Council (1998) *Forty Winters On*. London: South London Press.

Lampe, Armando. (2001) *Christianity in the Caribbean: Essays on Church History*. West Indies: University of the West Indies Press.

Lartey, Emmanuel Y. (1997) *In Living Colour: An Intercultural Approach to Pastoral Care and Counselling*. London: Cassell.

Lass, R. and J. Westergaard (1965) *London's Housing Needs: Statement of Evidence to the Committee on Housing in Greater London*. London: Centre for Urban Studies, University College.

Law, Ian (2002) *Race in the News*. Basingstoke: Palgrave.

Leech, Kenneth (1987) *Churches Fighting Racism in the '80s*. Cambridge: Great St. Mary's, the University Church.

Leibniz Gottfried, W. (2017). *Theodicy: Essays on the Goodness of God, the Freedom of Man, and the Origin of Evil*. Whithorn: Anodos Books.

Lincoln, C. Eric and Lawrence H. Mamiya (1990) *The Black Church in the African American Experience*. Durham: Duke University Press.

Lindsay, Ben (2019) *We Need to Talk About Race: Understanding the Black Experience in White Majority Churches*. London: SPCK.

Long Westfall, Cynthia and Bryan R. Dyer (2016) *The Bible and Social Justice: Old Testament and New Testament Foundations for the Church's Urgent Call*. Eugene: Pickwick Publications.

Mahler, Anne G. (2018) *From the Tricontinental to the Global South: Race, Radicalism, and Transnational Solidarity*. Durham: Duke University Press.

Marshall, Catherine and Gretchen B. Rossman (1989) *Designing Qualitative Research*. Newbury Park: Sage.

Marti, Geraldo. (2012) *Worship Across the Racial Divide: Religious Music and the Multiracial Congregation*. New York, New York: Oxford University Press.

Mazuri, Ali (1975) *The Political Sociology of the English Language*. The Hague/Paris: Mouton.

Mbiti, John S. (1975) *Introduction to African Religion*. New York: Praeger.

McClure, John S. (2011) *Mashup Religion: Pop Music and Theological Invention*. Waco: Baylor University Press.

McDonald, Chine (2021) *God Is Not a White Man and Other Revelations*. London: Hodder & Stoughton.

McGrath, Alister E. (1997) *Christian Theology: An Introduction*, Second edn., 300–401 Oxford: Blackwell Publishers.

McKenzie, Dulcie A. D. (2014) *The Future of the Past: Forging a Historical Context for Black Contemporary Gospel Music as a Tradition amongst African Caribbean Pentecostals in Post-War Britain*. PhD Thesis, University of Birmingham.

McLean-Farrell Janice. A. (2016) *West Indian Pentecostals: Living Their Faith in New York and London*. London: Bloomsbury Academic.

Medina, José (2013) *The Epistemology of Resistance: Gender and Racial Oppression, Epistemic Injustice and Resistant Imaginations*. New York: Oxford University Press.

Meister, Chad and James K. Dew Jr, eds (2017) *God and the Problem of Evil: Five Vies*. Westmont: IVP Academic.

Metz, Johann B. (1986) *The Emergent Church*. New York: Crossroad.

Mignolo, Walter D. (2000) *Local Histories / Global Designs: Coloniality, Subaltern Knowledges, and Border Thinking*. Princeton: Princeton University Press.

Mignolo, Walter D. and Catherine E. Walsh (2018) *On Decoloniality: Concepts, Analytics, Praxis*. Durham: Duke University Press.

Mignolo, Walter D. and Madina Tlostanova (2006) 'Theorizing from the Borders Shifting to Geo and Body-Politics of Knowledge'. *European Journal of Social Theory* 9: 205–21, 208.

Murrell, Nathaniel S., Adrian Anthony McFarlane and William Spencer, eds (1998) *Chanting Down Babylon: The Rastafari Reader*. Philadelphia: Temple University Press.

Murrell, Nathaniel S. and W. Spencer (1998) 'The Black Biblical Hermeneutics of Rastafari', in Nathaniel Murrell, S. McFarlane, A. Adria and William Spencer (eds), *Chanting down Babylon: The Rastafari Reader*, 326–49. Philadelphia: Temple University Press.

Murrell, S. (2000) 'Dangerous Memories: Underdevelopment, and the Bible', in Gemchand Gossai and Nathaniel S. Murrell, *Religion, Culture and Tradition in the Caribbean*. Basingstoke: Macmillan.

Neal, Mark A. (1999) *What the Music Said: Black Popular Music and Black Public Culture*. London and New York: Routledge Press.

Niebuhr, H. Richard (2006) *The Meaning of Revelation*. Louisville: Westminster John Knox Press.

Olofinjana, Israel O. (2010) *Reverse in Ministry and Missions: Africans in the Dark Continent of Europe: An Historical Study of African Churches in Europe*. Milton Keynes: AuthorHouse.

Olofinjana, Israel O. (2020) *World Christianity in Western Europe: Diasporic Identity, Narratives and Missiology*. Oxford: Regnum Books.

Ostwalt, Conrad (2012) *Secular Steeples: Popular Culture and the Religious Imagination*. London: Bloomsbury.

Otto, Rudolf (1959) *The Idea of the Holy: An Inquiry into the Non-Rational Factor in the Idea of the Divine and Its Relation to the Rational: Translated [from the German] by John W. Harvey*. Harmondsworth: Penguin Books.

Panayi, Panikos (2014) *An Immigration History of Britain: Multicultural Racism Since 1800*. London: Routledge.

Patten, Harold (2019) *The Spirituality of Reggae Dancehall Dance Vocabulary: A Spiritual, Corporeal Practice in Jamaican Dance*. Thesis (Ph.D.), Canterbury Christ Church University.

Paul, Kathleen (1997) *Whitewashing Britain: Race and Citizenship in the Postwar Era*. New York: Cornell University Press.

Perkinson, James W. (2004) *White Theology: Outing Supremacy in Modernity*. New York: Palgrave Macmillan.

Perry, Kennetta Hammond (2016) *London Is the Place for Me: Black Britons, Citizenship and the Politics of Race* (Transgressing Boundaries: Studies in black Politics and Communities). Oxford: Oxford University Press.

Phillipson, Robert (1992) *Linguistic Imperialism*. Oxford: Oxford University Press.

Pinn, Anthony B. (1999) *Why, Lord? Suffering and Evil in Black Theology*. New York: Continuum.

Pinn, Anthony B. (2014) *Writing God's Obituary: How a Good Methodist became a Better Atheist*. Amherst: Prometheus Books.

Portier-Young, Anathea and Gregory E. Sterling, eds (2018) *Scripture and Social Justice: Catholic and Ecumenical Essays*. Lanham: Lexington Books/Fortress Academic.

Preston, John (2019) *Grenfell Tower: Preparedness, Race and Disaster Capitalism*. London: Palgrave.

Public Health England (2020) *Disparities in the Risk and Outcomes of Covid-19*. London: PHE Publications.

Quebedeaux, Richard (1976) *The New Charismatics: The Origins, Development, and Significance of Neo-Pentecostalism*. Garden City: Doubleday.

Rachel, Daniel (2017) *Walls Come Tumbling Down: The Music and Politics of Rock Against Racism, 2 Tone and Red Wedge, 1976–1992*. London: Picador.

Ramdin, Ron (2017) *The Making of the Black Working Class in Britain* (updated version). London: Verso.
Reardon, Timothy W. (2021) *Politics of Salvation: Lukan Soteriology, Atonement, and the Victory of Christ*. London: T&T Clark, Bloomsbury Publishing Plc.
Reddie, Anthony G. (2006) *Dramatizing Theologies: A Participative Approach to Black God-Talk*. London: Routledge.
Reed, Teresa L. (2004) *The Holy Profane: Religion in Black Popular Music*. Lexington: The University Press of Kentucky.
Richardson, Brian, ed. (2005) *Tell It Like It Is: How Our Schools Fail Black Children*. London: Bookmarks Publications.
Riggins, Earl R. (2012) 'Black Theology and Human Purpose', in D. Hopkins and E. Antonio (eds), *The Cambridge Companion to Black Theology*, 132–3. Cambridge: Cambridge University Press.
Ritze, George (1995) *The McDonaldization of Society: An Investigation into the Changing Character of Contemporary Social Life*, second edn. Thousand Oaks: Pine Forge Press.
Roberts, Dan (2011) *Reading the Riots: Investigating England's Summer of Disorder*. London: Guardian Books.
Rodreguez, King-Dorset (2008) *Black Dance in London, 1730–1850: Innovation, Tradition and Resistance*. Jefferson: McFarland & Co.
Rollock, Nicola et al. (2014) *The Colour of Class: The Educational Strategies of the Black Middle Classes*. London: Routledge.
Rose, Tricia (1994) *Black Noise: Rap Music and Black Culture in Contemporary America*. Hanover and London: Wesleyan University Press.
Russel, Jesse and Ronald Cohn (2015) *Multicultural London English*. Lavergne: CPSIA.
Sakoda, Kent and Jeff Siegel (2003) *Pidgin Gramar: An Introduction to the Creole Language of Hawaii*. USA: Bess Press Incorporated.
Sanders, John (2016) *Theology in the Flesh: How Embodiment and Culture Shape the Way We Think About Truth, Morality, and God*. Minneapolis: Fortress Press.
Scott, Mark S. M. (2015) *Pathways in Theodicy: An Introduction to the Problem of Evil*. Minneapolis: Fortress Press.
Simpson, George E. (1978) *Black Religions in the New World*. New York: Columbia University Press.
Small, Stephen (2014) *Racialised Barriers: The Black Experience in the United States and England in the 1980's*. Routledge.
Smith, J. Mitzi, Angela N. Parker and Ericka S. Dunbar Hill (2022) *Bitter The Chastening Rod: Africana Biblical Interpretation After Stony the Road We Trod in the Age of BLM, SAYHERNAME and METOO*. Lanham: Lexington Books/Fortress Academic.
Smith, Mitzi J. (2018) *Womanist Sass and Talk Back: Social (in)Justice, Intersectionality, and Biblical Interpretation*. USA: Wipf and Stock Publishers.
Smith Pollard, Deborah (2008) *When The Church Becomes Your Party*. Detroit: Wayne State University Press.

Soji-George, James (2004) *The Contemporary Issues in the Nigerian Church: Healing, Signs & Wonders, Deliverance, Anointing Oil, Miracles, Prosperity*. Lagos: Fislol Nig.
Sölle, Dorothee (2007) *Creative Disobedience*. Eugene: Wipf & Stock Publishers.
Spencer, John M. (1990) *Protest & Praise: Sacred Music of Black Religion*. Minneapolis: Fortress Press.
Stewart, Dianne M. (2005) *Three Eyes for the Journey*. New York: Oxford University Press.
Stratton, Jon (2014) *Black Popular Music in Britain Since 1945*, 27ff. Farnham: Ashgate.
Stratton, Jon (2019) *When Music Migrates: Crossing British and European Racial Faultlines, 1945–2010*. London: Routledge.
Sturken, Marita and Lisa Cartwright (2009) *Practices of Looking: An Introduction to Visual Culture*, 2nd edn. New York: Oxford University Press.
Sugirtharajah, R. S. (1999) *Vernacular Hermeneutics*. Sheffield: Sheffield Academic Press.
Swinton, John (2018) Raging with Compassion: *Pastoral Responses to the Problem of Evil*. London: SCM Press.
Thomas, Oral A. (2014) *Biblical Resistance Hermeneutics within a Caribbean Context*. London: Routledge.
Thomas, Todne (2021) *Kincraft: The Making of Black Evangelical Sociality*. Durham and London Duke University Press.
Tomlin, Carol. (2019) *Preach It: Understanding African-Caribbean Preaching*. London: SCM Press.
Townes, Emilie M., ed. (1997) *A Troubling in My Soul: Womanist Perspectives on Evil and Suffering*. Maryknoll: Orbis Books.
Tracy, Carl. (2019) *Christian Sound Systems in Britain: Its Origins, Functions and Theology*. MA Thesis, Canterbury Christ Church University.
Turman, Ebony M. (2013) *Toward a Womanist Ethic of Incarnation: Black Bodies, the Black Church, and the Council of Chalcedon*. New York: Palgrave Macmillan.
Turner, Carlton. (2020) *Overcoming Self-negation: The Church and Jankanoo in Contemporary Bahamian Society*. UK: Pickwick.
Turner, Victor (1996) *The Ritual Process: Structure and Anti-Structure*. Aldine Transaction.
Vaughan, Alden T. (1995) *Roots of American Racism: Essays on the Colonial Experience*. Oxford: Oxford University Press.
Villafañe, Eldin (1993) *The Liberating Spirit: Toward a Hispanic American Pentecostal Social Ethic*. Grand Rapids: W.B. Eerdmans.
Waters, Anita M. (2017) *Race Class and Political Symbols: Rastafari and Reggae in Jamaican Politics*. London: Routledge.
Weaver, J. Denny (2001) *The Nonviolent Atonement*. Grand Rapids: Wm. B. Eerdmans Publishing Co.
Weber, Max (2014) *The Protestant Ethic and the Spirit of Capitalism*. New edn. Kettering: Angelico Press.

Welby, Justin (2021) *Reimagining Britain: Foundations for Hope*. London: Bloomsbury.
West, Cornel I. (1988) *Prophetic Fragments: Illuminations of The Crisis in American Religion and Culture*. Trenton: Africa World Press.
Whitford, David M. (2009) *The Curse of Ham in the Early Modern Era: The Bible and the Justifications for Slavery*. London: Routledge.
Whitla, Becca (2020) *Liberation, (De)Coloniality, and Liturgical Practices: Flipping the Song Bird*. London: Palgrave Macmilllan.
Wilkinson, John L. (1993) *Church in Black and White: The Black Christian Tradition in 'Mainstream' Churches in England: A White Response and Testimony*. Edinburgh, Scotland: Saint Andrew Press.
Williams, Jeremy (2021) *Climate Change Is Racist: Race Privilege and the Struggle for Climate Justice*. London: Icon Books.
Williams, Rowan (2012) *Faith in the Public Square*. London: Bloomsbury.
Wilmore, Gayraud S. (2007) 'Black Theology at the Turn of the Century', in D. N. Hopkins, *Black Faith and Public Talk: Critical Essays on James H. Cone's Black Theology and Black Power*. USA: Baylor University Press.
Woods, Rrobert and Brian Walrath, eds (2007) *The Message in the Music: Studying Contemporary Praise and Worship*. Nashville: Abingdon.
Woolverton, John F. (1984) *Colonial Anglicanism in North America*. Detroit: Wayne State University Press.
Yong, Amos (2010) *In the Days of Caesar: Pentecostalism and Political Theology*. Grand Rapids: W.B. Eerdmans Pub. Co.

Dissertations

Alexander, Valentina (1998) *Breaking Every Fetter'? To What Extent Has the Black Led Church in Britain Developed a Theology of Liberation?* PhD Dissertation, University of Warwick.
McKenzie, Dulcie A. (2014) *The Future of the Past: Forging a Historical Context for Black Gospel Music as a Tradition Amongst African Caribbean Pentecostals in Post-War Britain*. Dissertation, University of Birmingham.
Meunier, Jean-Baptiste (2012) *Trans-Atlantic Circulation of Black Tropes: Èsù and the West African Griot as Poetic References for Liberation in Cultures of the African Diaspora*. LSU Doctoral Dissertations.
Muir, P. E. (2018) *Sounds Mega: Musical Discourse in Black Majority Churches in London*. PhD Dissertation. London: Birkbeck, University of London.
Rhamie, Gifford (2019) *Whiteness, Conviviality and Agency: The Ethiopian Eunuch and Conceptuality in the Imperial Imagination of Biblical Studies*. Unpublished PhD Dissertation. UK: Canterbury Christ Church University.

Television and radio programmes

BBC (2020) *Subnormal*, BBC Documentary, TV. Lammas Park Productions.
Beckford, Robert (2016) *The Battle for Christianity*, TV Programme, BBC1, 8 April.
Beckford, Robert (2018) *Jamaican Bible Remixed*, [Radio Broadcast] BBC World Service.

Music production

Beckford, Robert (2017) *Jamaican Bible Remix*.
Clarke, Johnny (1976) 'Rockers Time Now', LP. London: Virgin Records.
Crouch, A. (1976) 'Soon and Very Soon', LP, Crouch Music Corp. Bud John Songs, Inc.
Manuva, Roots (1999) 'Brand New Second Hand', CD. London: Big Dada Records.
Niles, Joseph and the Consolers (1973) 'Gospel Ship' [LP] Redemption.
Rice, C. M. 'Great Is Thy Faithfulness' lyrics © Clumsy Fly Music, Hope Publishing Company, So Essential Tunes, Hill and Range Songs, inc.
Size, Roni (1997) 'New Forms', CD. London: Talking Loud.
Steel Pulse (1978) 'Klu Klux Klan', Handsworth Revolution, LP, UK: Island Records.
The Kingdom Choir (2018) 'Stand By Me', CD. UK: Sony Music.

Film production articles

BBC (2001) 'Black Messiah', TV Documentary. BBC 4.
Beckford, Robert (2022) 'After the Flood: Christianity, Slavery and Reconciliation', Film, Movement for Justice and Reconciliation.

Articles

Babarinde, Damiola M. (2019) 'Emergent Issues in the Hybridisation of Christian Gospel Music in South-West Nigeria'. *Cajolis-Calabar Journal of Liberal Studies* 21(1): 81–8.
Beaumont-Thomas, B. (2018) '"Stormzy aks" Theresa may, where's the Money for Grenfell? at Brit awards'. *The Guardian*, 21 February.
Beckles-Raymond, Gabriella (2020) 'African-Caribbean Women, (post)Diaspora, and the Meaning of Home'. *African and Black Diaspora: An International Journal* 13(2): 202–14.

Berger, Peter L. (1974) 'Some Second Thoughts on Substantive versus Functional Definitions of Religion'. *Journal for the Scientific Study of Religion* 13(2): 125.

Bourne, Jenny (2013) 'May We Bring Harmony'? Thatcher's Legacy on "race"'. *Race & Class* 55(1): 87–91.

Brackett, David (1994) 'The Politics and Practice of "Crossover" in American Popular Music, 1963 to 1965'. *The Musical Quarterly* 78(4): 774–97. JSTOR.

Carson, Marion L. S. (2014) 'Difficult Texts: Colossians 3.22 – Slaves, Obey Your Earthly Masters in Everything'. *Theology* 117(3): 203–5.

Chimene-Wale, Naomi C. (2019) 'Code Switching and Mixing in Nigerian Gospel Music'. *Scholarly Journal of Science Research and Essay* 9(1): 11–17.

Civil, David and Joseph J. Himsworth (2020) 'Introduction: Meritocracy in Perspective. The Rise of the Meritocracy 60 Years On'. *The Political Quarterly* 91(2): 373–78.

Claudrena, Harold (2012) 'Almighty Fire: The Rise of Urban Contemporary Gospel Music and the Search for Cultural Authority in the 1980s'. *Fire!!!* 1(1): 25–48.

Connolly, Michelle A. (2019) 'Antipodean and Biblical Encounter: Postcolonial Vernacular Hermeneutics in Novel Form'. *Religions* 10(6): 21.

Daniel, J. L., G. Smitherman-Donaldson and M. A. Jeremiah (1987) 'Makin' a Way Outa No Way: The Proverb Tradition in the Black Experience'. *Journal of Black Studies* 17(4): 482–508, 490.

Davis, Mark (2015) 'The Politics of Resurrection Hermeneutics – Luke 24:36–48'. *Political Theology Network online*. https://politicaltheology.com/the-politics-of-resurrection-hermeneutics-luke-2436-48/

Davis, Steven T. (2001) *Encountering Evil: Live Options in Theodicy*. Edinburgh: T&T Clark.

Duncanson-Hales, Christopher J. (2017) 'Dread Hermeneutics: Bob Marley, Paul Ricœur and the Productive Imagination'. *Black Theology* 15(2): 156–75.

Erskine, Noel Leo (2013). 'Di Jamiekan Nyuu Testiment'. *International Journal of Public Theology* 7(4): 389–97.

Feld, Steven. (1984) 'Sound Structure as Social Structure'. *Journal of Ethnomusicology* 28(3): 383–409.

Ferris, Lesley (2010) 'Incremental Art: Negotiating the Route of London's Notting Hill Carnival'. *Social Identities* 16(4): 519–36.

Fine, Gary A. (2003) 'Towards a Peopled Ethnography Developing Theory from Group Life'. *Ethnography* 4(1): 41–60.

Glendhill, R. (2016) 'The Remarkable Impact of London's Flourishing Megachurches'. *Christianity Today* 2. https://www.christiantoday.com/article/the-remarkable-impact-of-londons-flourishing-megachurches/99624.htm

Grant, Jacqueline (1994) '"Come to My Help Lord for I'm in Trouble": Womanist Jesus and the Mutual Struggle for Liberation'. *Journal of Black Theology in South Africa* 8(1): 21–34.

Grosfoguel R. (2007) 'The Epistemic Decolonial Turn'. *Cultural Studies* 21(2–3): 211–23.

Hall, Stuart (1984) 'Reconstruction Work: Stuart Hall on Images of Post War Black Settlement'. *Ten-8* 16(4): 2–9. https://rl.talis.com/warwick//items
Henriques, Julian (2008) 'Sonic Diaspora, Vibrations and Rhythms: Thinking through the Sounding of the Jamaican Dancehall Session'. *African and Black Diaspora* 1(2): 215–36.
Hoffman, A. (2017) 'Interview with Walter Mignolo/Part 2: Key Concepts."' *E-International Relations*. Available online: https://www.e-ir.info/2017/01/21/interview-walter-mignolopart-2-key-concepts/
Kala, Araya Araya (2014) 'Anancy Stories Beyond the Moralistic Approach of the Western Philosophy of Being'. *Boletín De Literatura Oral* (4): 43–52. Issn 2173-0695.
Kerwick, Jack (2011) '"Black Conservatism": The Philosophy of Thomas Sowell'. *E-LOGOS* 18: 1–2.
Kirk-Duggan, Cheryl. (2014) 'Sacred and Secular in African American Music', in *The Oxford Handbook of Religion and the Arts*. New York: Oxford University Press.
Law, Ian (2015) 'Scarman Report', in *The Wiley Blackwell Encyclopaedia of Race, Ethnicity, and Nationalism*. X. Smith et al. Oxford: Wiley, Blackwell.
Lindenbaum, J. (2013) 'The Neoliberalization of Contemporary Christian Music's New Social Gospel'. *Geoforum* 44: 112–19.
McMillan, Michael (2009) *The Front Room: Migrant Aesthetics in the Home*. London: Black Dog Publishing.
McMillan, Michael (2019) 'Dub in the Front Room: Migrant Aesthetics of the Sacred and the Secular'. *Open Cultural Studies* 3: 184–94.
Mignolo, Walter D. (2007) 'Introduction'. *Cultural Studies* 21: 2–3, 155–67.
Mignolo, Walter D. (2011) 'Geopolitics of Sensing and Knowing: On (de)coloniality, Border Thinking and Epistemic Disobedience'. *Postcolonial Studies* 14(3): 273–83, 274.
Ming, Dong Gu (2020) 'What is "decoloniality"? A Postcolonial Critique'. *Postcolonial Studies* 23(4): 596–600.
Morren, Ronald C. and Diane M. Morren (2007) *Are the Goals and Objectives of Jamaica's Bilingual Education Project Being Met?* SIL Electronic Working Papers. Online.
Morse, Janice M., Michael Barrett, M. Mayan and Jude Spiers (2002) 'Verification Strategies for Establishing Reliability and Validity in Qualitative Research'. *International Journal of Qualitative Methods* 1(2): 13–22.-
Muir, David (June 2018) 'From Tilbury to the Pew and Pulpit: How The Church Met the Empire Windrush'. *Church Times*. https://www.churchtimes.co.uk/articles/2018/29-june/features/features/from-tilbury-to-the-pews-how-the-church-met-the-empire-windrush
Mukherjee, S. Romi (2018) 'Make America Great Again as White Political Theology'. *Revue LISA/LISA e-journal* [En ligne] XVI(2) | 2018, mis en ligne le 24 septembre 2018, consulté le 08 décembre 2022.

Nealon, Jeffrey T. (1998) 'Refraining, Becoming-Black: Repetition and Difference in Amiri Baraka's Blues People'. *Symplokē* 6(1/2): 83–95.

Ngara, Constantine (2007) 'African Ways of Knowing and Pedagogy Revisited'. *JCIE* 2(2): 7–21.

Nketia, J. H. K. (1979) 'African Roots of Music in the Americas: An African View'. *Jamaica Journal* 42: 12–17.

Northcottm, Michael S. (1990) 'The Case Study Method in Theological Education'. *Contact* 103(1): 26–32.

Oakes, Edward T. (1992) 'Apologetics and the Pathos of Narrative Theology'. *The Journal of Religion* 72(1): 37–8.

Park, Wongi. (2021) 'The Blessing of Whiteness in the Curse of Ham: Reading Gen 9:18–29 in the Antebellum South'. *Religions* 12(11): 928.

Pathé News Report (1955) 'Our Jamaican Problem'. TV.

Pearce, Godwin L. (2019) 'Black Students in England 1950-2000: Representation, Identity and Barriers to Success'. *New Vistas* 45(2): 30–3. University of West London.

Quijano, Aníbal (2000) 'Coloniality of Power, Eurocentrism, and Latin America'. *Nepentla: Views From the South* 1(3): 533–80.

Riches, Tanya R. (2010) 'The Evolving Theological Emphasis of Hillsong Worship (1996-2007)'. *Australasian Pentecostal Studies* 13: 87–118.

Rogers, Andrew (2016) 'How are Black Majority Churches Growing in the UK? A London Borough Case Study'. *LSE Blogs*. Https://blogs.lse.ac.uk/religionglobalsociety/2016/12/how-are-Black-majority-churches-growing-in-the-uk-a-london-borough-case-study/

Rush, Anne (2007) 'Reshaping British History: The Historiography of West Indians in Britain in the Twentieth Century'. *History Compass* 5(2): 463–84.

Scarman, L. G. (1982) *The Scarman Report: The Brixton Disorders 10–12 April 1981: Report of an Inquiry*. London: Penguin.

Scott-Samuel, Alex, Clare Bambra, Chick Collins, David Hunter, Gerry McCartney and Kat Smith (2014) 'The Impact of Thatcherism on Health and Well-Being in Britain'. *International Journal of Health Services* 44(1): 53–71.

Shildrick, Tracy (2018) 'Lessons from Grenfell: Poverty Propaganda, Stigma and Class Power'. *The Sociological Review* 66(4): 783–98.

Smith, Anna Marie (1994) *New Right Discourse on Race and Sexuality: Britain, 1968–1990*. Cambridge: Cambridge University Press.

wa Thiong'o, Ngugi (1985) 'The Language of African Literature'. *New Left Review* 150 (March/April): 109–27, 125.

Tomlinson, Sally (2018) 'Enoch Powell, Empires, Immigrants and Education'. *Race Ethnicity and Education* 21(1): 1–14.

Walsh, Catherine, ed. (2017) *Pedagogias Decoloniales Tomo I. Practicas Insurgentes De Resistir (Re)Existir Y (Re)Vivir*, vol. 1, 443–68. Quito: Ediciones Abya-Yala.

Ward, Graham (2017) 'Decolonizing Theology'. *Stellenbosch Theological Journal* 3(2): 561–84.

Woodhead, Linda (2016) 'The Rise of "no religion" in Britain. The Emergence of a New Cultural Majority'. *Journal of the British Academy* 4(08): 245–61.

Wright, Jeremiah A. (1989) 'Music as Cultural Expression in Black Church Theology and Worship'. *Black Sacred Music* 1 (3): 1, 1–5.

Yin, Robert K. (2009) *Case Study Research, Design and Method*, 4 edn. London: Sage Publications Ltd.

Zahl, Simeon (2021) 'Beyond the Critique of Soteriological Individualism: Relationality and Social Cognition'. *Modern Theology* 37(2): 336–61.

Index of songs

Times

The Jamaican Language	3:15
Social Justice	5.43
Magnificat	4.50
Incarnation	7:25
Beatitudes	5:24
Manifesto	5:12
Go and Sin No More	3.52
Caesarea Philippi	4.38
Work of the Spirit	4:01
Pay Back	7:01
Resurrection	3:28

Credits

The Jamaican Language
Writer: Tony Bean/Robert Beckford
Publisher: 5AM Records
Copyright: Tony Bean/Robert Beckford
Vocals: Robert Beckford
Producer: Tony Bean/Robert Beckford
Studio: 5AM Records, West Midlands
Samples: David Starkey, BBC *Newsnight* 12 August 2011. Rev Courtney Stewart, BBC News, 24 December 2011.

Social Justice
Writer: Robert Beckford/Witness
Publisher: 5AM Records
Copyright: Tony Bean/Robert Beckford
Vocals: Robert Beckford/Witness
Producer: Tony Bean/Robert Beckford
Studio: 5AM Records, West Midlands
Samples: Luuk 4.18-19, Di Jamiekan Nyuu Testiment (JNT).

Magnificat
Writer: Tony Bean/Robert Beckford/Justice Inniss
Publisher: 5AM Records
Copyright: Tony Bean/Robert Beckford
Vocals: Justice Inniss
Producer: Tony Bean/Robert Beckford
Studio: 5AM Records, West Midlands
Samples: Rev. Rose Hudson-Wilkin, *ParliamentWeek* 6 November 2013. Luuk 1.48-54, Di Jamiekan Nyuu Testiment (JNT).

Incarnation: No Blacks, No Irish, No Dogs
Writer: Tony Bean/Robert Beckford/Darren Ellison
Publisher: 5AM Records
Copyright: Tony Bean/Robert Beckford
Vocals: Robert Beckford/Darren Ellison
Producer: Tony Bean/Robert Beckford
Studio: 5AM Records, West Midlands
Samples: British Pathé, 'Our Jamaican Problem', 1955. Jan 1.14, Di Jamiekan Nyuu Testiment (JNT).

Beatitudes
Writer: Tony Bean/Robert Beckford
Publisher: 5AM Records
Copyright: Tony Bean/Robert Beckford
Producer: Tony Bean/Robert Beckford
Saxophone: Soweto Kinch
Studio: 5AM Records, West Midlands
Sample: Matyu 5.3-10, Di Jamiekan Nyuu Testament (JNT). Jamaican National Anthem by the Children's Choir.

Manifesto
Writer: Tony Bean/Robert Beckford
Publisher: 5AM Records
Copyright: Tony Bean/Robert Beckford
Producer: Tony Bean/Robert Beckford
Vocals: Marlene Kerr
Studio: 5AM Records, West Midlands
Sample: Luuk 11.1-4, Di Jamiekan Nyuu Testament (JNT).

Go and Sin No More
Writer: Tony Bean/Robert Beckford
Publisher: 5AM Records
Copyright: Tony Bean/Robert Beckford
Producer: Tony Bean/Robert Beckford
Studio: 5AM Records, West Midlands
Samples: Francis Kress Welsing 'Black People Forgiving', on the COWS show with GUS T Renegad on 13 April 2015. Gee and Domonique Walker, 'Mother's Forgiveness' BBC Learning, 5 July 2012. Joseph Niles and the Consolers, 'Go and Sin No More' *Gospel Ship*, Redemption Records, 1973. Steel Pulse, 'Biko's Kindred Lament' *Tribute to the Martyrs*, Island Records, 1979. Jan 8.7, Di Jamiekan Nyuu Testament (JNT).

Caesarea Philippi
Writer: Juice Aleem
Publisher: 5AM Records
Copyright: Tony Bean/Robert Beckford
Producer: Tony Bean/Robert Beckford
Vocals: Juice Aleem
Studio: 5AM Records, West Midlands
Samples: Albert B Cleage Jr. 'That's a Creed: A Day of Remembrance Salute to Jaramogi' YouTube 22 February 2014. Hyung Kyung Chung, 'Image of God' YouTube 24 August

2011. Malcolm X, 1992. 40 Acres and a Mule Filmworks. Maak 8.27, Di Jamiekan Nyuu Testiment (JNT).

Work of the Spirit
Writer: Tony Bean/Robert Beckford
Publisher: 5AM Records
Copyright: Tony Bean/Robert Beckford
Producer: Tony Bean/Robert Beckford
Vocals: Abigail Kelly/Robert Beckford
Studio: 5AM Records, West Midlands
Samples: 'Anointing Fall on Me', *Lift Him Up with Ron Kenoly*, 1992, Ron Kenoly, Hosanna! Music, 1992. II Tesaluoniyan 2.6; Jan 14.16, Di Jamiekan Nyuu Testiment (JNT).

Pay Back
Writer: Tony Bean/Robert Beckford
Publisher: 5AM Records
Copyright: Tony Bean/Robert Beckford
Producer: Tony Bean/Robert Beckford
Vocals: Lez Henry
Studio: 5AM Records, West Midlands
Samples: BBC Radio 4, 'Start of the Week', 12.6.06. Jesse Jackson from 'Empire Pays Back,' Channel 4, 2005. Failiiman 1:18, Di Jamiekan Nyuu Testiment (JNT).

Resurrection
Writer: Robert Beckford
Publisher: 5AM Records
Copyright: Tony Bean/Robert Beckford
Producer: Tony Bean/Robert Beckford
Vocals: Jerome Bucknor
Studio: 5AM Records, West Midlands
Sample: Luuk 24.5-11, Di Jamiekan Nyuu Testiment (JNT).

Lyrics

The Jamaican Language

Robert – Welcome to the Jamaican Bible Remix.
It's a remix of the Jamaican New Testament, published in 2012.

We mix audio from the Jamaican New Testament with black urban music from Britain, and we provide a social and political-theological commentary on the audio.

So, when you mix it all together you end up with a powerful sonic fiction. You hear the Jamaican Bible come alive in the black urban context and you hear the Bible relate to real-life, social, political, historical and cultural concerns.

On another level, we are trying to demonstrate that translation is much more than grammar and syntax; it's also about communicating a peoples' worldview, their history, their hopes and their aspirations.

I guess you could say that we see language as being redemptive.
To say the Jamaican language is redemptive is to affirm the way in which Africans who were captured found ways of keeping their language and their culture alive in the way that they spoke.

But not everybody holds this view of the Jamaican language. For some, the Jamaican language is problematic:

David Starkey – This language, which is wholly false, which is a Jamaican patois.

Robert – But for others it's a legitimate language: a carefully retained expression of the history of the Africans on the island:

Rev. Courtney Stewart – It is patois, our language, and the critical part of this translation is that our language is what makes us who we are.

Robert – Now we're mixing this up from the location of the diaspora, the Jamaican diaspora in Britain.
And as a diaspora we have the gift of second sight: we live in two worlds.
So, we draw on ideas from the Caribbean, and we mix them with information, concerns and experiences that we have here in Britain.

This is a collaboration between 5AM Records (Tony Bean), The Bible Society and me, Robert Beckford.

On this album, we cover a variety of themes, all of them bound together by social justice.

Social Justice

Robert – Witness, good to see you.
Witness – And you too, Robert.
Robert – This is a project about social justice.

Witness – OK.

Robert – I've been going to church for 40 years, and I've not heard one decent sermon about social justice.

Witness – Wow!

Robert – Yet, social justice is at the heart of the gospel. Jesus begins His ministry talking about social justice.

Witness – Well it's funny that you should say that, you know Robert, because I don't believe that the church don't know it. I just think that they ignore it, 'cause Luke 4 declares it.

JNT – Luuk 4

'Di Spirit a di Laad de pan mi,

kaaz im pik mi out

fi kyari gud nyuuz go gi puo piipl.

Im sen mi fi mek di prizna dem nuo se dem a-go frii,

fi mek blain piipl nuo se dem a-go si agen,

fi mek piipl we a sofa nuo se dem naa go sofa fi eva.

An im pik mi out fi mek piipl nuo se dis a di taim wen di Laad a-go siev im piipl dem.'

Robert – This is one of the most important passages in the whole of the New Testament. Jesus begins his ministry, and what he says will determine how people understand him: what his life is about, what he is going to do. So, he needs to make an important impression on the people. He begins by using the language of Jubilee. For the people who were listening, the language of Jubilee was the language of revolution, revolution.

Chorus
We've got to know if we never touch this.
We don't have a faith if we don't have social justice.
We've got to know if we never touch this.
We don't have a faith if we don't have social justice. (x2)

Robert – Jesus is drawing on a long tradition that goes all the way back to the book of Leviticus. In Leviticus 25, there is a tradition called the Sabbatical. Every seven years, slaves were supposed to be set free, debts were cancelled, and poor people could go and feed off the land. It was a revolutionary statement by God that was intended to ensure that there was social justice. That people wouldn't want, that all people would be able to share in the blessings of the Promised Land.

Then every seven, seven years, or every 49 years, there was the Jubilee. All the land that had been taken from your ancestors was given back to you. It was a revolutionary statement by God, suggesting that all people are equal, and in the sight of God, all the resources of the land should be shared out equally amongst the people. Nobody should want, nobody should be poor, and nobody should be oppressed.
But the people couldn't do it, and they are still not doing it today.

Chorus
We've got to know if we never touch this.
We don't have a faith if we don't have social justice.
We've got to know if we never touch this.
We don't have a faith if we don't have social justice.

Witness – Ah ha, ok then, you tell me you're preaching the gospel, but is it the gospel or a good-spell? Binding the people making them unwell. Some of you need go and spell, as you're theologically unstable and still unable to meet the needs of the people. Some of you are so feeble. Kingsley (Burrell) died under police brutality, and only a few marched with me, church community, still sitting in their ivory singing their song, 'Close to Thee'. Hypocrisy, He came to set the captives free, those that are blind and cannot see. But what you see is not real to me. You need to be relevant to the point of people's needs, not your own needs. More social justice is what we need. So many mouths to feed. This empire building with egos to please, oh please! It's time to release, true social justice chorus please.

Chorus
We've got to know if we never touch this.
We don't have a faith if we don't have social justice.
We've got to know if we never touch this.
We don't have a faith if we don't have social justice.

Robert – Many of us within the church were taught to ignore social justice. But it was bad advice. The Jubilee means social justice. To serve God means being involved in making a difference in this world, a difference in your country, a difference in your community.

Chorus
We've got to know if we never touch this.
We don't have a faith if we don't have social justice.
We've got to know if we never touch this.
We don't have a faith if we don't have social justice. (x4)

Magnificat

Rev. Rose Hudson-Wilkin – I believe we need to hear more women's voices in public life, in particular for the next generation. If we are going to change the dynamics of what we have today, where it is still sort of a man's world. Then women today need to step forward, to enable their children and their grandchildren, in particular girls and actually boys, too. Boys need to see that their counterparts can be equally respected in terms of the contribution that they bring to the table.

JNT – Luuk 1

... mi a Gad-bles uman,
kaaz di Muos Powaful Gad du da mirikl ya fi mi —
im uoli!
Gad gud kyaahn don.

Chorus

Justice – Oh hear me ladies, oh hear me girls, 'cause God has chosen you to save the world.
All black women of the earth, skin like dirt, you need to know your worth.

JNT – Im tek im an du som powaful sitn;
im skyata skyata buosi piipl.
Gad aal dong ruula aafa dem ai chuon
an lif op piipl we nobadi neva tingk se mata.

Justice – I said its time for action, them slavery chains have a chain reaction, oh yes.

I am a fighter resister, a daughter, a sister, I am a fraction of progress.
Some don't lift a finger, but I ride the storm like the queen Masinga.
Because all through the process, trust me its mommy that knows best.
Yo, we need justice and equal rights, want to rest in peace when we sleep at night.
Fight for the children, they use and abuse them, world of confusion enough so we lose them to the streets.
Ain't no one to keep eyes out for them, no one to protect or vouch for them, let's reach out to them
mothers of the earth, we do more than give birth, lets show what we worth.

JNT – Im gi onggri piipl uol iip a gud sitn,
bot rich piipl im sen we wid dem tuu lang an.
Gad elp im sorvant dem, Izrel.
Im memba fi bi gud an kain tu dem.

Chorus

Justice – Oh hear me ladies, oh hear me girls, 'cause God has chosen you to save the world.
All black women of the earth, skin like dirt, you need to know your worth.

Justice – Armed with a pen and a paper and strong mind.
I read for those who couldn't, and there was a long line.
I'm too tall, the sky ain't the limit, a jungle sometimes, I got a panther spirit.
With or without a husband, I am freeing minds like Harriet Tubman.
The fact is, they deported and killed the activists, but they are a part of us, so we are attached to this.
Teacher, go teach the youth. Ananci, defend our people like the queens of Ashanti, bridge the gap for future generations, download our history and make our own stations. So many sayings left to be said, and so many books left to be read, we need to wake up the mentally dead, we need to lead so we won't be led, 'nough said.

Rev. Rose Hudson-Wilkin – For young women today who say that politics is rather boring and not for them,
I would like them to think of politics, as something that is going to impact on their lives,
whether they like it or not. So, in other words, they will need to ask themselves, 'Do I want to just sit and have something done to me, or do I want to be right there, at the cutting edge, making decisions, contributing to the decisions that are going to impact on society of which they are a part?'

Justice – I want to shout-out all my womanists:
Valentina Alexander
Caroline Redfern
Dulcie McKenzie
Maxine Howell
Lynette Mullings
Let's go
Let's go
Let's go . . .

Incarnation

BBC News – In 1954 about 10,000 West Indians came to Britain. In 1955, it is believed another 15,000 will make the long journey. Already their coming has caused a national controversy.

But one point must always be borne in mind. Whatever our feelings, we cannot deny them entry, for all are British citizens, and as such, are entitled to the identical rights of any member of the (British) Empire.

JNT – Jan 1

Nou, di wan we a di Wod ton man, im kom kom liv mongks wi, kom liv mongks wi. (x2)

Robert – John 1:14 tells the story of Jesus' incarnation. That the Word becomes flesh and lives amongst us.
It means that God who is fully God and fully man, takes on human form.
The incarnation means that unequivocally, all creation is good and that all flesh, no matter what colour, no matter what tone is good. My parents believed in this meaning of the incarnation, that their flesh was good.
They were immigrants from Jamaica who came to work in Britain after the Second World War.
But they soon came to realise that not everybody thought the same.
When they went to look for places to live, they were greeted with signs that said, 'No blacks, no Irish and no dogs.'

Darren – Sailed 5000 miles with the sun way off behind me. They said it's gonna be a while till I feel that warm again. Staring at the grey skies as the cold rain starts to soak me. Faces that I recognize but no one I'd call a friend. Just one class above how my fathers sailed before me. Still no wiser 'bout the days that lay ahead. Hands and feet are free but shackled by economy. Just a possibility of a better life instead. Maybe if you give me time just to let me tell my story. 'Bout how I came to be in the land of hope and glory. Moment that I touched the ground all I see is consternation. You never let me explain that I'm here by invitation.

Chorus

Came expecting arms to open wide. No blacks, no Irish, and no dogs inside. The sign is plain, and you don't try to hide. No blacks, no Irish, and no dogs inside.

BBC News – Much of the outcry against the immigrants arises from the Colour-Bar, which legally does not exist in Britain, does not exist in Britain.

JNT – im kom kom liv mongks wi, kom iiv mongks wi.

Darren – 5 years 3 days to go till I get back to my family. Got to find a place to stay with a people playing games. There's a lot of empty rooms and I know I've got the money.

Funny how my currency doesn't seem to be the same. Working from 5-to-5 and the guys are always on me. Now the fight to stay alive, never figured in my plans. Tried to find the house of God, only made the people angry. Sadly, realised that I'm seen as less than just a man. Maybe if you give me time just to let me tell my story. 'Bout how I came to be in the land of hope and glory. Moment that I touched the ground all I see is consternation. You never let me explain that I'm here by invitation.

Robert –The strange thing is that in church history the brilliant minds of the church have spent a great deal of time trying to explain the doctrine of the incarnation, that Jesus had to be fully God and had to be fully man and use that as a way of countering heresy. But less time has been spent on the *meaning* of the incarnation, what it means to *practice* the equality of all humanity. If the church had spent more time on the meaning and the practice of the incarnation, we wouldn't have this terrible Post-War story: No blacks, no Irish and no dogs.

Chorus

Came expecting arms to open wide. No blacks, no Irish, and no dogs inside. The sign is plain, and you don't try to hide. No blacks, no Irish, and no dogs inside.

Darren – God is not dead, He's still alive. (x2)

I can feel him in my hands,
I can feel him in my feet,
I can feel him all over,
Feel him all over me . . . (x3)

Beatitudes

JNT – Matyu 5, Gad bles unu . . .

Aal a unu we nuo se unu niid Gad iina evri wie, Gad bles unu,
kaa di gud sitn dem we Gad gi wen im ruul piipl laif iina evri wie, a unu a-go get dem.

Chorus

Gad bles unu. (X6)

JNT – Aal a uu a baal nou, Gad bles dem,
kaaz di taim a-go kom wen Gad a-go osh dem an mek dem api agen.
Aal a uu ombl demself, Gad bles dem,
kaa yu si di ort, a dem piipl de a-go kom get it.

Chorus

Gad bles unu. (X6)

JNT – Uu waahn du wa rait iina Gad yai so bad, dat it komiin laik se a ded dem a ded fi onggri an dem chuot jrai laik se dem no jringk waata ou lang, Gad bles unu,
kaa unu a-go get unu beli ful
Unu we paadn piipl, Gad bles unu,
kaaz im a-go paadn unu tu.

Chorus

Gad bles unu. (X6)

Children's Choir – Eternal Father bless our land.

JNT – Aal a uu onggl waahn fi du di sitn dem we mek Gad api, Gad bles unu,
Kaaz wan die, wan die, unu a-go get fi si Gad.
Gad bles aal a uu elp piipl fi liv iina piis,
kaaz a piipl laik dem de Gad a-go kaal fi im pikni dem.

Chorus

Gad bles unu. (X6)

JNT – Di piipl dem we ada piipl mek sofa jos kaaz dem liv ou Gad waahn piipl fi liv, Gad bles unu,
kaa di gud sitn dem we Gad gi wen im ron piipl laif ou im waahn ron it, a dem sitn de unu a-go get.

Chorus

Gad bles unu. (X18)

Manifesto

Robert – And now, a party-political broadcast on behalf of the Jesus Party from Luke Chapter 11.

Chorus

Marlene Kerr – Manifesto, need you to know. (x 2)

JNT – Luuk 11

Wan die Jiizas did de somwe a prie. Afta im don, wan a im speshal falara dem se tu im se, 'Laad, shuo wi ou fi prie.'

Robert – This isn't really an issue of prayer.
Every Jew knew how to pray.
They were taught how to pray three times a day.
Instead, what's at stake here is what they are meant to pray for?
What are Jesus' disciples meant to stand for?
Jesus obliges them, and introduces *five* commitments that form to make up his manifesto.

Chorus

Marlene Kerr – Manifesto, need you to know.
If there is hope, then we got to show it in the way that we live today.
More than words let the hungry know it, we got to wipe all the debt away.
Manifesto, need you to know.

Commitment number 1

JNT – Laad, shuo wi ou fi prie, laik ou Jan shuo fi im falara dem ou fi prie.
Jiizas tel dem se, 'Wen unu prie, unu fi se:"Faada, Faada, Faada."'

Robert – This is a god for all, a god for all.
A god who is not partial and a god who is inclusive.

Commitment number 2

JNT – mek piipl av nof rispek fi yu an yu niem,
Mek di taim kom wen yu ruul iina evri wie.

Robert – Respect God's name, you do God's business here on earth.
But what is that business?

Commitment number 3

JNT – Evridie gi wi di fuud we wi niid.
Robert – Feed the poor.

Commitment number 4

JNT – Aadn wi fi aal a di rang we wi du,
kaa wi paadn piipl we du wi rang tu.

Robert – Cancel the debts.

And finally, commitment number 5

JNT – An no mek wi fies notn we wi kaaz wi fi sin.

Robert – Never ever give up on the struggle!

Chorus

Marlene Kerr – Manifesto, need you to know.
If there is hope, then we got to show it in the way that we live today.
More than words let the hungry know it, we got wipe all the debt away.
Manifesto, need you to know.

Robert – Could it be that this is much more than just a simple prayer?
For the people who were listening to Jesus, who were experiencing hunger.
Who found themselves in debt to the Roman administration. Who found themselves in debt to the Temple authorities.
That this was a manifesto: a proposal for change in their lives introduced by God *herself*.

Chorus

Marlene Kerr – Manifesto, need you to know. (x2)
If there is hope, then we got to show it in the we live today.
More than words let the hungry know it, we got wipe all the debts away. (x6)

Go and Sin No More

JNT – Jan 8

Frances Cress Welsing – I think that ah this automatic forgiveness ah when it comes to black people being harmed or killed or injured by people who classify themselves as White. We don't hear people who are White if they have, ah feel they have sustained some injury or harm from a black person, we don't hear them saying, 'I forgive, I forgive I forgive.'

Chorus

Neither do I condemn you.
I'll never forgive. (X4)
Go and sin no more.

Gee Walker – When I expect the law to work for me, it's not up to me to take revenge. Forgive those who sin against you, as we forgive, we expect to be forgiven, that's why I chose to forgive.

JNT – Eni wan a unu we neva sin yet,
fling di fos stuon. (x2)

Chorus

Neither do I condemn you.
I'll never forgive. (X4)
Go and sin no more.

Dominique Walker – I was approached by a reporter, and he asked me if I could find in my heart to forgive the killers of Anthony, knowing that I am a woman. . . . Obviously, a woman of God, woman of faith. And I said, I stopped for a second, and I was just like. I actually had to think. For me for me it probably seemed like I lifetime, I had to think, but it must have been less than a few seconds, and I said to him, I said, 'The Bible taught us and Jesus said seventy times seven we must forgive and that is what we must do.'

JNT – Eni wan a unu we neva sin yet,
fling di fos stuon. (x4)

Chorus

Neither do I condemn you.
I'll never forgive. (X4)
Go and sin no more.

Frances Cress Welsing – So I think that it is a part of black peoples' tradition, tradition from the time of enslavement. Do you see when the slave master could beat the black person and I can just envision the black person being beaten and the slave master or the slave mistress would be saying, 'Say that you forgive me,' do you see and then giving them another lash. 'Say that you forgive me.' And so, the black person doesn't have a choice but to say 'I forgive master, I forgive, I forgive, I forgive.'

Chorus

Neither do I condemn you.
I'll never forgive.
Go and sin no more. (X8)

Caesarea Philippi

Juice – Yes indeed, this is Juice Aleem.
South Birmingham.

Just chilling with my big brother Jesus.
Jamaican Bible Remix.
Listen good, listen good . . .

JNT – Maak 8

Chorus

'Uu piipl se mi bi?' (x4)
uu unu tingk mi bi?

Juice – Was a baby, born in a manger predicted?
Three Wise Guys knew the Sun had been evicted?
Essenes said: He would be in war
with the wicked.
Others said he joined this very same group of mystics.
Black or White?
Nazareth or Nazarite?
Jasper skin.
Eyes glow in a di night.
Feet like burnt brass,
turn water walker.
Gospels, Apostles,
Really who's the author?
So many books.
Took a look in Revelation.
Black as the night.
Is the first in creation
Really Son of God?
With dem African features?
Lesson for the learned
A poor righteous teacher.

Albert Cleage – I believe that Jesus is the black messiah, is a revolutionary teacher send by God, sent by God. (x3)

Chorus

'Uu piipl se mi bi?' (x4)
uu unu tingk mi bi?

Juice – Young in the temple.
Some simple essentials.

Eighteen years.
Left studying the mental.
Lost in Egypt?
Must look the same like.
Black Madonna.
Dear Mama
Birthed a Kushite.
Middle Eastern?
When there was no Middle East.
Picture that you seen
Portrait of a beast?!
Maybe got married had a couple babies.
(**Robert** – Is he speculating that Jesus got married?
Tony – Yes but it's OK, he is just being historical critical).

Juice – Searchin' the histories
Can mek a man crazy.
I guess you were
Lookin' for a Yeshua,
Ha-Mashiakh.
Yes, you were convinced of that.
Messiah stats.
Covered in oils and fats.
Moisturize.
A trait known amongst the Blacks.
Son of Man.
Known in his habitat. (x3)

Chung Hyun Kyung – My image of God now is like a middle-aged Korean woman looking like my mother, very warm, and affirming. Very available, and strong and down to earth.

Chorus

'Uu piipl se mi bi?' (x4)
uu unu tingk mi bi?
Juice – So many words
Said about but never said by
The Logos.
Standing with the stars on his right side.
Peace!
He spoke as a sword

So, remember.
Two edges
One for the law and the lenders.
For revolution
A true rebel leader.
Smashed up the markets.
To Rah
He's a geezer.
Hunted by Romans.
Flippin' over tables.
Real livin' life
As opposed to the fables.
Hair like lamb's wool
skin pure sable.
Research in the works
If you true and livin' able.
But only if your able.

Malcolm X, The Movie – Just a moment, just a moment. God is White, isn't it obvious, isn't it obvious. (x3)

Chorus
'Uu piipl se mi bi?'
uu unu tingk mi bi? (x4)

Work of the Spirit

Abigail Kelly – What is the work, what's the work of the Spirit?

JNT – II Tesaluoniyan 2

Nou, unu don nuo aredi di wan we a uol im bak, an im a-go gwaan uol im bak so im kyan kom wen a fi im taim fi kom. Kaaz wan wikid sitn de bout we a wok anda di kwaiyat fi kaaz piipl fi go gens Gad Laa. Bot sumadi a uol it bak. An di wan we a uol it bak a-go gwaan uol it til im get muuv outa di wie.

Robert – In church people sing many songs about the Holy Spirit.
None of them more evocative than, *'Anointing Fall on Me.'*
In this song, the Holy Spirit is presented as a personal empowerment for people.
Something they can call upon to strengthen them.
It is very personal and very individual.
But this isn't the only image of the Spirit.

II Thessalonians paints a picture of the Spirit as a defensive force, restraining the evil within the world, and keeping it in check.

Chorus

What's the work of the Spirit?
Bot sumadi a uol it bak. (x4)

Robert – The work of the Spirit isn't just about individual empowerment.
It's also about holding back the terror within this world.
The Spirit is a dam against a tide of wickedness.

Chorus

What's the work of the Spirit?
Bot sumadi a uol it bak. (x4)

Robert – But the Spirit's work isn't just about defence; it's also about attack.
We need to take this in a different direction.

JNT – Jan 14

An mi a-go aks mi Faada fi sen wan neda sumadi fi elp unu an de wid unu aal di taim.
fi elp unu. (x2)

Robert – Before Jesus goes back to heaven, he says to the disciples, he is not going to leave them alone.
He will send the comforter; the comforter is going to be there to help them.
And be there to drive them forward.

Chorus

Work of the Spirit. (x5)

Robert – The work of the Spirit is an offensive force in this world, puts people who believe in God on the attack.
To 'mash up' the forces of wickedness in this world.

Chorus

Work of the Spirit. (x4)

Robert – So what's the work of the Spirit within this world? Within this world. (x2)
Defence and attack. (x 24)

Pay Back

Lez – Introducing Dr Lesley Henry lyrics, on the Jamaican Bible Remix.

JNT – Paal leta tu Failiiman

Andrew Marr – Should Britain pay reparations and make a formal apology to the descendants of slaves? Much of our imperial and business strength has its origins in the Slave Trade of the 18th and early 19th Century and the academic Robert Beckford, argues in a new television programme that the Empire should pay back.

Chorus

JNT – Ef im did du notn rang tu yu ar im uo yu, ... wi pie yu bak , pie yu bak. (x2)

Andrew Marr – Let's start with the scale of slavery, you compare it in the programme to the Nazi Holocaust.

Robert Beckford – For several decades of the Slave Trade it was cheaper to bring in Africans, work them to death and then replace them. So, we are looking at genocidal conditions on the Caribbean plantations.

Lez – The complexity of our condition is what you fail to comprehend, historically turned into chattels, beasts of burden less than men, thinking the only way to survive is to pretend to be you, mocking our very existence, animals in your human zoo.

Chorus

JNT – Ef im did du notn rang tu yu ar im uo yu, ... wi pie yu bak pie yu bak. (x2)

Andrew Marr – There are two almost instant default defences made by a lot of British people when this is raised. The first is, that actually, the Slave Trade was something that was driven from Africa itself, that it was Muslim, Arab slave traders moving down south and that people in the centre ground of West Africa in particular were behind the Slave Trade.

Robert – What we focus on is what the British did. I am not that concerned with what one ethic group did to another ethnic group in Africa. I am interested in how the British participated in it, the huge profits that were made, and the incredible economic benefit to this country, and also the underdevelopment of Africa. And more so, the brutalization of African people in the Caribbean.

Lez – Wearing your names in our brains, African cultures disrespected, educated against ourselves is why we wind up disaffected. The saddest case, in the saddest place, even these words leave a bitter taste in my mouth cos as an African to you I'm human waste.

Chorus

JNT – Ef im did du notn rang tu yu ar im uo yu, . . . wi pie yu bak pie yu bak. (x2)

Andrew Marr – The second defence mechanism people say is well it was Britain which ended the Slave Trade, it was Wilberforce and then it was the Royal Navy and that Britain's got a lot be proud of in stopping the Slave Trade.

Robert – When I was taught history, I was always told to approach it from a multi-dimensional perspective to look at what happened in the subjugated histories, and not just read history like TV history from the good and the great. In the Caribbean, they talk about the slaves who ended slavery, the fact that there were rebellions across the Caribbean in the 1830s that made slavery economically impossible and just not viable. So, we know that Britain ended the trade in 1807, we know that slavery was ended in 1834/38 – took a little bit of a while for it to work through. But we cannot discount the influence and the work of Africans in the Caribbean who helped to undermine slavery. So, it's a much more complex picture.

Lez – You try to confuse telling the world you set us free. Good old England, don't you know, we were anti-slavery. The Clapham sect should get respect because they showed a lot of class, another historical distortion like your William '*Wilber farce*'.

Chorus

JNT – Ef im did du notn rang tu yu ar im uo yu, mi . . . wi pie yu bak. (x2)

Andrew Marr – and probably most controversially, you say that there should be payback, there should be reparation.

Robert – I believe that as a mature, sophisticated post-industrialized nation, that we are in a very strong and dynamic position, and to be able to apologies for the past is not a sign of weakness but a sign of strength. And I also believe that things like compensation and an apology are psychosocial in their impact; they help to heal the nation and enable people to move on.

Lez – We've seen through your deception, and speak our truth in redemption songs, reparations transcends money it's about repairing historical wrongs. Britain as a nation needs to face one brutal fact, we need more than just a band aid to put the African on the map.

Chorus

JNT – Ef im did du notn rang tu yu ar im uo yu, mi . . . wi pie yu bak pie yu bak. (x2)

Rev. Jesse Jackson – There must be repay for damage done, repair for damage done. It's not a foreign concept: Israel is a state of reparations for damage done, justifiably so. The African victims of the Slave Trade, we must demand repay for damage done. It may take many forms, but the concept is legitimate and the need is great.

Chorus

JNT – Ef im did du notn rang tu yu ar im uo yu, mi . . . wi pie yu bak pie yu bak. (x2)

We've got to know if we never touch this.
We don't have a faith if we don't have social justice. (x4)

Resurrection

JNT – Luuk 24

'Wa mek unu a luk fi di wan we a liv mongks di wan dem we ded? Im no de ya, im kom bak alaiv!, im kom bak alaiv!'

Jerome – Resurrection revolution.
Christ is risen, sin and shame done.
Satan can't win.
Christ is risen. (x2)

JNT – Afta dem kom bak fram di tuum, di uman dem tel Jiizas ilevn apasl an aal di res a falara dem wa did apm. Nou a did Mieri Magdaliin, Juowana, Mieri we a Jiemz mada, an di ada uman dem, uu did tel di apasl dem wa dem si. Bot di apasl dem neva biliiv di uman dem, kaaz we dem did a se soun laik fuulinish.

Jerome – Resurrection revolution.
Christ is risen, gun and gang done.
No vexation immigration.
Christ is risen. (x2)

JNT – Piita get op an ron go a di tuum. Im ben dong, bot di onggl ting im si a di piis a linin klaat wan, so im go we, a wanda wa apm.

Jerome – Resurrection revolution.
Christ is risen, end pollution.
Palestinian peace solution.
Christ is risen. (x2)

Jerome – Up from the grave He arose.
With a mighty triumph for His foes.
He arose the victor from the dark domain.
And He lives forever with the saints to reign.
Christ is risen. (x4)

Index

Note: Page numbers followed by 'n' refer to notes

Ackah, W. 17
Adkins, I. 8
affective narrative epistemology 46
African Caribbean Apostolic Church 76
African Caribbean diaspora Christianity 31, 110
African Traditional Religion 127–9, 169
age of discovery 55
Airborne 132
Akerman, Roy 168
Aleem, Juice 133
Alexander, Valentina 31–2, 105
Allen-McLaurin, L. 19
Amazing Grace (1972) 88
Anancy tradition of stories in Jamaica 46
Andrae Crouch 31
Anglican Church 17, 36, 72
anti-blackness 7, 40, 55, 68, 150
antiphonal communicative strategies 46
anti-racism 70, 82, 100
anti-slavery 36, 69, 110, 112
anti-theodicy 155–6
assertive nativism 138, 146
atonement 141–8
   in Christian tradition 142–3
   Christus Victor atonement 144
   decolonial/theological register of Jamaican Patwa 141
   hegemony of Standard English in Jamaica 146–7
   JNT version 146–8
   liberation atonement 145–7
   linguistics of the enslaved 147
   penal substitution 142–5
   resurrection and Reformation 142–3
   riots of 2011 142
Augustine's Legacy (2019) 91
Aulén, Gustaf 142

Babylon the Bandit 100

Bailey, Randall 49, 53–4, 106
Baptists 36
Barrett, David 7
The Battle for Christianity (BBC1 documentary) 15–16
Bean, Tony 26–7
'Beatitudes' 12, 26, 138, 147–9, 220
BeBe and CeCe Winans 88
Beckford, Robert 25, 28, 110–11, 168
Beyond Belief, BBC's flagship ethics programme 37
Bhogal, Inderjit 54
Biggar, Nigel 37
Black
   British contemporary gospel songs 1, 79
   British Pentecostalism 8, 90
   Church tradition of testimony 118
   conservativism 85–6
   experience in evangelical churches, study of 72
   heritage 2
   liberation theology 19–24, 155–6
   preaching 139
   theodicy 155–6
   theology 8–9, 22, 54, 58, 103, 168, 179 n.41
Black African Caribbean Christian conservatism 84
Black Atlantic culture/community 3, 33, 84, 133
Black biblical studies 113–14, 116, 157, 161, 172
   biblical validity 106
   'Incarnation: No Blacks, No Irish, No Dogs', illustration 107–9
   incarnation's constructive social meanings 107
   inter(con)textual interpretation 106, 116

JNT   137, 141, 148–9
  methods   107
Black Church reception theory   2–5
  African American Spirituals   3
  experience of colonial citizens in
    Second World War   4
  'Go Down Moses'   3
  Jamaica Theological Seminary   5
  'Magnificat'   5
  post-war racism(s)   3
  theological ideas and meanings   3
Black history   7, 55, 76, 113–14, 118, 150,
    158, 161, 172
  Kemitic religion   109
  loving blackness   110
  'Pay Back', illustration   110–13
Black Learning Achievement and Mental
    Health UK CIC (BLAM
    UK)   139
Black suppressionsism   151, 153–4, see
    also dangerous memories
  horrors of the slave past   154
  obstacle for Black Christian
    communities   153
Black vernacular
  assertive nativism   138
  atonement (see atonement)
  'Beatitudes', illustration   147–9
  Black British English (BBE)   139
  Black preaching   139–40
  code-switching in Windrush-era   139
  Jamaican Language Movement   142
  Jamaican Patwa (patois)   137–8, 141
  JNT   141, 146–8
  language use among African
    peoples   138–9
  liberation   145–7
  political issue in Anglophone
    Caribbean   139
  suppression of   139
  vernacular hermeneutics   140–1
Blair, Tony   89
Blakitecture   124–5
  Christian spirituality   125
  physical sanctification   125
  politics of absences   124–5
  respectability   124
'The Blessing Song'   35
Blue-Spot   125

Bogle, Paul   158
Bonhoeffer, Dietrich   107
Boone, Pat   75
border thinking   97–9
'Born Born, Born Again'   74
Bourne, R.   8
Bristol hip-hop sounds   42
British Nationality Act of 1948   185 n.15
Brit Awards   20
Brixton Riots of 1981   84
Brown, Gordon   89
Bucknor, Jerome   173
Butler, Melvin L.   20

'Caesarea Philippi'   11, 121–2, 132–5
Callahan, Dwight Allen   110
CalledOut Music   132
CARD, see Co-ordinating Committee
    Against Racial Discrimination
    (CARD)
Caribbean diaspora   2, 8–9, 15, 18, 31,
    47, 97, 101, 110
Caribbean Melodies   73
Caribbean Revival   73
Carter, J. Kameron   55
The Celebration Club   82
'Chant Down Babylon'   100
Charles, Monique   64
Christian Aid   167
Christian slavery, practice of   36–40, 157
Church songs, colonial influence in   73–7
  Caribbean choruses   73
  first Black gospel bands   75–6
  Overcomers   76
  Pentecostal eschatology   74
  pop songs, Euro-American
    Christian   75
  Redemption Hymnal   7
  *Sacred Songs and Solos by Ira D.
    Sankey*   74
  'Sankey' and the *Redemption
    Hymnal*   73
  Singing Stewarts   76
  songwriting   75–6
  three Rs' of gospel hymnody   75
  US hymnals   73
Civil Rights Movement   7, 33, 70, 110, 170
Clapton, Eric   82
Clarke, Johnny   8

The Clash   82
Cliff, Jimmy   127
A Closer Walk with Thee (1957)   75
code-switching   137, 139
Cole, Nat King   127
colonial Christianity in the songs of Windrush generation
  arrival of *Empire Windrush*   64
  Black Church   68, 71–2
  Black women's leadership   70, 71
  CARD   70
  Christianized sociobiological racism   67–8
  colonial influence (*see* church songs, colonial influence in)
  cultural racism   67
  discrimination   68–70 (*see also* discrimination)
  historiography   64
  'Incarnation: No Blacks, No Irish, No Dogs', illustration   77–9
  influence of songs   73
  interracial friendship   70
  mobilization   70
  post-war contemporary gospel music   63
  problematization of colonial citizens   65–6
  racialization   67–8
  resistance, reasons for   70, 72–3
  social justice campaigns   72
  West Indian's arrival   65–6
  WISC   70
colonial Christian negative Black ontology   55
colonial Christian thinking   2, 6, 10, 48, 56, 92, 94, 172–3
coloniality within contemporary gospel music
  action or decolonial praxis   41
  active radicalism   32–3
  Caribbean's racial capitalism   36
  Christian slavery   36–7
  colonial Christianity, theological reflection   35–40
  Covid-19 pandemic   34–5
  evangelization without manumission   37
  New World   36

passive radicalism   32–3
pastoral spiral, stages   41
political decision-making   36
protest songs   33
racial hierarchy   36
scriptures to support   38
'Social Justice', illustration   41–4
'Soon And Very Soon', experience of singing   31–2
soteriology   39
'The Colony' (1964)   76
communal blackness   9
Community Gospel Choir   86, 167
Cone, James   145
Connolly, Michele   140
Cooke, Sam   127
Co-ordinating Committee Against Racial Discrimination (CARD)   70
Copeland, Kenneth   86
Covid 19   34–5, 172–3
Cress Welsing, Frances   159–60
Crusaders   159
Curry, Rev Dr Michael   115–17
'Curse of Ham' narrative   38, 40, 157
cut 'n' mix   15

Dadzie, Stella   40
dangerous memories   117–18, 150–60
  Black suppressionsism   151, 153–4
  enslavement in song writing   150
  false equivalency   152
  'Go and Sin No More', illustration   159–60
  horrors of the slave past   154
  intellectual neglect   152–3
  New World   153
  prayer   156–7
  pseudo-scientific racial theory   157
  racialisation of Christian tradition   157–8
  theodicy (*see* theodicy)
  White saviourism   151
Davis, Mark   173
Day, Keri   46
decolonial categories for Black Christian decolonial thinking
  affective narrative epistemology   46
  affirmation of Black life and Black being   55–6

characteristics 46–8
Christian scripture 47–8
colonial frames in Christian music 56
concordism and spiritual interpretation 52
contextual interpretation 53
decolonial turn 45
emancipation 48
first testimony 48–9
hermeneutical templates for meaning of God 46
loving blackness 53–6
'Manifesto', song illustration 56–8
narrative theology 46–7
pastoral care 48
social soteriology 49–51
strategies of Rastafari and Christianity 49, 52
testimony 46
value of Black people's experience 55
decolonial gospel music 88, 137, 172–3
decoloniality 8, 12, 41, 44, 97–8, 137, 141, 149, 166–8
decolonization 2, 7, 11, 21, 24, 30, 45, 97–8, 132, 137, 166–7
delinking contemporary gospel music 98–101
'Babylon', delinking 100
Black biblical studies 105–7
biblical validity 106
'Incarnation: No Blacks, No Irish, No Dogs', illustration 107–9
incarnation's constructive social meanings 107
inter(con)textual interpretation 106
Black history 109–10
Kemitic religion 109
loving blackness 110
'Pay Back', illustration 110–13
border thinking 97–8
'divide and rule' of Black peoples in Britain 101
'geo- and body-politics' of knowledge 99
Handsworth revolutions 100–1
Jahaziel, leaving statement 101–2
post-war Windrush generation 101
Rastafari theomusicology 99–100

Steel Pulse 100
womanist soteriology 102–3
experience of Black women 102–3
'Magnificat', illustration 103–5
Derricks, Cleavant 73
Desmond Dekker and the Aces 128
diagnostic of Black Pentecostal extemporaneous prayer 150
Different Lifestyles (1991) 88
Di Jamiekan Nyuu Testiment (JNT) 11, 24, 107, 124, 146, 197 n.30
discrimination 68–70
in church life 69–70
in employment 68–9
in health services 34
in housing 68–9
racial 34, 69–70, 83, 123
'divide and rule' of Black peoples in Britain 101
Dixon, Marcia 122
doctrine of 'Powellise' 81
Drane, John 19
Duggan, Mark 91, 143
'Duppy Conqueror' theology 8
Durkheim, Émile 131

economic (global) crash of 2008 89
Edwards, Jackie 74
Elementary Forms of Religion (1912) 131
Elim Pentecostal Church 74
Ellison, Darren 77, 107
emancipation 6, 48
Empire Windrush 64–5, 67, 72, 172
'Employment in the U.K. of Surplus Colonial Labour' 67
environmental degradation 1, 100, 173
Esu (Eshu-Elegba) 129, 194 n.29
ethical theodicy 150, 158–9
'Ethics of Empire' project, University of Oxford 151
Ethiopianism 110
Eurocentric Christian historiography 45
Everywhere+Nowhere (2001) 132
The Evolution of Gospel (1991) 88
Exorcism: Resisting the Bewitchment of Colonial Christianity (2014) 23

Fanon, Frantz 7, 116
F. D. Maurice lectures at Kings College London 5

'Feels Like Summer' 167
'Fill My Cup' (1984) 86
Fishbane, Michael 25
Floyd, George 153, 177 n.10
Frankin, Aretha 88

Garvey, Amy Ashwood 70–1, 158
Garvey, Marcus 7, 71, 158
Garveyism 110
Gaye, Marvin 165, 167, 172
gender oppression 40, 102
geopolitics 99, 101
Gerbner, Katherine 39
'Get Real,' Black apologetics
 organization 154
'Ghetto Cry' (1999) 90
Gibson, Karen 165, 167
global warming 167
'Go and Sin No More' 12, 150, 159–60
Godwyn, Morgan 37, 39, 157
golden age of contemporary gospel
 music 82–6
 abundance 86
 Black British Christian
  conservatism 84–5
 Black Pentecostal songwriting 92–4
 crossover genre 87–9
 Holiness music 80–2
 impact of Powell's *racecraft* 81
 LCGC 86
 legislative changes in criminal justice
  system and policing 87
 mission, money and role models 87–8
 Nu Colours 87
 racism in postcolonial Britain 87
 re-inscription (*see* re-inscription)
 'The Rivers of Blood' speech 81–2
 success 85–6
 Thatcherite individualism (*see*
  Thatcherism)
 unemployment and distress 85–6
 Word of Faith Movement in
  America 86
'Work of the Spirit', illustration 92–4
Gordon, Lewis 2
Gospel Music Association of Great
 Britain 173
Gospel of Jesus 5–6, 17, 37, 87, 170–1,
 172–3
Graham, Elain 30, 152

Grant, Jacquelyn 47, 49, 53–4
Great Commission 87
'Greater Love' 88
'Great Is Thy Faithfulness' 34
Grenfell Tower tragedy 20–1, 168, 173
'griot' tradition 46
Grundy, Stanley 75
Guvna B 132

Hagin, Kenneth E. 86
Hall, Delroy 47
Hall, Stuart 66, 84
Handsworth Revolution (1978) 7–9, 11,
 34, 97–113, *see also* delinking
 contemporary gospel music
'The Harmonizers' 128, 131
Harris, Clive 68
Heaven 88
Hendricks, Obery 21, 57
Henry, Lez 110, 168
Hill, Clifford 35
Hinds, David 100
Hodges, Hugh 101
Huddleston, Trevor 151
Hudson-Wilkin, Rev Rose 103–5, 115–16
human trafficking 100

The Idea of the Holy (1917) 131
'I'm Not About That' (2017) 91
'Incarnation: No Blacks, No Irish, No
 Dogs' 4, 64, 77–9
individual blackness 9
Israelite (1968) 127
'I've Got to Get Away' (1968) 90

Jamaican Bible Remix 2, 3, 9, 23–7, 138
 audio samples from the JNT or
  scripture track 25
 impact, case studies on 167–70
 JNT translation 24–5
 Kingdom Choir (*see* Kingdom Choir)
 message track or verbal
  narratives 25–7
 music or instrumental track 25
 promotion 24
 racial justice/climate justice agenda of
  Christian Aid 167
 social justice 15, 27, 169
 sonic textures of Black music 165
 technical resource 25

tracks 25–7
West Indian Front Room (*see* West Indian Front Room' event (symposium))
'The Jamaican Language' 10, 27–8, 142–7
Jamaican Language Movement 142
Jamaican proverbs 101
James, C. L. R. 85
James, Winston 68
Jazz Warriors 148
Jim Crow, resistance to 33
JNT, *see Di Jamiekan Nyuu Testament* (JNT)
John Collins Lecture at Oriel College 4
John Holt and the Paragons 90
Johnson, Boris 35
Jones, Carmel 69
Joseph Niles and the Consolers 74, 131

Kelly, Abigail 92
Kerr, Marlene 57–8
Kilby, Karen 155
Kinch, Soweto 148
King, Ben E. 115
King, Martin Luther 70
Kingdom Choir 115, 121, 167–70
   African cosmology 168
   collaboration, for 'Mercy, Mercy Me' 167
   performance at Royal Wedding 115
   racial justice/climate justice agenda of Christian Aid 167
   religious influence 167–8
   social justice 169
'Ku Klux Klan' 34

Lammy, David 144
Lawrence, Stephen 87
LCGC, *see* London Community Gospel Choir (LCGC)
leitourgia 19
'Let My People Go' 132
Lincoln, C. Eric 22
Lindsay, Ben 72
London Community Gospel Choir (LCGC) 86
Lorde, Audre 138
'Lover's Rock' reggae genre 103
loving blackness 53–6, 110
   affirmation of Black life and Black being 55–6
   social modes of operation 55
   value of Black people's experience 55
Luuk 27, 41, 57, 173

McCartney, Paul 81
McClure, John 25
McClurkin, Donne 74, 122
McKenzie, Dr Dulcie 19–20, 166
McMillian, Dr Michael 124, 166
McQueen, Steve 52
'Magnificat' 5, 11, 98, 103–5, 166
Malcolm X (1992) 133
Mamiya, Lawrence 22
'Manifesto' 10, 45, 56–8
mantronics 127
Markle, Meghan 114–15
Marr, Andrew 110–12
Marvin Gaye Estate 167
Mashup Religion 25
Meade, Bazil 166
'Melting Pot' (1969) 81
'Mercy, Mercy Me' (environmental song) 12, 167–70, 172
Methodists 36, 54, 68
Middleton, Kate 144
The Mighty Diamond 8
Mignolo, Walter D. 98–9, 101
Milton Friedman Chicago School of Economics 83
Moody, Dwight Lyman 75
Morgan, Volney 132
Mouw 19
'Moving Out a Babylon' 100
Muir, David 66
Muir, Dr Pauline 19, 64, 166
multiculturalism 17, 81
Murrell, Nathaniel 38, 117
Music of Black Origin awards (MOBOs) 131
music production
   Black orality as tools for production 115–17
   Kingdom Choir, performance at Royal Wedding 114–15
   tool 1: crossover 115–16
      secular song's lyrics 115
      'Stand by Me' 116
   tool 2: Black vernacular 116–17
      inter(con)textual interpretation 116

JNT version 117
tool 3: dangerous memories 117–18
    slavery's memory 117–18
    spiritual and material 118
music selection
    African Traditional Religion 128–9
    broad vision of the sacred 127–30, 132
    hip-hop turntable technology 128
    narrow vision of the sacred 130–2
    neo-Pentecostal themes of spiritual overcoming 132
    pre-fundamentalist Christian phase 127
    sacred/profane binary 128, 130
    sonic migration 129

National Health Service (NHS) 34
The Negro's & Indian's advocate 39
neo-Nazis 34
New Labour project 89
New Testament Church of God 6, 17
New Testament pneumatology (Villafañe) 92
New World 36, 153, 157
Ngũgĩ wa Thiong'o 138
Niebuhr, H. Richard 47
Niles, Joseph 74, 127–8, 131, 159
non-violence 51
North Atlantic slavery 155
Notting Hill Carnival 70–1

'Ob-La-Di, Ob-La-Da' (1968) 81
Okafor, Ben 91, 98
Otto, Rudolf 131
Out of Darkness 91
The Overcomers (1969) 76

Palmer, Lisa 103
Pan African Congress 71
Park, Wongi 40
Patwa 24, 137–9, 141–2, 144–7
Paul's letter to the Colossians 38
'Pay Back' 11, 26, 98, 110–13
Pentecostal(ism) 8, 32, 46, 74, 90
    Christianity 54
    doctrine of the Holy Spirit 74, 86
    eschatology 74
    music in Jamaica 20
    Pentecostal Credit Union 69–70

performative knowledge 30–1
Perkinson, James 36
Perry, Kenyetta 67
Phillipson, Robert 139
Pilgrim Holiness Church 125
Pinn, Anthony 155
Policing the Crisis: Mugging the State and Law and Order (Hall) 83–4
pop songs, Euro-American Christian 75
positionality 9
postcolonial theology 139–40
post-Second World War racisms 107
Powell, Enoch 81–2, 143
power, coloniality of 46, 98, 138, 146
    interpretive component 40
    ontology 40
    pro-slavery reading 40
    race and racism 40
    soteriological component 39
    Zinzendorf's hermeneutical strategy 40
Prince Harry 114
Prince William 144
punishment theodicy 158

Quakers 36
Queen Elizabeth II 114–15
Quijano, Anibal 38

racial capitalism 3, 36–7, 88, 150
racial hierarchy 36, 39, 116
racialization 63, 67–70, 83
racialized discrimination 34, 123
racialized oppression 72, 102
racism 7, 20, 37, 40, 49, 52, 66–8, 74, 80, 88, 100, 102, 115, 126, 132, 145, 153, 156–7, 159, 169
    biological 67
    British 5, 33
    campaigns against 71
    Christian 72
    cultural 67
    'institutional racism' in the police 87
    plantocracy 116
    post-Second World War racisms in Britain 107
    religious 63
    Rock against Racism 82
    in the Royal household 115
    sociobiological 67–8

structural 5, 37, 49, 167
radicalism 32–3, 35–6, 40, 51, 72, 74, 76, 156
rap improvisation 35
Rastafari
  epistemology 100
  inspired reggae (*see* reggae music)
  in post-diaspora history 52
  religion 100
  strategies 52
  theomusicology 99–100
rationalization 19
Ready to Live (2007) 90
Reddie, Anthony 17, 23, 153
Redemption Hymnal 74
redemptive suffering 154, 156
Reeves, Jim 75, 127, 131
reggae music 7, 11, 25–7, 33, 41, 90, 94, 98–100, 103, 110, 113, 126–8, 131, 137, 168, 172, 191 n.6
rehabilitation 158
Reimagining Britain (Welby) 152
re-inscription 89–92
  'outlaw culture' 89
  redemption 90
  shooting of teenage girls 89
  systemic failure 89–90
  West African British contemporary gospel music 90
  White Christology 91
repetition and development, Black culture 193 n.8
resurrection 128, 141–3, 155, 173–4
'Revival Choruses' in Jamaica 3
Rhamie, Gifford 106
Richards, Jo-Ann 3
righteousness 1, 86
'Rivers of Blood' speech 81, 143
Robinson, Noel 167
Rock against Racism 82
Rogers, Andrew 18
Rollock, Nicola 50
Roots Manuva 10, 27, 42, 110
Royal Wedding 11, 114–15, 121–2, 144

Sabbatical 43
Sacred Songs and Solos by Ira D. Sankey 74
Sankey, Ira David 74–5
Second World War 4, 65, 77, 107–8

Secret World 132
Seventh-day Adventist Church 76
Shield, Marcus W. 40
Singing Stewarts, gospel group 76
Size, Ronnie 57
slave/post-slave country-folks oratory 50
slavery 3, 12, 26, 33, 56, 76, 100, 110, 117–18, 141, 149–50, 152–3, 155, 157, 159, 169, 197 n.6
  Caribbean 36, 39–40
  chattel 38–40
  Christian slavery 36–40, 157
  pro-slavery 40, 110
Smith, K. A. 46
Smith, Mitzi 53, 106
Smith Pollard, Deborah 15
'Social Justice' 1–2, 6–7, 10, 15, 17, 19, 27, 33, 41–4, 63, 172
social media manipulation 100
Sölle, Dorothee 50
songs about social justice, omission of
  Black Church music 19–20
  bridging the gap 23–7
  contested multiculturalism of Black British experience 16
  cut 'n' mix 15
  Grenfell Tower tragedy of 2017 20–1
  Jamaican Bible Remix (*see* Jamaican Bible Remix)
  liturgical/commercial/theological explanations 18–19
  message track or verbal narratives 25–7
  Pentecostal music in Jamaica 20
  worship service 17–18
sonic migration 129
soteriology 36, 39–41, 45, 80, 92, 102, 122, 132, 161, 170
  experience of Black women 102–3
  'Magnificat', illustration 103–5
  social 41, 56, 58, 75, 105
  womanist 51, 105, 113–14, 121, 172
Spirit baptism 73
'Stand by Me' 21, 115–16
Starkey, David 142–5
Steel Pulse 7, 11, 33–4, 98–100, 113, 159
Stewart, Rod 82
Stormzy 20, 168
Stratton, Jon 81

Strummer, Joe   82
Sugirtharajah   140

Thames Valley University   168
Thatcher, Margaret   83–4, 86
Thatcherism   83–4
   Brixton Riots of 1981   84
   Lord Scarman Report (1981)   84
   marketplace politics   84
   neoliberal economics   83
   new right ideology   83
   oppressive policing   83
theodicy   154–6
   Black liberation theology   155–6
   discussion of God's goodness 154–6
   ethical theodicy   159
   feature of biblical narrative   154
   punishment theodicy   158
   redemptive suffering   156
   rehabilitation   158
   for remembering slavery   158–9
   resolutions   155–6
   soul-making theodicies   156
Tlostanova, Madina   101
Tomlin, Carol   139
trans-Atlantic
   Black theological dialogue   49, 54
   slave trade   110, 152
Tribute to the Martyrs (1979)   100
Trojan label artists   126–7
Turman, Eboni Marshall   107
Turner, Carlton   55

UK grime music genre   92
United Nations Cop26 Global Conference on Climate Action   165
United Nations Summit on Climate Change   167
Urban Theology Unit, University of Sheffield   43

vernacular hermeneutics   139–1, *see also* Black vernacular
Villafañe, Eldin   92
violence   47, 87, 89, 90, 143–4
von Zinzendorf, Count Ludwig   39–40
Vybz Kartel, *see* golden age of contemporary gospel music

Walker, Anthony   159
Walrath, Brian   19
Walton, Heather   30
Ward, Graham   152
Weber, Max   84–5
Welby, Justin   72, 152
West African neo-Pentecostal prosperity doctrine   90
West Indian front room crossover
   broad vision of music selection   128–30, 132 (*see also* music selection)
   'Caesarea Philippi', illustration   132–6
   controversial musical strategy   121
   dwelling space and racialized discrimination   123
   Euro-American and African Caribbean gospel albums   126
   features of the front room   124 (*see also* Blakitecture)
   home entertainment   125–6
   local Black music record shops   125
   music selection   126
   narrow vision of the sacred   130–2 (*see also* music selection)
   participant observation   121–2
   racialized stereotypes of Black family life   124
   rituals of purification   126
   selector   126–7
   traditional and progressive, debate on   122–3
   transcendence   126
   womanist soteriology   121
West Indian front room event (symposium)   165–7
   heritage of Black Christian music   166
   positive response   167
   songs of praise and worship   167
   sonic textures of Black music   165
West Indian Standing Conference (WISC)   70
We Thank Thee (1962)   75
White, Del   87
White American Pentecostal and Evangelical mission   6
White Christology   91
White conservative American missionary parent denominations   6

White saviourism 151–3, *see also* dangerous memories
    false equivalency 152
    intellectual neglect 152–3
Wilberforce, William 112, 151
Williams, Clare 154
Williams, Jeremy 167
Williams, Rowan 152
Willoughby, Governor of Barbados/Leeward 36
Wilmore, Gayraud 22
Windrush generation, *see also* colonial Christianity in the songs of Windrush generation
    Black Church testimony 45
    Churches 59
Womanist Sass and Talk Back: Social (In)justice, Intersectionality and Biblical Interpretation (Smith) 106
Woodhead, Linda 16
Woods, Robert 19
Word of Faith Movement in America 86
'Work of the Spirit' 11, 92–4
World's Midnight (1982) 85

'you sing so well' genre 3–5, 7